SYSTEMS ANALYSIS AND DESIGN

SYSTEMS ANALYSIS
AND DESIGN

SYSTEMS ANALYSIS AND DESIGN

TECHNIQUES, METHODOLOGIES, APPROACHES, AND ARCHITECTURES

ROGER H.L. CHIANG
KENG SIAU
BILL C. HARDGRAVE
EDITORS

ADVANCES IN MANAGEMENT
INFORMATION SYSTEMS
VLADIMIR ZWASS SERIES EDITOR

LONDON AND NEW YORK

References to the AMIS papers should be as follows:

Henderson-Sellers, B. Agent-oriented methods and method engineering. In Roger H.L. Chiang, Keng Siau, and
Bill C. Hardgrave, eds., *Systems Analysis and Design: Techniques, Methodologies, Approaches, and Architectures.* Volume 15, *Advances in Management Information Systems* (Armonk, NY: M.E. Sharpe, 2009), 118–138.

ISBN 978-0-7656-2352-2 (hbk)
ISSN 1554–6152

ADVANCES IN MANAGEMENT INFORMATION SYSTEMS

AMIS Vol. 1: Richard Y. Wang, Elizabeth M. Pierce, Stuart E. Madnick, and Craig W. Fisher
Information Quality
ISBN 978-0-7656-1133-8

AMIS Vol. 2: Sergio deCesare, Mark Lycett, and Robert D. Macredie
Development of Component-Based Information Systems
ISBN 978-0-7656-1248-9

AMIS Vol. 3: Jerry Fjermestad and Nicholas C. Romano, Jr.
Electronic Customer Relationship Management
ISBN 978-0-7656-1327-1

AMIS Vol. 4: Michael J. Shaw
E-Commerce and the Digital Economy
ISBN 978-0-7656-1150-5

AMIS Vol. 5: Ping Zhang and Dennis Galletta
Human-Computer Interaction and Management Information Systems: Foundations
ISBN 978-0-7656-1486-5

AMIS Vol. 6: Dennis Galletta and Ping Zhang
Human-Computer Interaction and Management Information Systems: Applications
ISBN 978-0-7656-1487-2

AMIS Vol. 7: Murugan Anandarajan, Thompson S.H. Teo, and Claire A. Simmers
The Internet and Workplace Transformation
ISBN 978-0-7656-1445-2

AMIS Vol. 8: Suzanne Rivard and Benoit Aubert
Information Technology Outsourcing
ISBN 978-0-7656-1685-2

AMIS Vol. 9: Varun Grover and M. Lynne Markus
Business Process Transformation
ISBN 978-0-7656-1191-8

AMIS Vol. 10: Panos E. Kourouthanassis and George M. Giaglis
Pervasive Information Systems
ISBN 978-0-7656-1689-0

AMIS Vol. 11: Detmar W. Straub, Seymour Goodman, and Richard Baskerville
Information Security: Policy, Processes, and Practices
ISBN 978-0-7656-1718-7

AMIS Vol. 12: Irma Becerra-Fernandez and Dorothy Leidner
Knowledge Management: An Evolutionary View
ISBN 978-0-7656-1637-1

AMIS Vol. 13: Robert J. Kauffman and Paul P. Tallon
Economics, Information Systems, and Electronic Commerce: Empirical Research
ISBN 978-0-7656-1532-9

AMIS Vol. 14: William R. King
Planning for Information Systems
ISBN 978-0-7656-1950-1

AMIS Vol. 15: Roger H.L. Chiang, Keng Siau, and Bill C. Hardgrave
Systems Analysis and Design: Techniques, Methodologies, Approaches, and Architectures
ISBN 978-0-7656-2352-2

Forthcoming volumes of this series can be found on the series homepage.
www.mesharpe.com/amis.htm

Editor-in-Chief, Vladimir Zwass (zwass@fdu.edu)

Advances in Management Information Systems

Advisory Board

Eric K. Clemons
University of Pennsylvania

Thomas H. Davenport
Accenture Institute for Strategic Change
and
Babson College

Varun Grover
Clemson University

Robert J. Kauffman
Arizona State University

Jay F. Nunamaker, Jr.
University of Arizona

Andrew B. Whinston
University of Texas

CONTENTS

SERIES EDITOR'S INTRODUCTION

VLADIMIR ZWASS, EDITOR-IN-CHIEF

The field of Information Systems (IS) shares a disciplinary interest in systems analysis and design (SA&D) with computer science (CS) and, in particular, with its subfield of software engineering. The IS discipline focuses on behavioral, cognitive, organizational, economical, and social issues along with the business-facing technological issues of systems development.

The present volume of *Advances in Management Information Systems* (*AMIS*) addresses this broad set of concerns. Edited and written by some of the leading authorities, the volume's aim—consistent with objectives of the *AMIS* series—is to bring together research work that forms our thinking about the processes and products of SA&D. For this reason, the volume is organized around the influential tiered framework that systematizes IS development methodologies (Iivari, Hirschheim, and Klein, 2000–2001). Thus organized, the work of the volume's editors and the researchers who contributed to it makes visible a coherent view of the approaches underlying SA&D (such as structured development, object orientation, or sociotechnical design), specific methodologies relying on these approaches, and techniques deployed to develop systems using these methodologies. The distinct architectural principles for designing complex artifacts that are IS are discussed and exemplified in the context of satisfying the varied requirements of system stakeholders.

Demonstrably, we are able to develop and implement ever larger, more complex, and more pervasive systems. Equally demonstrably, our systems development processes are subject to severe time and budget overruns as well as implementation failures, and the resulting systems suffer from a wide array of vulnerabilities and maintainability deficiencies. These facts alone call for the deeper study of fundamentals of our SA&D approaches, methodologies, and techniques. Well beyond these factors, the drastically changing environment of software development calls for a fundamental review and reassessment of our methodologies for this development. The examination of foundations that is undertaken in the present *AMIS* volume is thus very important.

The changes are profound and striking, since I last had an opportunity to write my assessment of the entire SA&D arena some twenty-five years ago (Zwass, 1984). Some of the current principal overlapping aspects of the ongoing change include:

1. Contemporary information systems are widely distributed. This distribution occurs in many senses of the word: geographical, organizational, across heterogeneous systems software and hardware, across diverse enterprise systems, and across heterogeneous databases and data warehouses.

2. The overall functionality of major IS is actually delivered by systems of systems. These supersystems have an emergent quality: they have not been (and cannot be, in most cases) planned and developed as an entity. The obvious example is the Internet–Web compound; other examples include supply chain management systems that emerge to support the changing constellations of

business partners, and the sense-and-control systems that will support the work of corporations and other organizations with ubiquitous sensors and actuators, feeding voluminous data into the event-driven IS. Such systems "are 'unbounded' because they involve an unknown number of participants or otherwise require individual participants to act and interact in the absence of needed information" (Fisher and Smith, 2004, p. 1). The emergent systems of systems act in a manner unforeseen at the time the individual systems were being designed, acquiring vulnerabilities that emerge during execution and system interaction.

3. Reuse of software components of various degrees of complexity and functionality has become an objective of development. This complicates the design of individual components, as developers need to determine the level of component granularity and achieve the necessary degree of generality, documentation, and imperviousness to misuse (De Cesare, Lycett, and Macredie, 2006). It also calls for the supporting systems of discovery, integration, secure deployment, and intellectual property management. Components and subsystems are provided by diverse suppliers under different organizational arrangements, including open source under various licenses. With the availability of software components, such as commercial-off-the-shelf (COTS) products or Web services, development becomes integration-oriented. Stability of the integration environment underwrites the stability of the systems developed with its use. The stability of the environments, or its absence, is an outcome of the general competitive jockeying for the standardization rents conducted by technology companies.

4. Execution paths in some systems are nondeterministic, owing to the runtime binding of services discovered via directories. The fact that different code entities may be invoked to handle the same transactions at different times magnifies other vulnerabilities and lowers system reliability considerably.

5. A highly dynamic competitive environment on a global scale results in mergers and acquisitions, as well as spin-offs and other divestments, and thus necessitates continuing and thoroughgoing evolution of organizational systems.

6. A variety of modes of system provisioning and governance, including outsourcing, offshoring, software as a service, grid computing, singly and in various combinations, presents a variety of alternatives in the continuing supply of organizational information services. When governance changes are enacted, extensive software (r)evolution in organizational IS results.

7. The open source mode of software production and maintenance, with support provided by software vendors, offers an enticing alternative to the traditional licensing of software products. Beyond that, when internalized by firms it offers a new working paradigm for organizational IS. For instance, the Progressive Open Source program aims to gradually introduce open-source methods into large corporations by going from the intraorganizational deployment of open source gradually to include outside developers (Dinkelacker et al., 2002). Intellectual property issues come to the fore in various forms, including the variety of copyleft licenses under which various parts of the emerging composite systems have been produced. The Open Source Initiative lists seventy-two different licenses compliant with its review criteria (Open Source Initiative, 2006). Security exposures due to the use of third (and further) -party code require coherent handling.

A number of fundamental advances in SA&D have been directed at managing the growing complexity of information systems and their development processes. These advances include: the growing understanding of modular system design with information encapsulation and hiding; layered system development with strictly limited interfaces; progression of modeling tools with a gradual movement from the business-process level of abstraction to the solution level of detail; semantically powerful programming languages with typing facility and, in some cases, platform neutrality; supportive software development environments and the means of system composition, such as service-oriented architecture (SOA). All of these enhance our ability to dynamically align an organization's IS with its capabilities and business processes.

Research in the SA&D domain continues apace. New modeling approaches are being developed with service orientation to support the highly dynamic business environment, sometimes dubbed "on-demand business," with the modular definition of business components supported by IS components (Cherbakov et al., 2005). The elicitation of requirements, a key part of systems analysis, is being studied in a generalized way, to tighten the mapping between what the users want and what the system delivers (Hickey and Davis, 2004). The effectiveness of various prototyping strategies is being investigated empirically (Hardgrave, Wilson, and Eastman, 1999). Cost–benefit analysis of the use of unified modeling language (UML) documentation during the maintenance of object-oriented software is being performed through controlled experiments with actual developers (Dzidek, Arisholm, and Briand, 2008). As evidenced by the contents of the present volume, agent-oriented architectures are of the particular moment with the advent of ubiquitous computing; design with autonomous agents leads to new approaches being grafted onto object-oriented development (Garcia and Lucena, 2008). Work continues on developing quantitative methods of predicting the characteristics of the system development process at its inception (Curtis et al., 2008). The means of alignment between corporate software development processes and strategic initiatives are being studied (Slaughter et al., 2006). The empirics of the cognitive transition of developers to new development methodologies surface the tactics for success (Armstrong and Hardgrave, 2007).

Within the IS research area, the development of software artifacts is being studied in a disciplined manner, using the precepts of design science. The aims of this research stream were articulated about two decades ago (Nunamaker, Chen, and Purdin, 1990–91). Viewing IS as a discipline of applied research, design science aims to empirically surface the principles undergirding the processes of development and implementation of successful organizational IS (Hevner et al., 2004; Peffers et al., 2007–2008). The work on design science is part of a more general interdisciplinary project of "designing the design" (Baldwin and Clark, 2006).

The ability to actively create systems is, without a doubt, a vital subject of IS research, practice, and teaching. The volume editors, authors, and I fully expect that the appearance of this *AMIS* volume, addressing the foundations of these efforts, will stimulate further work that will lead to more creative, resilient, and organizationally fit IS.

REFERENCES

Armstrong, D.J., and Hardgrave, B.C. 2007. Understanding mindshift learning: the transition to object-oriented methodologies. *MIS Quarterly,* 31, 3 (September), 453–474.

Baldwin, C.Y., and Clark, K.B. 2006. Between "knowledge" and "the economy": notes on the scientific study of designs. In B. Kahin and D. Foray (eds.), *Advancing Knowledge and the Knowledge Economy.* Cambridge, MA: MIT Press, 299–328.

Cherbakov, L.; Galambos, G.; Harishankar, R.; Kalyana, S.; and Rackham, G. 2005. Impact of service orientation at the business level. *IBM Systems Journal,* 44, 4, 653–668.

Curtis, B.; Seshagiri, G.V.; Reifer, D.; Hirmanpour, I.; and Keeni, G. 2008. The case for quantitative process management. *IEEE Software,* May/June, 24–28.

De Cesare, S.; Lycett, M.; and Macredie, R.D. (eds.). 2006. *Development of Component-Based Information Systems,* Vol. 2. *Advances in Management Information Systems.* Armonk, NY: M.E. Sharpe.

Dinkelacker, J.; Garg, P.K.; Miller, R.; and Nelson, D. 2002. Progressive open source, *Proceedings of the Twenty fourth International Conference on Software Engineering.* New York: ACM Press, 177–184.

Dzidek, W.J.; Arisholm, E.; and Briand, L.C. 2008. A realistic empirical evaluation of the costs and benefits of UML in software maintenance. *IEEE Transactions on Software Engineering,* 34, 3 (May/June), 407–432.

Fisher, D.A., and Smith, D. 2004. Emergent issues in interoperability. *News @ SEI,* 3. Available at www. sei.cmu.edu/news-at-sei/columns/eye-on-integration/2004/3/eye-on-integration-2004–3.htm (accessed on July 10, 2008).

Garcia, A., and Lucena, C. 2008. Taming heterogeneous agent architectures. *Communications of the ACM,* 51, 5 (May), 75–81.

Hardgrave, B.C.; Wilson, R.L.; and Eastman, K. 1999. Toward a contingency model for selecting an information system prototyping strategy. *Journal of Management Information Systems,* 16, 2 (Fall), 113–136.

Hevner, A.; March, S.; Park, J.; and Ram, S. 2004. Design science research in information systems. *MIS Quarterly,* 28, 1 (March), 75–105.

Hickey, A.M., and Davis, A.M. 2004. A unified model of requirements elicitation. *Journal of Management Information Systems,* 20, 4 (Spring), 65–84.

Iivari, J.; Hirschheim, R.; and Klein, H.K. 2000–2001. A dynamic framework for classifying information systems development methodologies and approaches. *Journal of Management Information Systems,* 17, 3 (Winter), 179–218.

Nunamaker, J.F. Jr.; Chen, M.; and Purdin, T.D.M. 1990–91. Systems development in information systems research. *Journal of Management Information Systems,* 7, 3 (Winter), 89–106.

Open Source Initiative. 2006. Licenses by Name, September 18. Available at www.opensource.org/licenses/alphabetical (accessed on July 17, 2008).

Peffers, K.; Tuunanen, T.; Rothenberger, M.A.; and Chatterjee, S. 2007–2008. A design science research methodology for information systems research. *Journal of Management Information Systems,* 24, 3 (Winter), 45–77.

Slaughter, S.; Levine, L.; Ramesh, B.; Pries-Heje, J.; and Baskerville, R. 2006. Aligning software processes and strategy. *MIS Quarterly,* 30, 4 (December), 891–918.

Zwass, V. 1984. Software engineering. In A.H. Seidman and I. Flores (eds.), *The Handbook of Computers and Computing.* New York: Van Nostrand Reinhold, 552–567.

ACKNOWLEDGMENTS

The editors would like to thank the series editor of *Advances in Management Information Systems (AMIS)*, Dr. Vladimir Zwass, for inviting us in February 2005 to submit a proposal as editors of a research-oriented volume on systems analysis and design. With his continuous support and guidance, we have finally completed editing this work. We are grateful to the executive editor, Harry Briggs, and associate editor, Elizabeth Granda, of M.E. Sharpe, Inc. for their assistance in innumerable ways in preparing the manuscripts for publication. Many reviewers have contributed by providing excellent and constructive comments to improve the quality and readability of these submissions. Finally, we would like to express our sincere and deepest gratitude to the contributing authors, who have spent a lot of time and effort in writing these wonderful chapters. Further, their great patience in collaborating with us during this long editing process needs to be acknowledged. Without their state-of-the-art research in the area of systems analysis and design, it would have been impossible for us to complete this volume.

SYSTEMS ANALYSIS AND DESIGN

CHAPTER 1

THE STATE OF SYSTEMS ANALYSIS AND DESIGN RESEARCH

JOHN ERICKSON AND KENG SIAU

INTRODUCTION

Successful implementation of information systems depends heavily on a thorough and well-executed systems analysis and design (SA&D) effort. While organizations have been building information systems for nearly fifty years, information systems failure is still a common occurrence (Avison and Fitzgerald, 2006; Hardgrave, Davis, and Riemenschneider, 2003; Schmidt et al., 2001; Siau, Wand, and Benbasat, 1997; Smith, Keil, and Depledge, 2001). The field of systems analysis and design remains very much an art rather than a precise science. Traditionally, the area of systems development has suffered from abysmally low success rates, typically cited in the range of 25–35 percent. Even though David Rubinstein (2007) cited an overall doubling in success rates between 1994 and 2006, the success rates claimed in Rubinstein's summary of a Standish Report still stand at about 35 percent. While the apparent improvement is welcome news, 65 percent of systems efforts are still considered failures. The stubbornly high failure rates in systems development projects highlight the continuous need for quality research in nearly every area of systems development.

Over the past twenty years or so, a number of different ideas regarding systems development have revolutionized the field. One such revolution involves the movement from structured systems development to the object-oriented perspective (Armstrong and Hardgrave, 2007) triggered by a more or less wholesale move toward object-oriented programming in the 1980s. Another trend is forward engineering, where models developed can be automatically translated into programming codes. While the goal of complete executable modeling remains tantalizingly out of reach, some progress toward that end has made it possible in some cases to make more than 40 percent of code executable. More recent trends in systems development promote the idea of arranging existing program code modules rather than writing the code itself, such as Web services or service-oriented architectures (SOA) (Erickson and Siau, 2008); they also highlight a desire to move beyond the programming function itself. In addition, new ideas and emphases such as agility (Erickson, Lyytinen, and Siau, 2005), extreme programming, agent-oriented approach, and cognition (Siau and Tan, 2005a, 2005b; Wei, Chiang, and Wu, 2006) in the context of systems analysis and design have assumed increasing importance to academicians and practitioners. Continuing research into these areas, especially concentrating on the analysis and design efforts of the larger systems development process, remains a high priority, with a goal of reducing systems development failure. This volume consists of chapters that address these concerns.

VARIOUS CLASSIFICATION SCHEMES FOR SYSTEMS ANALYSIS AND DESIGN RESEARCH

One issue the editors of this volume needed to resolve was the classification of the chapters. Several perspectives or dimensions were considered, and these are briefly reviewed below.

Iivari, Hirschheim, and Klein (2001) used a framework consisting of paradigms, approaches, methodologies, and techniques. In the social sciences, the term "paradigm" is usually used to describe the basic assumptions underlying coexistent theories (Burrell and Morgan, 1979). An approach can be viewed as the basic principles, goals, and concepts that anchor the way systems development is understood and developed. Examples are the object-oriented approach and the structured approach (e.g., data flow diagram). Methodologies, which are composed of specific procedures, are closely related to the more general and goal-driven approaches. An example is the unified process. The methodologies are used to guide information systems development. Finally, techniques can be seen as "well-defined sequence(s) of basic operations." Examples of techniques are class diagram and use case diagram. If the techniques are properly completed, they can lead to specific (and measurable) results.

One common classification of research is pure research versus applied research. Pure research aims at expanding human knowledge, but does not necessarily find immediate application in practice or the real world. Development of new techniques or methodologies in systems analysis and design fall under this category. Applied research not only expands the knowledge base, but also can be applied to problems in the real world. Examples are the fine-tuning of an existing methodology and technique for use in an organization. With the goal of obtaining new knowledge, pure research can move in any direction and is not constrained by the issue of whether the result is immediately useful or not. Later events may show that pure research becomes useful in unexpected places and unexpected ways. For example, while SIMULA I and Simula 67, the first two object-oriented languages, were developed in the 1960s, object-oriented programming only became popular in the 1980s.

Another way to classify research is to look at the underlying philosophies of the approaches, methodologies, or techniques. Hirschheim, Klein, and Lyytinen (1995) distinguished between the ontology and epistemology perspectives. Ontologies are ways to classify the world in terms of its unchangeable, foundational, and universal structures. The world of ontologies can be further decomposed into two separate perspectives, realism and nominalism. Whereas realism proposes that a set of absolute laws and structures underlies the universe, the nominalism perspective posits that there is no absolute set of law and structures, and that those that exist are created by humans via social networks and structures. The epistemology perspective of the world proposes to set a basis for what constitutes knowledge, how new knowledge is acquired, and what investigations into the world may be and how they should be conducted. The two endpoints of the epistemology dimension are positivism and interpretivism. Positivism proposes that the scientific method can be used to explain relationships between entities in terms of their causes, and to discover the universal truth underlying the world. Interpretivism, on the other hand, assumes that no absolute truths, if they exist at all, can be scientifically proved or disproved.

Avison and Fitzgerald (2003) classified systems development methodologies into time-based eras, in which popular methodologies reflected the state of the art in terms of systems development in the general time frame or era. They described the 1960s and 1970s as the Pre-Methodology Era, during which the attention was focused mostly on the technical and hardware limitations. Examining the business needs underlying development was nearly always secondary. The Early Methodology Era was the time period between the late 1970s and early 1980s. The Systems

Development Life Cycle is a well-known artifact of this time, during which the focus of systems development shifted from hardware and technical constraints to the process itself. Unfortunately, the focus still did not exert adequate effort in identifying business needs. The methodology era, encompassing the late 1980s through the late 1990s, saw an explosion of methodologies in a variety of genres. The methodologies were (more or less) squarely aimed at ameliorating the deficiencies of the methodological approaches to systems development characterized in the earlier eras. Finally, from the late 1990s through the present, developers have gradually come to the realization that strict adherence to any given methodology, no matter how efficacious it might have appeared in success stories about it, could not guarantee the success of the next project it was used for. They named this the Post-Methodology Era.

Hirschheim and Klein (1989) presented another concept of systems development: paradigmatic thinking. Their effort developed and created what they called the "four paradigms of systems development." They described the first paradigm as functionalism, in which systems development was driven from outside, using formal and well-defined plans and tools. The elements of each system were seen as physical entities, and the structured methodologies could be seen as examples. Their second paradigm was termed social relativism, which viewed systems development as happening from inside. Entities and structures were seen more as changing, dynamic, or evolutionary in nature. The various ethnographic systems development methodologies are examples of this paradigm. The third paradigm was radical structuralism, which emphasizes the need to overthrow or transcend the limitations placed on existing social and organizational arrangements. This underlines the structure and analysis of economic power relationships. The last paradigm, neohumanism, seeks radical change, emancipation, and potentiality, and stresses the role that different social and organizational forces play in understanding change.

CLASSIFYING CHAPTERS IN THIS VOLUME

The systems development chapters in this volume are grouped into three broad categories: techniques, methodologies, and approaches. This grouping relies on the Iivari, Hirschheim, and Klein (2001) classification scheme because of the fit between the scheme and the chapters presented here. While these authors used a four-level hierarchy that includes the above three levels as well as a paradigm level as an explanatory vehicle, this volume consists of chapters representing only the lower three levels—techniques, methodologies, and approaches.

The book has four sections based on three categories—techniques, methodologies, and approaches—because two chapters specifically discuss agent-oriented methodologies. Thus, there are two sections on methodologies.

Part I. Techniques for Systems Engineering and Requirements Elicitation

Techniques (Iivari, Hirschheim, and Klein, 2001) include the steps necessary for basic operations, and if properly executed, can deliver metrical results. The following chapters in the volume present exemplary research designed to specify the important components of requirements elicitation.

Chapter 2, "Flow-Service-Quality (FSQ) Systems Engineering: A Discipline for Developing Network-Centric Information Systems" proposes a new engineering framework for reasoning about and developing systems of systems: the flow-service-quality (FSQ) framework. This chapter provides rigorous, practical engineering tools and methods to reason about system flows as first-class objects of specification, design, implementation, and operation. System flows are realized as traces of system services, and their quality attributes are treated as dynamic, changing quantities that are measured during system execution.

Chapter 3, "Requirements Elicitation Techniques as Communication Channels: A Framework to Widen the Window of Understanding" investigates and highlights the criticality of communication —one of the foundations on which systems analysis and design rests—in the process of requirements elicitation. A broad reclassification of requirements elicitation techniques according to their communication emphasis is presented. This classification is used to develop a model that can be used to diagnose communication needs in a specific project setting and to provide guidance in the selection of requirements elicitation techniques best suited to that setting. This chapter offers suggestions for the practical application of the theoretic frameworks and identifies avenues for future research.

Part II. Methodology Foundation and Evolution of Systems Analysis and Design

Methodologies (Iivari, Hirschheim, and Klein, 2001) represent the specifics of how to implement the more abstract approaches. The following chapters examine or develop specific methodologies used in systems analysis and design.

Chapter 4, "Iteration in Systems Analysis and Design: Cognitive Processes and Representational Artifacts," examines the concept of iteration and how it has been applied to systems analysis and design. It distinguishes between two domains of iteration: iterations inherent in cognitive processes during design, and iterations over representational artifacts about designs. This chapter reviews how the past research on systems analysis and design has treated iteration within these different domains, what we know about these iterations, and how these iterations have been shown to affect design outcomes. It concludes with an observation that the differences between "iterative" or "agile" development and traditional methodologies lies not in the presence or absence of iteration, but in the locus of visibility and control, and the associated timing and granularity of what is being iterated.

Chapter 5, "A Framework for Identifying the Drivers of Information Systems Development Method Emergence," explores how unique and locally situated information systems development (ISD) methods unfold over time and why they emerge differently. The purpose is to identify the underlying process form and drivers of ISD method emergence. A theoretical framework is developed based on a synthesis of literature about contextualism, structuration theory, and change processes. This chapter reports a comparative analysis of two longitudinal case studies of method emergence in a Multimedia project and a Web project. It suggests that the theoretical framework is relevant for both researchers and practitioners to read a situation before project initiation, during development, and after project completion and to identify and leverage the dynamics inherent in or relevant to a particular situation and change process.

Chapter 6, "Transition to Agile Software Development in a Large-Scale Project: A Systems Analysis and Design Perspective," reports the implementation of Extreme Programming, one of the agile software development methods, in a large-scale software project in the Israeli Air Force. The chapter also describes the transition from a plan-driven process to an agile one as it is perceived from the systems analysis and design perspective. Specifically, during the first eight months of transition, the project specifications and acceptance tests of the agile team are compared with those of a team that continues working according to the previous plan-driven method. This chapter discusses the role of systems analysts during the transition process and different development models with respect to systems analysis and design.

Part III. Agent-Oriented Systems Analysis and Design Methodologies

The two chapters in this section deal specifically with agent-oriented (AO) methodologies. Agent methodologies are gaining popularity, and we are pleased to present two exemplary research chapters in this area in the volume.

Chapter 7, "Agent-Oriented Information Systems Analysis and Design: Why and How," argues that emerging applications such as e-business, peer-to-peer, and ubiquitous computing require new software development paradigms that support open, distributed, and evolving architectures. This chapter presents the Tropos methodology for agent-oriented software development and compares it with other proposals in the same family. The Tropos methodology is currently supported by a range of formal analysis tools, and its application has been explored along a number of fronts: design of Web services and business processes, design of autonomic software, and also design of Web sites and user interfaces.

Chapter 8, "Agent-Oriented Methods and Method Engineering," surveys a number of contemporary agent-oriented methodological approaches and examines their evolution from and relationship to earlier object-oriented methodologies. This chapter proposes an approach that is based on the ideas of situational method engineering (SME). The author argues this as a better approach than attempting to create a "one-size-fits-all" AO methodology. A brief case study is included in the chapter.

Part IV. New Approaches and Architectures for Information Systems Development

Approaches (Iivari, Hirschheim, and Klein, 2001) exist at a relatively abstract level and as such propose the basic principles, goals, and concepts that provide a basis for explaining how systems development is understood and developed. At the same time, however, approaches are concrete enough to allow research to proceed. Conceptual and domain-based research represent the efforts in this section.

Chapter 9, "Application of the Fact-Based Approach to Domain Modeling of Object-Oriented Information Systems," identifies a number of problems associated with the text analysis approach and proposes the use of the fact-based approach (also known as Object Role Modeling) as an alternative technique. This chapter shows how the fact-based approach can be used effectively, in conjunction with the use case approach, in the construction of domain models for object-oriented information systems. In particular, this chapter demonstrates (a) how the order of data entry dependency can be used in identifying and organizing the fact types; (b) how the conceptual schema (that is, the fact-type model) can be validated in several simple but effective ways; and (c) how to convert the conceptual schema into a domain class model.

Chapter 10, "Systematic Derivation and Evaluation of Domain-Specific, Implementation-Independent Software Architectures," presents a systematic process and a supporting tool, Reference Architecture Representation Environment, for deriving and evaluating a high-level software architecture, the Domain Reference Architecture (DRA). The proposed architecture reflects quality goals prioritized by the architect, including reusability, maintainability, performance, integratability, reliability, and comprehensibility. The DRA is an implementation-independent architecture composed of Domain Reference Architecture Classes, each of which specifies some portion of domain data and functionality.

Chapter 11, "OO-Method: A Conceptual Schema-Centric Development Approach," examines the foundation of Model-Driven Architecture (MDA) and discusses its weak points. It introduces an approach based on the formal specification language OASIS that sets the foundation for delivering on the promises of MDA. The chapter also presents a strategy to define and eventually automate the transformation of conceptual models into software systems. In addition, this chapter introduces OLIVANOVA Model Execution as an implementation of the OO-Method.

CONCLUSIONS AND POST HOC ANALYSIS

Reviewing and selecting chapters to include in the volume were difficult tasks for the three volume editors. The job entailed much more perspiration than inspiration. There is much more frustration than fun in the process. Nevertheless, now that the volume is ready, the editors emphasize that editing the volume was a challenging, but at the same time, rewarding experience. The chapters represent state-of-the-art research in the field and serve to inform readers of potential and future areas of research. Further, many of the contributing authors are internationally well-known researchers in the area.

REFERENCES

Armstrong, D., and Hardgrave, B. 2007. Understanding mindshift learning: the transition to object-oriented development. *MIS Quarterly,* 31, 3, 453–474.

Avison, D., and Fitzgerald, G. 2003. Where now for development methodologies? *Communications of the ACM,* 46, 1, 78–82.

———. 2006. *Information Systems Development: Methodologies, Techniques and Tools,* 4th ed. Maidenhead, UK: McGraw-Hill.

Burrell, G., and Morgan, G. 1979. *Sociological Paradigms and Organizational Analysis.* London: Heineman.

Erickson, J., and Siau, K. 2008. Web services, service oriented computing, and service oriented architecture: separating hype from reality. *Journal of Database Management,* 19, 3, 42–54.

Erickson, J.; Lyytinen, K.; and Siau, K. 2005. Agile modeling, agile software development, and extreme programming: the state of research. *Journal of Database Management,* 16, 4, 88–100.

Hardgrave, B.; Davis, F.; and Riemenschneider, C. 2003. Investigating determinants of software developers' intentions to follow methodologies. *Journal of Management Information Systems,* 20, 1, 123–151.

Hirschheim, R., and Klein, H. 1989. Four paradigms of information systems development. *Communications of the ACM,* 32, 10, 1199–1216.

Hirschheim, R.A.; Klein, H.K.; and Lyytinen, K. 1995. *Information Systems Development and Data Modeling: Conceptual and Philosophical Foundations.* Cambridge: Cambridge University Press.

Iivari, J.; Hirschheim, R.; and Klein, H.A. 2001. Dynamic framework for classifying information systems development methodologies and approaches. *Journal of Management Information Systems,* 17, 3, 179–218.

Rubinstein, D. 2007. Standish Group Report: There's less development chaos today. *SD Times,* March 1. Available at www.sdtimes.com/content/article.aspx?ArticleID=30247 (accessed on March 8, 2008).

Schmidt, R.; Lyytinen, K.; Keil, M.; and Cule, P. 2001. Identifying software project risks: an International Delphi study. *Journal of Management Information Systems,* 17, 4, 5–36.

Siau, K., and Tan, X. 2005a. Improving the quality of conceptual modeling using cognitive mapping techniques. *Data and Knowledge Engineering,* 55, 3, 343–365.

———. 2005b. Technical communication in information systems development: the use of cognitive mapping. *IEEE Transactions on Professional Communications,* 48, 3, 269–284.

Siau, K.; Wand, Y.; and Benbasat, I. 1997. The relative importance of structural constraints and surface semantics in information modeling. *Information Systems,* 22, 2/3, 155–170.

Smith, H.J.; Keil, M.; and Depledge, G. 2001. Keeping mum as the project goes under: toward an explanatory model. *Journal of Management Information Systems,* 18, 2, 189–227.

Wei, C.; Chiang, R.; and Wu, C. 2006. Accommodating individual preferences in the categorization of documents: a personalized clustering approach. *Journal of Management Information Systems,* 23, 2, 173–201.

PART I

TECHNIQUES FOR SYSTEMS ENGINEERING AND REQUIREMENTS ELICITATION

CHAPTER 2

FLOW-SERVICE-QUALITY (FSQ) SYSTEMS ENGINEERING

A Discipline for Developing Network-Centric Information Systems

ALAN HEVNER, RICHARD LINGER, MARK PLESZKOCH,
STACY PROWELL, AND GWENDOLYN WALTON

Abstract: Modern enterprises are irreversibly dependent on large-scale information systems built from components whose function and quality attributes are not necessarily known a priori. The ad hoc and network-centric nature of these systems means that a complete static analysis of such systems is difficult or impossible. These systems grow and interconnect with other systems in ways that exceed current engineering techniques for intellectual control. We propose a new engineering framework for reasoning about and developing such systems of systems: the Flow-Service-Quality (FSQ) framework. Our aim is to provide rigorous, practical engineering tools and methods to reason about system flows as first-class objects of specification, design, implementation, and operation. System flows are realized as traces of system services, and their quality attributes are treated as dynamic, changing quantities that are measured during system execution.

Keywords: Systems Engineering, System Integration, Flows, Services, Qualities, Information Systems, Systems of Systems, System Analysis and Design, System Specification

MOTIVATION

Much of the complexity of modern information systems arises not from their size (e.g., lines of code, function points, objects), but from their adaptive, component-based, and network-centric natures. Such systems may exhibit indeterminate boundaries, as components and services come and go and other systems connect and disconnect during execution. For this reason, the development of large-scale, modern information systems is largely a matter of systems-of-systems integration.

Assembling diverse commercial-off-the-shelf (COTS) components and network services to accomplish a particular mission has become fundamental to information systems engineering. These systems exhibit extensive asynchronous behaviors as a virtually unknowable interleaving of communications among system components. Components may be homogeneous, as with database and server pooling, or heterogeneous, as with Web browsers and sensor networks. To accomplish a particular mission, the system may use one collection of components. Later, to accomplish the *same* mission, the system may use a *different* collection of components. Because the boundaries of the system can change, perhaps as mobile devices move in and out of range, the system's boundary, and thus its capabilities, can change over time.

The fundamental challenge is to identify stable, dependable anchors for system specification, analysis, design, and implementation on which we can build a unified engineering discipline for large-scale network system development. The Flow-Service-Quality (FSQ) framework provides these anchors (Hevner et al., 2002; Linger et al., 2002). The FSQ approach does not solve all these problems; rather it provides a rigorous framework with which to understand and reason about such systems. In the remainder of this chapter we introduce the FSQ approach and its underlying framework and semantic model as a discipline for engineering complex, network-centric systems. A central concept in this discussion is the treatment of mission task flows of system service uses as first-class artifacts for specification and design under intellectual control, despite the structural and functional uncertainties that characterize large-scale network systems. Other methods that focus on component and architecture specification and design often lose sight of the mission-driven dynamic behavior that network systems are required to provide. FSQ engineering focuses on dynamic flow behavior and provides a stable framework within which these other methods can be employed to best advantage.

SERVICES, FLOWS, AND QUALITIES

Information systems can be viewed as networks of asynchronously communicating components, each of which provides some set of system services. These services are combined in various patterns to satisfy business requirements, which are structured into mission-centric user tasks called flows. The *flow structures* of FSQ provide the bridge between mission requirements and the services provided by various system components. Qualities of flow structures are determined from the qualities of the services invoked and the engineering of the flows on the network systems.

Services

A *service* is the basic abstraction in the FSQ framework. One or more components may provide a service in a variety of ways. The service may even be accomplished by invoking another large, networked system. For our purposes a service is simply a function provided by a system component or set of components.

For example, user authentication may be viewed as a service. Authentication of users may be done in a variety of ways, against different sources, using multiple components. Figure 2.1 shows two examples of authentication services. On the left is a simple authentication service that maintains an internal database of encrypted passwords for comparison. On the right is a more complex authentication service that itself depends on other services. For example, if biometrics is available, it may be preferred. Because biometrics may not be available in every circumstance, other authentication mechanisms are also provided, such as a Lightweight Directory Access Protocol (LDAP) server and even simple password hashing. This component also provides a database of access rules that can provide user rights based on both the user to be authenticated and the form of authentication used.

A given service may participate in multiple asynchronous requests or even in multiple concurrently operating systems. The response of a service to a request may depend not only on the request but also on the complete history of prior requests. We treat services as black boxes (Prowell et al., 1999) whose response to any given request can depend not only on the request but also on the history of use of the service. This history of prior requests is captured as state information internal

Figure 2.1 **Authentication Services**

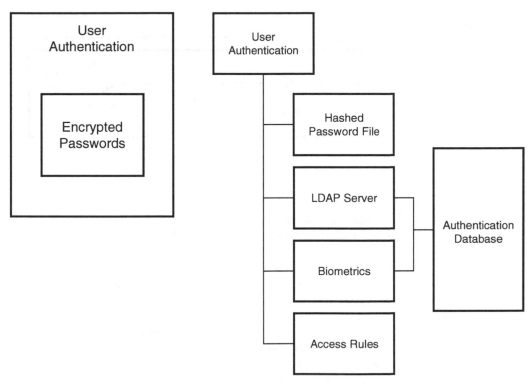

to the service. The full history of use and the specific internal state of the service are seldom available from the point of view of a given system or user task. Because of this fact, it is necessary to consider all possible responses resulting from all possible service states. Relational specifications must be used to define the complete set of potential responses for any given request (Janicki and Sekerinski, 2001), and effective abstractions may be used to manage the complexity of any such specification (Prowell and Poore, 2003).

Flow Structures

Accomplishing a mission-centric user task may require the invocation of several services, and these service invocations may be sequenced in a variety of ways. For example, a task might begin by invoking a service to authenticate a user, and proceed only if the user is properly authenticated. Exactly how a task is accomplished may change from one attempt to the next. If a required service X is unavailable, other service invocations may still run while the system waits for service X to become available.

While the specific sequence of service invocations to accomplish a task may remain unknown until the task is actually performed, we can establish constraints on the allowable sequences. For example, we may always require successful user authentication before other services are invoked.

The specifics of which sequence of service invocations is to be performed at any given time and system environment are abstracted away by the concept of a flow structure. A *flow* is a mission-centric user task that can be accomplished by sequencing service invocations in

Figure 2.2   **A System-of-Systems User Flow**

Gas purchase flow:

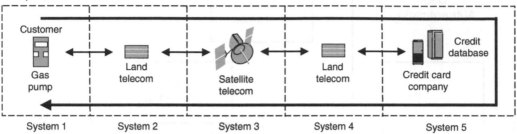

certain ways. The specific sequence of service invocations used at runtime is the flow *instance*. Flow *structures* constrain the potential sequencing of services, but typically do not determine a particular sequence.

We can express an overall information system design as a set of flow structures, where each flow represents some end-to-end user capability along with its quality requirements. Each flow is then further expressed as a sequence of service invocations in some order. For example, in Figure 2.2 we see a user flow for a gasoline purchase transaction that invokes computation and communication services of many different components through the roundtrip trace from a gas pump via a satellite communication system to a customer database and back again. This flow provides a framework for discussing the function and quality requirements of all participating systems, and provides insights into system dependencies and design risks.

Qualities

System requirements impose demands on reliability, performance, availability, responsiveness, security, survivability, and many other quality attributes. Because of the dynamic nature of network-centric systems, an a priori static estimate of these qualities may not be sufficient. These quality attributes must be defined as functions whose values can be measured in near-real-time in order to make decisions about the mapping of flows onto the available services. In FSQ engineering we require that such attributes be characterized in such a way that they can be computed and used in decision making as dynamic characteristics of system operation. We wish to define these characteristics as functions to be computed rather than simply as capabilities to be achieved. Such a function is a *computational quality attribute* (CQA). Each CQA is a mathematical function mapping current usage information, status of required services, and network environmental information to an attribute value that represents the current relevant measure of quality. This approach supports the description of any set of quality attributes and any models for describing each attribute, provided each model yields a representative numerical value for the quality attribute.

As an example, the prior user flow for a gas transaction in Figure 2.2 may implement survivability as a CQA. The status of relevant system services such as transmission site bandwidth and satellite position, along with any detected intrusion activities, would be used to produce a completely specified flow containing decision logic based on outcomes (desired or undesired) of service invocations in order to maintain survivability for critical flows where possible (Mead et al., 2000).

A SEMANTIC MODEL FOR FSQ

In large-scale network systems, flows can engage in extensive traversals of network nodes and communication links, where the behaviors of invoked services cannot always be known and predicted. In this environment, a variety of uncertainty factors must be managed, including:

1. Unpredictable function—a service may be provided by commercial off-the-shelf (COTS) vendors or external service providers (ESP) without complete behavior definitions. Thus, components of unpredictable function and reliability may not perform expected operations every time or anytime it is invoked.
2. Compromised function—a service may have been compromised or disrupted by an intrusion or physical attack and may not be able to perform its function correctly or at all.
3. High-risk function—a service may not be able to provide adequate levels of quality attributes as required by a flow.
4. Modified function—a service may be modified or replaced as part of routine maintenance, error correction, or system upgrade, with intentional or inadvertent modification of its function.
5. Asynchronous function—a service may be used simultaneously and asynchronously by other flows, and thus produce results dependent on unpredictable history of use, both legitimate and illegitimate.

These factors are pervasive behavioral realities of network-centric systems (Schneider, 1999). Dealing with them is an enterprise risk management problem with potentially serious consequences. It is vital to take appropriate actions to continue system operations in the environments they create. FSQ engineering is intended to provide a systematic means for defining information system flows, services, and quality attributes despite these persistent uncertainties.

The mathematical semantics of the FSQ framework are defined to support development and verification of flows for such uncertain environments as a standard engineering practice. To allow for unpredictable behavior of services, flow semantics require specification of only the processing that a flow itself performs and not the processing of the services it invokes. Flow specification requires definition of appropriate actions by a flow for all possible responses of key services, both desired and undesired. Thus, if the behavior of an invoked service changes for any reason, the specification and verification of the invoking flow need not change. This approach accommodates the realities of today's network systems and offers important advantages. It requires for mission survivability that the uncertainty factors be dealt with explicitly in specification, design, and dynamic execution, thereby addressing important aspects of enterprise risk management. It permits flows and reasoning about them to be localized yet complete. And it permits flow structures to be defined by simple deterministic structures despite the underlying asynchronous behavior of their constituent services. These deterministic structures can be refined, abstracted, and verified using straightforward compositional methods for human understanding and intellectual control.

It turns out that these objectives require extension of the traditional functional semantics model. The FSQ semantic model is based on the well-known concept of services as rules for mathematical functions (or relations if flows include concurrent operations), that is, mappings from domains (inputs, stimuli) to ranges (outputs, responses) (Hoffman and Weiss, 2001; Linger, Mills, and Witt, 1979; Mills, Linger, and Hevner, 1986; Prowell et al., 1999). The key extension required to deal systematically with uncertainty is to make the histories of service invocations themselves part of the specified behavior of flows. Mathematically, this is achieved by including the invocation

Figure 2.3   **Flow–Service Semantics**

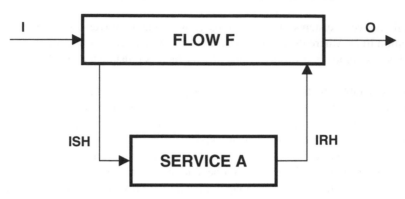

stimulus history (ISH) of every service in the range of the function that represents the specification of a flow. In addition, because subsequent flow processing can depend on the responses from these invocations, the invocation response history (IRH) must be part of the domain of the mathematical function that represents the specification of a flow. The diagram of Figure 2.3 illustrates these semantics for a flow F invoking a service A.

I is the set of possible inputs to flow F, and O is the set of possible outputs from flow F. Thus, the semantics of F can be given by a mathematical function f with domain I x IRH and range O x ISH. It is this counterintuitive inclusion of service responses in the domain of F and service stimuli in the range of F that allows flows to manage uncertainty. In particular, IRH represents the range of possible service responses and thus embodies the uncertainty issues that must be recognized in flow behaviors. *Flows must assess and act upon all possible responses, desired and undesired, that service invocations can produce.* Of course, no semantics can force such informed design, they can only illuminate the desirability of doing so and provide means for it to be accomplished.

In this semantic model, the specification of flow F is not required to account for the behaviors that result due to invocation of service A. Rather, it simply defines the invocation of service A with certain parameters, and how the response from that invocation affects subsequent processing of F. This means, for example, that any lower-level services invoked by service A need not be part of the ISH and IRH of flow F. If this were not the case, the specification of F would change if service A was modified, for example, to invoke different lower-level services. This approach differs from traditional functional semantics, where the specification of F would be required to include the full effects of all lower-level service invocations by service A as a part of its functional specification.

This innovative approach to specification is essential to maintain intellectual control over flow specification and design. As noted, deterministic flows that invoke nondeterministic, asynchronous services can be modeled by deterministic mathematical functions, making human reasoning and analysis much simpler. Alternately, if the behavior of flows were nondeterministic, then the flows themselves would become far more complicated, and their semantics would need to be expressed as a mathematical relation from domain I x IRH to range O x ISH. This complex situation is avoided by our FSQ semantic model.

The flow-service semantic model described above is particularly suited to the common situation where service A already exists on a network, or is provided by COTS or ESP components with complex and possibly unknown functions. In cases where service A is new and must be designed as part of the implementation of flow F, these flow semantics can be combined with more traditional design and verification methods (e.g., Mills, Linger, and Hevner, 1986) to support reasoning about the combined behaviors of the system consisting of F and A together. In this way, the desired behavior of F and A can be used to guide the construction of A.

FSQ Systems Engineering

Figure 2.4 shows the use of flows, services, and qualities for both developing new systems and for understanding the behaviors of existing systems. Across the top we see the process of system design using flows. On the left, a set of flows defines the functionality and quality attributes that a network and its services must provide to support user requirements. These flows can be defined as structured sequences of service invocations. Moving right, the flows are refined in terms of services and their quality attributes. These services may be preexisting services on the network or may be newly developed if no existing service provides the proper functionality and quality. For example, in the figure, two services on the left are further refined in the middle, in each case into sequences of two lower level services that carry out the required operations. In addition, the initial conception of a flow may be modified to conform to the available architecture. Finally, the flows are mapped onto the network at the right-hand side of Figure 2.4.

Existing systems may be understood in the FSQ framework by abstracting from the network and service details to obtain the critical flows, as shown across the bottom of Figure 2.4. The resulting flows can become the basis for further system reengineering work or can be analyzed for their survivability, reliability, or other critical quality aspects.

DYNAMIC FLOW MANAGEMENT ARCHITECTURE

The right-hand side of Figure 2.4 shows the network. Some parts of the network may arise from the flows, but much of the network may be preexisting and independent of the original user flow set. The precise topology of the network and the quality attributes of the links and nodes are all time dependent. Some network links may become saturated with traffic, some service providers may become unreliable or fail altogether, and mobile devices may move in and out of range.

In such a system, there must be a dynamic system control to continually monitor the real-time availability and quality of system services. The precise implementation of a flow in terms of sequencing of particular flows and services is a dynamic task. An FSQ *manager*, either as a centralized component or decentralized across the network, must manage these dynamic aspects and provide flow instantiation and management to assure that mission goals are met. This dynamic management to provide "self-healing" and to assure reliability (e.g., connectivity and availability) is already a common idea in networking; what we propose here is to extend these ideas to the entire system (hardware and software) to ensure survivability and robustness.

A dynamic *flow management architecture* (FMA) must be defined to provide such an FSQ manager. The FSQ manager accepts a demand from outside the system, perhaps from a user or from another system. This demand initiates a flow request, which may be queued based on priority. The FSQ manager evaluates the queued flow requests in terms of available services, other active flows, and computational quality attributes. Each flow request is then *instantiated* as a sequence of service invocations. The details of the instance execution are not static; services may be executed more than once, and the evolution of the flow instance may depend on the responses from various services. If the instance is unable to proceed because a given service becomes unavailable during the instance's execution, the FSQ manager may suspend the flow until the service is available, or it may try to find a new mapping to comparable services to allow the instance to complete.

This dynamic management of flow instances should not be understood to alleviate the need

18

Figure 2.4   **Systems Engineering with FSQ**

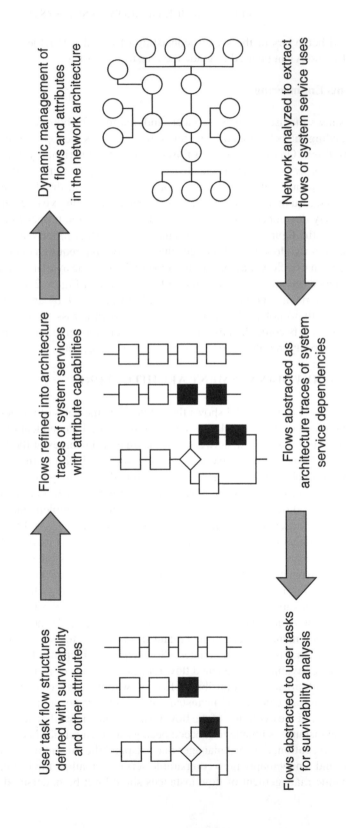

Development of New Systems
(Refinement of Flows)

Dynamic management of
flows and attributes
in the network architecture

Network analyzed to extract
flows of system service uses

Flows refined into architecture
traces of system services
with attribute capabilities

Flows abstracted as
architecture traces of system
service dependencies

Analysis of Existing Systems
(Abstraction of Flows)

User task flow structures
defined with survivability
and other attributes

Flows abstracted to user tasks
for survivability analysis

for system design. In fact, in order for the FSQ manager to correctly map each flow request to an appropriate flow instance that meets all requirements, each flow must be characterized in terms of services, their responses, and the appropriate next actions. This requires the definition of a flow structure language in which flows can be specified. Such a specification includes the necessary services, an ordering of these services, and their quality attributes. The services should be described at the highest level of abstraction possible and treated as "black boxes" in order to allow the maximum flexibility to implement the flow. These services may themselves be refined recursively into flows and lower-level services as necessary. By treating services as black boxes and writing flow specifications in terms of service responses, however obtained, such a system achieves referential transparency and provides an appropriate level of abstraction for managing systems-of-systems development and integration.

MANAGING COMPUTING QUALITY ATTRIBUTES

A CQA's value is another responsibility for the FSQ manager. Local values for attributes must be combined to determine the end-to-end values for each flow. Alternately, a flow may impose particular attribute requirements on a service. The process of measuring, predicting, or estimating quality attribute values and then generating a modified set of flows that takes the attributes into account can adversely affect system performance. However, in a large networked system there is no other way to assure that each flow meets its quality requirements. Future research is needed to find better ways to monitor the state of quality attributes and to dynamically compute the system qualities available for the execution of flow instances.

When a flow demand is presented to the FSQ manager, the manager must assemble a collection of candidate flow instances and evaluate the CQA values for each instance. Flows that satisfy the required CQA values are selected, and one is chosen from among them, perhaps based on user-specified priorities. Note that since the flow will unfold over time it is necessary that the FSQ manager *predict* the relevant CQA values at the time each given service will execute. Such a prediction may be simple (assume no change from current value) or may employ various estimation techniques (assume some time distribution and extrapolate). The only essential aspect is that the CQA values are used to choose an appropriate flow instance from among the possibilities.

CONCLUSION AND RESEARCH DIRECTIONS

FSQ systems engineering recognizes flows, services, and computational quality attributes as first-class concepts for understanding, developing, operating, and maintaining large-scale, network-centric information systems. These concepts provide a unifying framework around which systems development methods, practices, and tools can be developed. The concept of dynamically mapping flows to available services relying on real-time computational quality attributes provides the ability to manage dynamic systems whose available services and network properties cannot be known a priori.

Theoretical foundations developed in this research can prescribe engineering practices that will improve system management, acquisition, analysis, development, operation, and evolution. The following observations summarize our research and development vision.

- FSQ supports complexity reduction and survivability improvement in development and operation of large-scale network systems composed of any mix of newly developed and COTS/ESP components.

- FSQ provides systematic, scale-free semantic structures for requirements, specification, design, verification, implementation, and maintenance.
- FSQ supports seamless decomposition from user flows, services, and quality attribute requirements to flow structures, services, and quality attribute implementations, with intrinsic traceability.
- User flows of services and quality attributes permit system development in terms of user views of services, as opposed to strictly functional decomposition or object-based composition.
- Flow structures are deterministic for human understanding and analysis, despite the uncertainties of complex, network-centric behaviors, thus enabling compositional methods of refinement, abstraction, and verification.
- Flow structures reflect the realities of network-centric systems in dealing with the uncertainty factors, to support enterprise risk management and system survivability.
- Flow structures support the definition of attack and intrusion flows for assessing system vulnerabilities and compromises, as a basis for security and survivability improvements.
- Computational quality attributes reflect the realities of network-centric systems, in assessing and reconciling quality requirements and capabilities as an intrinsically dynamic process.
- Computational quality attributes provide a scale-free, computational use-centric (rather than system-centric) view of quality.
- Flow management architectures provide systematic and uniform methods for managing user flow instantiation and quality attribute satisfaction in execution.
- Foundations of flow structures can stimulate research on representation and analysis of flows at the requirements level within enterprises, and at the implementation level within system architectures.
- Foundations of computational quality attributes can stimulate research in modeling and dynamic evaluation of important quality attributes and metrics.

We are aggressively pursuing research directions to build the foundation theories, engineering processes, and automated tools to support the development of complex, network-centric systems with FSQ concepts.

REFERENCES

Hevner, A.; Linger, R.; Sobel, A.; and Walton, G. 2002. The flow-service-quality framework: unified engineering for large-scale, adaptive systems. Paper presented at the *Thirty-fifth Hawaii International Conference on System Sciences (HICSS'35)*, Kona, Hawaii, January 7–10.

Hoffman, D., and Weiss, D. 2001. *Software Fundamentals: Collected Papers by David L. Parnas.* Upper Saddle River, NJ: Addison-Wesley.

Janicki, R., and Sekerinski, E. 2001. Foundations of the trace assertion method of module interface specification. *IEEE Transactions on Software Engineering,* 27, 7, 577–598.

Linger, R.C.; Mills, H.; and Witt, B. 1979. *Structured Programming: Theory and Practice.* Reading, MA: Addison-Wesley.

Linger, R.; Pleszkoch, M.; Walton, G.; and Hevner. A. 2002. *Flow-service-quality engineering: foundations for network system analysis and development.* CMU/SEI-2002-TN-019, June.

Mead, N.; Ellison, R.; Linger, R.; Longstaff, T.; and McHugh, J. 2000. *Survivable network analysis method.* CMU/SEI-2000-TR-013, September.

Mills, H.; Linger, R.; and Hevner. A. 1986. *Principles of Information System Analysis and Design.* San Diego, CA: Academic Press.

Prowell, S., and Poore, J. 2003. Foundations of sequence-based specification. *IEEE Transactions on Software Engineering,* 29, 5, 417–429.

Prowell, S.; Trammell, C.; Linger, R.; and Poore, J. 1999. *Cleanroom Software Engineering: Technology and Process.* Reading, MA: Addison-Wesley.

Schneider, F. (ed). 1999. *Trust in Cyberspace.* Washington, DC: National Academies Press.

CHAPTER 3

REQUIREMENTS ELICITATION TECHNIQUES AS COMMUNICATION CHANNELS

A Framework to Widen the Window of Understanding

ROBERT M. FULLER AND CHRISTOPHER J. DAVIS

Abstract: *This chapter highlights the criticality of communication in requirements elicitation. Using the concept of channel expansion, a broad reclassification of requirements elicitation techniques according to their communication emphasis is presented. This classification is used to develop a model that can be used to diagnose the communication needs in a specific project setting and to provide guidance in the selection of requirements elicitation techniques best suited to that setting. The chapter offers suggestions for the practical application of the theoretic frameworks and identifies fruitful avenues for future research.*

Keywords: *Elicitation, Communication, Intersubjectivity, Channel Expansion Theory*

INTRODUCTION

Requirements elicitation remains one of the most important and challenging steps in systems analysis and design. Difficulties in accurately identifying and capturing system requirements continue to be encountered and have been identified as a major factor in the failure of 90 percent of large software projects (Hayes, 2004; Standish Group, 1994). In this chapter, we explore communication—one of the foundations on which systems analysis and design rests—in the process of requirements elicitation. The focus on this phase of the analysis and design process is prompted by the frequency and persistence of concerns about the adequacy of the tools and techniques used and the important role requirements elicitation plays as a foundation for success in subsequent design phases (Marakas and Elam, 1998; Roberts et al., 2005).

For requirements elicitation, a primary indicator of success is that requirements meet end-user needs. However, this outcome has proved difficult to achieve because users frequently experience difficulty in fully articulating their needs—they either cannot explain them in a manner that is readily intelligible by the analyst, or they have not been directly addressed by the analysts' inquiries (Moores, Change, and Smith, 2004; Siau, 2004).

This dialogue between the analyst and the user during requirements elicitation is critical to the success of information technology (IT) projects. As "gatherers" of requirements, systems analysts assume that users know their business. However, ineffective communication during requirements elicitation has persistently been blamed for information systems that disappoint end users, resulting in unused, poorly used, or misused systems. As the range of "businesses" that information systems support becomes wider and more specialized, these communication challenges increase.

Prior research has identified the need for effective collaboration between the analysis and design and user communities (Berry and Lawrence, 1998; Browne and Ramesh, 2002; Davis, 1982; Kim and Peterson, 2001). Communication between users and analysts is accomplished using a range of methodologies, tools, and techniques. In this chapter, we consider the efficacy of user–analyst communication at the elicitation tool/technique level. This work was prompted by the persistence of communication difficulties in requirements elicitation despite both the growing maturity of systems analysis as a professional field and the wide range of communication tools and techniques available.

Recent research shows that communication persists as a principal locus of the issues and concerns in requirements elicitation (Roberts et al., 2005; Smith, Keil, and Depledge, 2001). Clearly, as the range of information systems applications and development methodologies, tools, and techniques expands, effective communication becomes an increasingly critical imperative for effective requirements elicitation.

Over the past thirty years, research and development efforts have explored the potential of a range of techniques to facilitate user–analyst communication. A review of this work identifies three broad communication emphases, from providing methods to help the analyst ask questions to providing methods to help users frame their responses to the analyst. Although they strive for the common goal of optimizing the identification, description, and capture of user requirements, there are substantial variations in the purpose of the communication they facilitate.

A review of the requirements engineering literature highlights the introduction of elicitation techniques such as interviews, brainstorming sessions, scenario analysis, use case modeling, contextual inquiry, and even ethnography (Alter, 2004). These more qualitative, interpretive techniques are drawn from the social sciences. They contrast with the more traditional engineering origins of elicitation techniques and represent attempts to provide analysts with deeper insight into, and understanding of, the user's world (Somerville and Ransom, 2005). However, the inherent differences between these elicitation techniques as a means of communication between users and analysts have remained largely unexplored. This has given rise to communication technique (or "channel") compatibility issues: misinterpretations, misconceptions, and mistakes in requirements elicitation have arisen from their injudicious use (Boehm and Huang, 2003).

Despite attempts to complement traditional engineering techniques (e.g., flow charting, note boards, etc.), analysts face a continuing dilemma. They need robust and reliable inquiry techniques, but ones that do not constrain their ability to understand the end user's world or limit the opportunities for innovation and invention. Likewise, these techniques need to be as effective, efficient, and appropriate as possible given the business context and the understanding required.

Effective requirements elicitation thus remains a central and critical activity in the systems analysis and design process: this chapter explores the nature of the communication challenges that confront analysts and users during requirements elicitation. The chapter begins by providing a review and classification of requirements elicitation techniques that highlight their differing communication emphases. The classification is used to develop a conceptual model of the user–analyst communication process that identifies the communication characteristics of a range of task (requirements elicitation) contexts. We explain how the model can be used to identify communication issues that give rise to ambiguity and misunderstanding during requirements elicitation. Following discussion of the range and nature of these issues, we map a range of requirements elicitation techniques into the framework. The main body of the chapter provides analysis of the "fit" between various requirement elicitation techniques and the communication demands of the contexts in which they might be applied.

The chapter concludes by showing how the framework can be used to provide guidance on the selection of requirements elicitation techniques by practitioners. It also identifies a number of communications "gaps" and conflicting agendas—areas where further research might enhance the tools and techniques used for requirements elicitation.

COMMUNICATION

Communication has been defined as "a process in which participants create and share information with one another in order to reach a mutual understanding" (Rogers, 1986, p. 199). Creating and sharing information is inherently a social exchange process, in which developing understanding about information received from others requires both information transfer and processing. Developing a mutual understanding requires that individuals pass information about how they understand and interpret the world around them, as well as processing to make sense of the passed information itself. Thus an important outcome of successful communication is the development of mutual understanding about the information and the meaning that each participant attaches to it (Daft and Lengel, 1986; Miranda and Saunders, 2003; Rogers, 1986; Te'eni, 2001).

Communication channels facilitate or enable individuals to communicate with others to develop mutual understandings (Rice et al., 1990). These channels include many of the media that are used to communicate today, such as telephone systems and voice mail, as well as other computer-supported media, such as videoconferencing, bulletin boards, instant messaging, and e-mail. However, in a more general sense, a communication channel could be any device or technique that facilitates, guides, or otherwise enables individuals to communicate with one another. While much of the recent research into communication has focused on newer media such as e-mail and videoconferencing, other more commonplace communication methods, such as reports, documentation, interview scripts, and agendas are also communication channels that in some way impact the nature of how individuals communicate.

Considering the interaction between user and analyst, the methods, tools, and techniques employed by the analyst serve as channels that simultaneously guide, constrain, and facilitate communication as the analyst attempts to understand the requirements of the business situation at hand. In common with other communication channels, the techniques employed by the analyst may be more or less effective dependent on the context and manner in which they are used (Daft and Lengel, 1986; Dennis and Valacich, 1999; Dennis, Wixom, and Vandenberg, 2001).

A significant amount of research has examined how communication channels can impact the communication performance (development of shared understanding) between two individuals. In general, this stream of research has focused on the prediction of performance from using certain communication channels for certain types of communication-oriented tasks. The findings from this research, while often ambiguous, do acknowledge that characteristics of the communication task, certain salient characteristics of the channel, and characteristics of the individuals communicating can influence performance of a particular medium for a task (Dennis and Kinney, 1998; Mennecke, Valacich, and Wheeler, 2000; Rice and Shook, 1990). Furthermore, to the degree that individuals have greater or lesser levels of familiarity with the communication task or topic, the individuals involved in the communication, and the channel that supports or guides the communication, differential results in communication performance can arise (Carlson and Zmud, 1999; Dennis and Valacich, 1999; McGrath, 1991).

To understand how the use of communication channels can support the development of shared understanding between individuals, we use the theoretical lens of channel expansion theory— CET—(Carlson and Zmud, 1999). CET identifies certain experiences as important in shaping how an individual may perceive (and use) a certain communication channel as being rich enough to facilitate the communications necessary for efficient development of shared understanding. Specifically, it proposes that an individual's experiences with the communications channel (e.g., communications method or technique), message topic, organization context, and communication partner can influence the perception and use of the communication channel. CET proposes that as levels of experience across these four knowledge bases increase, individuals will be able to more efficiently send (ask) and receive (interpret) messages with leaner communication channels, and still be able to develop understanding. Conversely, it suggests that if an individual has less experience with the message topic, the organizational context, or the communication partner, they will require a richer communication channel to enable efficient communications to develop understanding.

Here, we apply channel expansion theory to suggest that individuals (e.g., analysts) with lesser degrees of experience across three of the knowledge bases central to requirements elicitation— message topic, organization context, and communication partner—would benefit from the use of a richer elicitation technique or "channel"[1] to efficiently send and receive messages and develop understanding more than would individuals with greater experiences in these knowledge bases. In the context of requirements elicitation, this accords with previous research findings suggesting that the quality of the requirements elicitation process varies according to the analysts' level of experience with the specific domain (the message topic) that the information systems is attempting to address, the organizational context in which the information system will be implemented, and the communication partner with whom they are interacting. CET leads us to propose that, based on these levels of experience, elicitation techniques will vary in their effective support of user–analyst dialogue. Furthermore, we propose that this variation also directly affects both users' and analysts' capacity to learn from their experience of systems analysis and design activities, processes, tools, and techniques. In turn, crucially, this affects the degree to which they are able to expand their other three knowledge bases (topic, context, and partner).

For requirements elicitation, we focus specifically on the empirical significance of two of these knowledge bases, experience with the topic and experience with the organizational context in which the topic exists. These two components of CET are at the core of the communication activities performed between user and analyst during requirements elicitation, since they represent the analyst attempting to better understand the requirements for an information system—the topic domain—within the context of use—the organizational environment. Since the analyst is interested in understanding the requirements for an application in a specific context, these two knowledge bases are fundamental to the process of analysis and design: they strongly influence the characteristics of the elicitation techniques best suited to elicit requirements.

From a communication perspective, elicitation techniques fall into three broad categories, each characterized by differences in the organizational context and application domain as noted in Table 3.1, on page 26.

Verification (Nonrefutation) Focus

Certain elicitation techniques employed by analysts during requirements elicitation are geared toward the verification of requirements as understood by the analyst. These techniques are driven by the analyst in terms of the questions asked. Typically, the emphasis is on nonrefutation. The range of responses that can be provided by the user is constrained so as to provide auditable "proof" of the dialogue. While they are less expensive and easier for distribution, they are limited in the richness of the responses that could be received from the user, and provide little control over the potential (mis)interpretation of questions. The primary assumptions of these types of elicitation techniques are that the analyst knows the right questions to ask, that a relatively finite set of questions can develop an understanding of the business scenario, and that the user is able to understand and appropriately respond to the questions. These elicitation techniques exploit the analysts' high level of experience with an organizational context or application domain, and focus on the provision of effective methods to verify these experiences. Techniques such as questionnaires and structured interviews exemplify this class of elicitation techniques.

Collaboration Focus

Other elicitation techniques are less structured, controlled, and driven by the analyst, and place greater emphasis on collaborative—rather than confirmatory—communication between user and analyst. We categorize these techniques as collaborative since they tend to be less formal and allow users some latitude to negotiate the focus or agenda of the analysis within the structural constraints of the technique. Unlike verification techniques, these techniques allow the user to provide requirements in various formats and even allow the user some degree of control over the elicitation process. As a result, the format of the requirements elicited often requires additional work on the part of the analyst to condense and understand. They also tend to require a more iterative process between user and analyst to make sure that understanding of the requirements has occurred. These techniques generally assume some level of knowledge by the analyst of the organizational context and/or application domain, but more information is necessary to enhance understanding. Therefore, collaborative techniques allow the analyst to retain some control over the elicitation process to develop understanding in those areas that are less understood, while allowing for some verification where prior knowledge does exist. Techniques such as semistructured interviews, scenario analysis, and use cases are exemplars.

Generation Focus

Our final category encompasses those techniques that are much more free-form in nature and allow for maximum variation in user responses with potentially significant loss of control over the interaction from the perspective of the analyst. These types of techniques we identify as exploratory, as they tend to be free of bias and overall control from the part of the analyst, and there tends to be less structure involved in the interaction. The focus is on learning as much as possible about potential requirements, and the direction of the interaction is not driven by the analyst. Given the lack of experience with the organizational context and application domain, these techniques are designed to provide a rich set of information to allow the analyst to more effectively develop these knowledge bases and understand the requirements specific to the business scenario of interest. Techniques such as observation, RepGrid analysis, and contextual inquiry exemplify these types of techniques.

The knowledge bases and communication foci discussed above raise questions about the efficacy of requirements elicitation techniques as communication channels in the wide range of organizational contexts in which systems analysis and design is undertaken.

Table 3.1

Classification of Requirements Elicitation Techniques by Communication Focus

Communication emphasis	Characteristics	Examples	Prior research
Verification	Confirmatory Deterministic Bounded Objective Parsimonious	Questionnaires Structured interviews Technical document review Workflow, flowcharts	Browne and Rogich (2001) Pitts and Browne (2004) Gilbert (2003); Neill and Laplante (2003) Laguna, Marques, and Garcia (2003); Jones (2003); Marakas and Elam (1998)
Collaboration	Negotiative Semistructured	Scenario analysis Use case modeling Focus groups What-if analysis Semistructured interview	Hsai et al. (1994); Damas et al. (2005) Marttiin et al. (1995); Some (2006) Ramesh and Jarke (2001) Liang and Hung (1997) Coughlan, Lycett, and Macredie (2003)
Generation	Creative Constructive Unbounded Subjective Epigenetic	Brainstorming Contextual inquiry Cognitive mapping Observation RepGrid analysis Ethnography	Connolly, Jessup, and Valacich (1990); Ramos, Berry, and Carvalho (2005) Beyer and Holzblatt (1995) Siau (2004); Brooks, Davis, and Lycett (2005) Viller and Somerville (1999); Somerville and Ransom (2005) Gutierrez (1987) Alter (2004)

COMMUNICATION FOR REQUIREMENTS ELICITATION

Prior research attempting to improve on the requirements elicitation process focuses on the two primary populations involved in this process, the user and the analyst. Much of this research has usually attempted to overcome the challenges faced by analysts in eliciting requirements from users by focusing either on the cognitive limitations within these populations of information processors, by examining the conflicts that occur among these populations, or by examining the obstacles in communications between them (Byrd, Cossick, and Zmud, 1992; Davis, 1982; Siau and Tan, 2005; Valusek and Fryback, 1987).

Research focused on overcoming challenges within individuals and resolving conflicts among the two populations has been instrumental in the larger context of requirements elicitation. Within issues such as memory limitations, bias, and bounded rationality have generated research into methods and techniques to overcome these cognitive limitations, leading to the introduction of various techniques such as devil's advocacy and what-if analyses into the systems analyst's repertoire (Browne and Ramesh, 2002). Likewise, research considering the conflicts between these populations has examined and developed techniques to minimize or rationalize the conflicts that occur from elicitation, as the requirements may themselves be complex, contradictory, too large, or impossible to satisfy (Valusek and Fryback, 1987). The research from this stream of literature has introduced methods and techniques such as requirements interaction management (Robinson, Pawlowski, and Volkov, 2003), multiviewpoint analysis (Horai, 1996), and requirement collaboration systems (Chen and Nunamaker, 1991).

Our focal interest in this chapter is on the fundamental communication-based techniques and methods available for use by an analyst that underlie the acquisition and understanding of system requirements. This research on the interaction between users and analysts considers more closely the communication challenges that can impede the requirements elicitation process (Davis, 1982; Valusek and Fryback, 1987). These problems often come about due to variations in the richness of the knowledge bases between users and analysts, and by the inherent complexities of the information that is needed by both parties to define and articulate the business context and requirements. To illustrate the range of communication challenges that arise from variations in the knowledge bases of users and analysts, we use personal construct theory (Gaines, 2003; Hudlicka, 1996; Kelly, 1955) and elements of the Johari window (Luft, 1970) to classify them.

Personal construct theory (Kelly, 1955) suggests that individuals construct their own interpretations of the world around them. As such, individuals may differ in their interpretations of the world through this construction process. It is through a social process that these constructions are shared between individuals to develop what may be called communality, where two individuals share a similar construction of a particular event or world subject. In the systems development process, it is through the social process of requirements elicitation where the analyst attempts to develop this communality, by understanding and capturing the constructions of a user that identify potential requirements for the information system.

The Johari window is a depiction of the states of awareness between two individuals. It suggests that two individuals have four states of awareness in any interaction. These four states come about due to differences in each individual's knowledge of him/herself and the other individual involved in the interaction. Figure 3.1 identifies four states of awareness on the degree of mutuality in the knowledge bases of user and analyst. The four quadrants (each a classification of intersubjective experience) indicate how these two types of individuals may share understanding and interpretations about the business context of interest. It also enables a categorization of the communication

Figure 3.1 **The Requirements Appreciation Model**

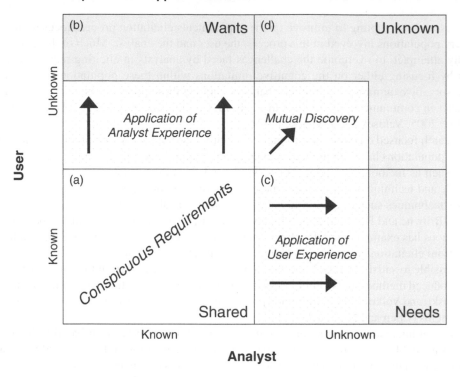

challenges faced by the user and analyst when attempting to come to a mutual understanding regarding a business situation of interest.

In requirements elicitation, there is often a common ground (a) where requirements are known by both parties—what we call conspicuous requirements. These requirements are known and understood by both the user and analyst due to their shared prior experiences in the domain of interest. However, requirements outside this shared area represent a number of challenges to both the analyst and the user.

One set of communication challenges exists when there are likely some potential requirements (b) that are known by the analyst but not known by the user. These potential requirements come about due to the unique experience the analyst has in the system domain that is not shared by the user. Increasing the size of the shared area (a) usually comes about through the application of the analyst's experience and skills to identify patterns (Bolloju, 2004) or common system requirements, effectively enlarging area (a) upward. The analyst must be able to effectively communicate these potential requirements to the user to determine whether they are also requirements in the current context (Davis, 1982). This application of the analyst's experience in requirements elicitation seeks to exploit the opportunity to reuse some previously derived design artifact (Purao, Storey, and Han, 2003).

Another set of communication challenges exists when there are potential requirements (c) known by the user, but not known by the analyst. These potential requirements come about due to the unique experience the user has in the system domain that is not shared by the analyst. Unless the user—typically an expert of some kind—can identify and articulate these requirements, they may go unidentified and unshared with the analyst, limiting the functionality of the system. To identify these requirements and increase area (a) to the right generally involves the analyst's attempt to get at the information that is known by the user (Browne and Ramesh, 2002; Gaines, 2003). To identify and capture these requirements, it is generally assumed that the analyst can ask the right questions and prod for more information, and that the user can understand and answer the questions. It is hoped that such questioning prompts the user's recognition of unknown (to the analyst) needs, thereby eliciting these additional requirements.

Finally, a set of communication challenges exists when there are potential requirements (d) that are not known about by the analyst to ask, and not known by the user to request. These requirements are outside the immediate experience of both the user and analyst and represent opportunities arising from completely new concepts. These requirements are often neither "captured" nor even realized during typical requirements elicitation, but may be realized later, for example, when the system has been implemented and is in use. Such unrealized requirements frequently manifest themselves as change requests, system enhancements, or, euphemistically, as "lessons learned." To successfully elicit these requirements demands communication techniques that facilitate mutual learning or co-discovery (Purao, Storey, and Han, 2003; Siau, 2004). In turn, the enriched communication facilitated by these techniques can result in design innovation and further experiential learning for both the analyst and user.

REQUIREMENTS ELICITATION TECHNIQUES AS COMMUNICATION CHANNELS

The prior sections explain that in a given systems development project, the analyst and user will have some level (higher or lower) of shared understanding of the given business scenario of interest. Depending on the knowledge that the analyst may have about the business scenario, the analyst will benefit from certain types of interactions (facilitated through elicitation techniques) with the user to increase his or her understanding about the business context. However, it is evident that different elicitation techniques will likely yield different requirements information about the business scenario (Marakas and Elam, 1998).

From channel expansion theory, we highlight two knowledge bases that are particularly relevant to the efficacy of elicitation techniques in increasing analyst understanding: the analyst's experience with the message topic (application domain) and the analyst's experience with the organizational context. These bases directly affect the ability of analysts to articulate the essence of the user(s) requirements—a mutual understanding of the context-specific focus of the analysis and design effort. The framework in Figure 3.2 uses these bases to provide a conceptual model of the "location" of the requirements elicitation techniques categorized in Table 3.1 (see page 26).

Figure 3.2 elaborates the classification set out in Table 3.1, incorporating the knowledge bases proposed by Carlson and Zmud (1999). The result is a conceptual model, the horizontal boundaries of which indicate the interdependence of the analyst's domain and application experience. The model highlights the need for balance between the conceptual "repertoires" of analyst and user in order to elicit mutually understandable requirements. For instance, an analyst with a wealth of application experience might feel able to reconceptualize users' wants in terms of previously delivered systems (or "solutions"). However, if the analyst's experience with the specific organizational context is modest, there is—as our conceptual model suggests—a need to move out of the "comfort zone" of the focus on verification. Figure 3.2 highlights the communication tradeoffs that need to be considered during systems analysis and design in order that requirements are elicited—rather than usurped—from their context.

Figure 3.2 extends from Figure 3.1 in that it takes the perspective of the analyst in the require-

Figure 3.2 **Knowledge Bases and Communication Focus**

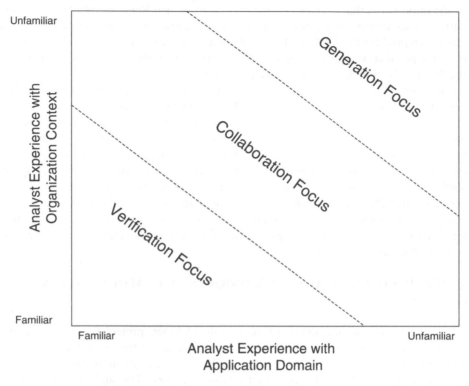

ments elicitation process and is based on the analyst's understanding of the application domain and organizational context (usually where the user is expert). As a result, it highlights the types of communication interaction and focus given the analyst's understanding and experience within context and domain where requirements are to be understood. Where the organizational context and application domain is well understood, the communication is more focused on a verification of the conspicuous requirements. Where there is a hybrid or mix of understandings, the communication must take on a more collaborative focus, where the analyst must both apply his or her own experience and rely on experiences of the user to understand requirements. Finally, where there are higher levels of unfamiliarity with the organization context and/or application domain, the communication must have a more generative focus, enabling mutual discovery of requirements.

In combination, Figures 3.1 and 3.2 highlight the need for awareness of both communication constraints and opportunities in requirements elicitation. They can be used as a framework for the selection and combination of requirements elicitation techniques. Consider the following brief scenario. An experienced systems analyst is invited to undertake a project to develop a Web-based front end to the database system in use in a general medical practitioner's office. Although competent in both database and Web design, and familiar with the business processes of an HMO through experience as a patient, the analyst would almost certainly be unfamiliar with the meaning and use of the clinical coding schema central to the diagnostic, treatment, reporting, and billing procedures. The analyst's preliminary work with the users should identify a need to apply the users' experience—individually and collectively—to increase his/her contextual knowledge. Thus, this project would be located in quadrant (c) of Figure 3.1.

Figure 3.3   **Requirements Elicitation Techniques Mapped to Knowledge Bases and Communication Focus**

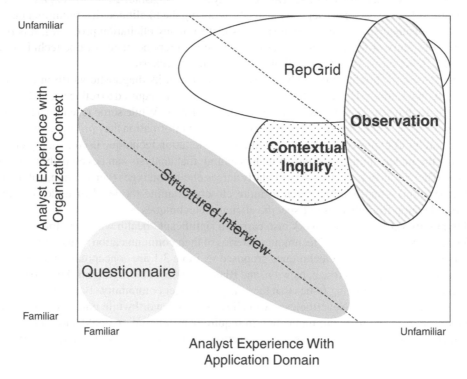

In order to develop the contextual knowledge required to address the clinical coding process in the local context, the analyst could use Table 3.1 to select a combination of elicitation techniques that will provide the collaborative, negotiative, and/or generative capacity to optimize communication with the users and thus to fully appreciate the significance of the otherwise "inconspicuous" clinical coding scheme.

Without this insight, there is a strong possibility that analysts might choose to use questionnaires, structured interviews, and other techniques with which they are familiar. However, this example suggests that rather than relying exclusively on these more verification-focused techniques, the requirements elicitation process would be enhanced by incorporating contextual inquiry, cognitive mapping, or one of the other "generation" techniques in order to increase the "bandwidth" of the communication channel between the analyst and users.

IMPLICATIONS FOR REQUIREMENTS ELICITATION PRACTICE AND RESEARCH

Our review of requirements elicitation techniques—summarized in diagrammatic form in Figure 3.3—shows that they have potential to constrict or narrow the focus of the requirements elicitation process. The predetermined content of questionnaires and other verification techniques can be compared to newspapers: although they do not tell you what to think, they do direct what analysts and users think about.

It is our hope that the conceptual framework presented in Figure 3.3 will enable researchers and practitioners to better appreciate the capacity of epigenetic requirements elicitation techniques such as cognitive mapping (Brooks, Davis, and Lycett, 2005; Siau, 2004) to "expand" the communication channel between users and analysts, reducing the likelihood that requirements will be missed or misunderstood. Likewise, it suggests that for many elicitation processes, it is possible that a healthy mix of these techniques as opposed to the preponderance of one technique would provide a richer basis for understanding the development scenario.

The framework briefly outlined here has already proved its diagnostic worth in a number of organizational settings. However, further empirical research is required to refine it and demonstrate its utility: such research will be undertaken in the near future. While some research has examined the use of various elicitation techniques and the resultant information they provide, little comparative research has explored the degree to which the elicitation technique used actually constrains or limits the understanding or types of understanding that analysts can develop about a business context. There is an opportunity—particularly across elicitation types (verification, collaboration, and generation)—for future research to more closely examine the level of understanding that analysts develop from their use of specific elicitation techniques.

Despite its value, our framework also carries a significant "health warning" for practitioners. Although superior to traditional techniques in terms of their communication "bandwidth," the more collaborative and generative techniques proposed in Table 3.1 are conceptually rather "alien" to requirements engineers (Lerouge, Newton, and Blanton, 2005). This highlights the need to consider the development and training issues that face the practitioner community (Bajaj et al., 2005; Kim, Hahn, and Hahn, 2000). Nevertheless, we believe this is a worthwhile enterprise. Overcoming some of the mis- and mal-communication in requirements elicitation could substantially reduce information systems failures, users' dissatisfaction with systems, and, ultimately, development costs.

NOTE

1. We use the term elicitation technique to refer to user–analyst communications channels or tools in a more general sense.

REFERENCES

Alter, S. 2004. Possibilities for cross-fertilization between interpretive approaches and other methods for analyzing information systems. *European Journal of Information Systems: Special Issue: "Interpretive" Approaches to Information,* 13, 3, 173–185.

Bajaj, A.; Batra, D.; Hevner, A.; Parsons, J.; and Siau, K. 2005. Information technology and systems—I: Systems analysis and design: should we be researching what we teach? *Communications of the Association for Information Systems,* 15, 1, 478–493.

Berry, D.M., and Lawrence, B. 1998. Requirements engineering. *IEEE Software,* 15, 2, 26–29.

Beyer, H.R., and Holzblatt, K. 1995. Apprenticing with the customer. *Communications of the ACM,* 38, 5, 45–52.

Boehm, B., and Huang, L. 2003. Value-based software engineering: re-inventing "earned value" monitoring and control. *Software Engineering Notes (ACM SIGSOFT),* 28, 1–7.

Bolloju, N. 2004. Improving the quality of business object models using collaboration patterns. *Communications of the ACM,* 47, 7, 81–86.

Brooks, L.; Davis, C.; and Lycett, M. 2005. Organizations and information systems: investigating their dynamic complexities using repertory grids and cognitive mapping. *International Journal of Information Technology and Human Interaction,* 1, 4, 39–55.

Browne, G., and Ramesh, V. 2002. Improving information requirements elicitation: a cognitive perspective. *Information and Management,* 39, 8, 625–645.

Browne, G., and Rogich, M. 2001. An empirical investigation of user requirements elicitation: comparing the effectiveness of prompting techniques. *Journal of Management Information Systems,* 17, 4, 223–249.

Byrd, T.A.; Cossick, K.L.; and Zmud, R.W. 1992. A synthesis of research on requirements analysis and knowledge acquisition techniques. *MIS Quarterly,* 16, 1, 117–138.

Carlson, J.R., and Zmud, R.W. 1999. Channel expansion theory and the experiential nature of media richness perceptions. *Academy of Management Journal,* 42, 2, 153–170.

Chen, M., and Nunamaker, J.F. 1991. The architecture and design of a collaborative environment for systems definition. *ACM SIGMIS Database,* 22, 1–2, 22–29.

Connolly, T.; Jessup, L.; and Valacich, J. 1990. Effects of anonymity and evaluative tone on idea generation in computer mediated groups. *Management Science,* 36, 6, 689–703.

Coughlan, J.; Lycett, M.; and Macredie, R. 2003. Communication issues in requirements elicitation: a content analysis of stakeholder experiences. *Information and Software Technology,* 45, 8, 525–537.

Daft, R., and Lengel, R. 1986. Organizational information requirements, media richness and structural design. *Management Science,* 32, 5, 554–571.

Damas, C.; Lambeau, B.; Dupont, P.; and van Lamsweerde, A. 2005. Generating annotated behavior models from end-user scenarios. *IEEE Transactions on Software Engineering,* 31, 12, 1056–1073.

Davis, G.B. 1982. Strategies for information requirements elicitation. *IBM Systems Journal,* 21, 1, 4–30.

Dennis, A.R., and Kinney, S.T. 1998. Testing media richness theory in the new media: cues, feedback, and task equivocality. *Information Systems Research,* 9, 3, 256–274.

Dennis, A.R., and Valacich, J.S. 1999. Rethinking media richness: towards a theory of media synchronicity. *Proceedings of the Thirty-second Hawaii International Conference on System Sciences,* 1–10.

Dennis, A.R.; Wixom, B.H.; and Vandenberg, R.J. 2001. Understanding fit and appropriation effects in group support systems via meta-analysis. *MIS Quarterly,* 25, 2, 167–193.

Gaines, B. 2003. Organizational knowledge acquisition. In C. Holzapple (ed.), *Handbook on Knowledge Management 1: Knowledge Matters.* Berlin: Springer, 317–347.

Gilbert, C. 2003. Documents as prototypes: designing written drafts for communication across cross-disciplinary teams. *IEEE Transactions on Professional Communication,* 46, 4, 327–330.

Gutierrez, O. 1987. Some aspects of information requirements analysis using a repertory grid technique. In R. Galliers (ed.), *Information Analysis: Selected Readings.* Reading, MA: Addison-Wesley, 347–363.

Hayes, F. 2004. Chaos is back. *Computerworld,* 38, 45, 70.

Hickey, A., and Davis, A. 2004. A unified model of requirements elicitation. *Journal of Management Information Systems,* 20, 4, 65–84.

Horai, H. 1996. Multi viewpoint analysts in requirements process. *Joint Proceedings of the Second International Software Architecture Workshop* and *International Workshop on Multiple Perspectives in Software Development,* 175–179.

Hsia, P.; Samuel, J.; Gao, J.; Kung, D.; Toyosh-Ma, Y.; and Chen, C. 1994. Formal approach to scenario analysis. *IEEE Software,* 11, 2, 33–41.

Hudlicka, E. 1996. Requirements elicitation with indirect knowledge elicitation techniques: comparison of three methods. *Proceedings of the Second International Conference on Requirements Engineering* (ICRE96), Colorado Springs, April 15–18, 4–11.

Jones, C. 2003. Variations in software development practices. *IEEE Software,* 20, 6, 22–27.

Kelly, G.A. 1955. *The Psychology of Personal Constructs.* New York: Norton.

Kim, C., and Peterson, D. 2001. Developers' perceptions of information systems success factors. *Journal of Computer Information Systems,* 41, 2, 29–35.

Kim, J.; Hahn, J.; and Hahn, H. 2000. How do we understand a system with (so) many diagrams?" Cognitive integration processes in diagrammatic reasoning. *Information Systems Research,* 11, 3, 284–303.

Laguna, M.; Marques, J.; and Garcia, F. 2003. DocFlow: workflow based requirements elicitation. *Information and Software Technology,* 45, 6, 357–369.

Lerouge, C.; Newton, S.; and Blanton, J.E. 2005. Exploring the systems analyst skill set: perceptions, preferences, age and gender. *Journal of Computer Information Systems,* 45, 3, 12–23.

Liang, T.P., and Hung, Y. 1997. DSS and EIS applications in Taiwan. *Information Technology & People,* 10, 4, 303 315.

Luft, J. 1970. *Group Processes: An Introduction to Group Dynamics.* Palo Alto, CA: National Press Books.

Marakas, G., and Elam, J. 1998. Semantic structuring in analyst acquisition and representation of facts in requirements analysis. *Information Systems Research,* 9, 1, 37–63.

Marttiin, P.; Lyytinen, K.; Rossi, M.; Tahvanainen, V-P.; Smolander, K.; and Tolvanen, J.P. 1995. Modeling requirements for future CASE: modeling issues and architectural consideration. *Information Resources Management Journal,* 8, 1, 15–25.

Mennecke, B.E.; Valacich, J.S.; and Wheeler, B.C. 2000. The effects of media and task on user performance: a test of the task-media fit hypothesis. *Group Decision and Negotiation,* 9, 6, 507–529.

McGrath, J.E. 1991. Time, interaction, and performance (TIP): a theory of groups. *Small Group Research,* 22, 2, 147–174.

Miranda, S.M., and Saunders, C.S. 2003. The social construction of meaning: an alternative perspective on information sharing. *Information Systems Research,* 14, 1, 87–106.

Moores, T.; Change, J.; and Smith, D. 2004. Learning style and performance: a field study of IS students in an analysis and design course. *Journal of Computer Information Systems,* 45, 1, 77–85.

Neill, C.J., and Laplante, P. 2003. Requirements engineering: The state of the practice. *IEEE Software,* 20, 6, 40–45.

Pitts, M., and Browne, G. 2004. Stopping behavior of systems analysts during information requirements elicitation. *Journal of Management Information Systems,* 21, 1, 203–226.

Purao, S.; Storey, V.; and Han, T. 2003. Improving analysis pattern reuse in conceptual design: augmenting automated processes with supervised learning. *Information Systems Research,* 14, 3, 269–290.

Ramesh, B., and Jarke, M. 2001. Toward reference models for requirements traceability. *IEEE Transactions on Software Engineering,* 27, 1, 58–93.

Ramos, I.; Berry, D.; and Carvalho, J. 2005. Requirements engineering for organizational transformation. *Information and Software Technology,* 47, 7, 479–495.

Rice, R.E., and Shook, D. 1990. Relationships of job categories and organizational levels to use of communication channels, including electronic mail: a meta-analysis and extension. *Journal of Management Studies,* 27, 2, 195–229.

Rice, R.E.; Grant, A.E.; Schmitz, J.; and Torobin, J. 1990. Individual and network influences on the adoption and perceived outcomes of electronic messaging. *Social Networks,* 12, 27–55.

Roberts, T.; Cheney, P.; Sweeney, P.; and Hightower, R. 2005. The effects of information technology project complexity on group interaction. *Journal of Management Information Systems,* 21, 3, 223–247.

Robinson, W.; Pawlowski, S.; and Volkov, V. 2003. Requirements interaction management. *ACM Computing Surveys,* 35, 2, 132–190.

Rogers, E. 1986. *Communication Technology: The New Media in Society.* New York: Free Press.

Siau, K. 2004. Evaluating the usability of a group support system using co-discovery. *Journal of Computer Information Systems,* 44, 2, 17–28.

Siau, K., and Tan, X. 2005. Technical communication in information systems development: the use of cognitive mapping. *IEEE Transactions on Professional Communications,* 48, 3, 269–284.

Smith, H.; Keil, M.; and Depledge, G. 2001. Keeping mum as the project goes under: toward an explanatory model. *Journal of Management Information Systems,* 18, 2, 189–228.

Some, S. 2006. Supporting use case based requirements engineering. *Information and Software Technology,* 48, 1, 43–58.

Somerville, I., and Ransom, J. 2005. An empirical study of industrial requirements engineering process assessment and improvement. *ACM Transactions on Software Engineering and Methodology,* 14, 1, 85–117.

Standish Group, The. 1994. The high cost of chaos. *Computerworld,* December 12, 20.

Te'eni, D. 2001. Review: a cognitive-affective model of organizational communication for designing IT. *MIS Quarterly,* 25, 2, 251–312.

Valusek, J., and Fryback, D. 1987. Information requirements determination: obstacles within, among, and between participants. In R. Galliers (ed.), *Information Analysis: Selected Readings.* Reading, MA: Addison-Wesley, 139–151.

Viller, S., and Somerville, I. 1999. Coherence: an approach to representing ethnographic analyses in systems design. *Human-Computer Interaction,* 14, 9–41.

PART II

METHODOLOGY FOUNDATION AND EVOLUTION OF SYSTEMS ANALYSIS AND DESIGN

CHAPTER 4

ITERATION IN SYSTEMS ANALYSIS AND DESIGN

Cognitive Processes and Representational Artifacts

NICHOLAS BERENTE AND KALLE LYYTINEN

Abstract: *The concept of iteration is fundamental to systems analysis and design practice and methods. In this chapter we explore the notion of iteration and distinguish two domains of iteration: iterations associated with cognitive processes that take place during design and iterations over representational artifacts about the design. Cognitive iterations can be concerned with the design, the design process, or stages within the design process. Representational artifacts can take the form of descriptive documentation of the system or the executable code itself. We discuss the claimed impacts of "iterative development" and compare these impacts to empirical findings on the effects of iterative methods. The findings are generally consistent with expected outcomes. We conclude with the observation that the differences between "iterative" or "agile" development and traditional methodologies lie not in the presence or absence of iteration, but in the locus of visibility and control, and the associated timing and granularity of what is being iterated.*

Keywords: *Iterative Development, Design Iteration, Evolutionary Prototyping, Evolutionary Enhancement, Software Prototyping, Agile Methodologies, Rapid Application Development*

INTRODUCTION

Recent agile methods recognize "iterative development" as a fundamental design principle (Cockburn, 2002). Yet, the idea of iteration is not new—system analysis and design has always been iterative! From the earliest development methodologies, the concept of iteration has been inherent in discussions about system design, though not always explicitly. Therefore, for those researching and developing systems it is important to understand what is iterated during design, why it is iterated, and what the impacts of this iteration are.

In this chapter we explore the concept of iteration and how it has been applied to systems analysis and design. We distinguish between two domains of iteration: iterations inherent in cognitive processes during design, and iterations over representational artifacts about designs. Cognitive iterations are concerned with the design object itself, the design process, or stages in the design process. Iterations of representational artifacts take place across descriptive documentation associated with the system and its components or the executable code. Table 4.1 depicts the framework. Our goal is to review how past research on systems analysis and design has treated iteration within these different domains, what we know about these iterations, and how these iterations have been shown to affect design outcomes. We do this by surveying the main streams of the systems analy-

Table 4.1

Iteration Framework

Cognitive iterations	
The design	• evolving perspectives of the design in the minds of the designers
The design process	• conceptions of design practices in the minds of the designers
Stages in the design process	• conceptions of progress or location within the design practices

Iterations of representational artifacts	
Documentation	• material artifact representing some aspect of the design or design process
Software code	• the design object itself, which acts as both a representational artifact and the fundamental component of the anticipated system

sis and design literature and soliciting the main findings through a literature review. We aim to offer readers an understanding of how iteration has been defined and treated in both prescriptive and empirical studies of design in order to determine what we know and do not know about the impacts of different types of iterations under different design contingencies.

The remainder of the chapter is organized as follows. First, we provide a description of our sampling of the theoretical literature associated with this framework and then review the sparse empirical body of research on the effects of iteration. We observe that empirical research on iteration focuses almost entirely on one type of iterating artifact: the evolutionary prototype. The findings associated with evolutionary prototyping are generally consistent with expected outcomes.

We conclude the chapter with a new perspective on iteration in systems analysis and design. As iteration forms a fundamental property of all systems analysis and design, then we must ask what, exactly, is the difference between iterative or agile, and traditional, "noniterative" development? If it is not the presence or absence of iteration, we need to have a more refined vocabulary to analyze differences among iterations and the criteria that can be used to spell out those differences. We accordingly suggest that these differences lie in the criteria that define the content and outcomes of iterative behavior as defined by notions of (a) iteration visibility—who can observe it? (b) control—who can control it? (c) granularity—what is being iterated and at what level of detail? and (d) timing—when do the iterations occur?

This insight challenges researchers to be mindful of the perspectives that designers and other stakeholders assign to various forms of documentation and to the executable code itself. The timing and level of detail where evolving artifacts are made visible affect the perspectives of the various stakeholders associated with the project, and these perspectives, in turn, affect project outcomes. We stress that iteration must be understood in terms of multidimensional, dynamic behaviors that are central to design, not as an unproblematic "thing" that either exists or does not.

ITERATION DEFINED

We need to carefully explore the concept of iteration because it underpins all systems development practices. The term "iteration" is common in a variety of disciplines. It can be defined as "the repetition of a process" in computer science, "a specific form of repetition with a mutable state" in mathematics, and in common parlance it is considered synonymous with repetition in general (Wikipedia, 2007). The "iterative method" describes a problem-solving methodology in many fields, including computer science and mathematics. These methods share the description of techniques "that use successive approximations to obtain more accurate solutions . . . at each step" (Barrett et al., 1994). The problem-solving system is said to converge when a solution that satisfies the problem criteria is reached through successive iterations.

It is no wonder the term "iteration" is not used consistently to refer to the same aspect of systems design in the extant literature. For example, for software designers, iteration commonly refers to the cyclical generation and testing of increasingly functional software code (Beck, 2002), but it can also describe the repetition of a phase of development due to rework (Davis, 1974), or successive subphases within a main phase (Iivari and Koskela, 1987). Less common applications also abound. For example, Checkland and Scholes (1999) indicate that the cyclical comparison of conceptual models to the real world represents a form of iteration. Iterative activities also often go by different names such as "prototyping" when designers iteratively elicit user input (Alavi, 1984), "rounds" when designers iteratively search for a design solution to reduce functional or implementation risk (Boehm, 1988), or even a "dance" of interactions among designers and users toward increased mutual understanding (Boland, 1978).

Although all of these uses bear a Wittgensteinian family resemblance (Blair, 2005), the fundamental aspect of iteration relates to a question of whether iteration is goal-driven or mere repetition. Dowson illustrates the difference vividly when speaking of a choice between Sisyphus and Heraclitus while modeling software processes:

> The Greek mythic hero Sisyphus was condemned to repeatedly roll a rock up a hill, never to quite achieve his objective; the Greek philosopher Heraclitus maintained that "You can never step in the same river twice." That is, do we see iteration as repetition of the same (or similar) activities, or does iteration take us to somewhere quite new? (Dowson, 1987, p. 37)

Here we contend that equating iteration with mere repetition does not capture the most salient aspect in its common usage for systems analysis and design, computer science, or mathematics. For us, use of the term "iteration" implies a progression toward an objective, whereas repetition has no such implication. Software development activity accordingly involves work toward closure, which is the delivery of a product. Even if repeated activities bear a strong resemblance to each other, some learning in the development project can be reasonably assumed to take place within each step while the same development activity is carried out many times. Yet, no formal, single definition of the term "iteration" in systems analysis will be presented here. Rather, echoing the spirit of its many uses, we suggest that the key facets of iteration are: (1) looping operations through repeated activities, and (2) a progression toward a convergence or closure.

Systems design occurs within the minds of individual developers, among developers, and between developers and other groups. Consequently, iterations take place cognitively, within the minds of developers, and socially or communicatively across individuals. Cognitive iterations imply repeated mental activity as a designer converges on a solution that is deemed adequate— the perfecting of the design idea. Likewise, any object, or artifact, can be iterated during design while it evolves in discrete steps toward some notion of completion as recognized by the rules of the genre that define its completeness. As noted above, we suggest that there are two fundamental forms of iteration during systems analysis and design process: (1) iterative cognitive processes in the minds of the developers; and (2) iterations over representational artifacts that are used and shared by designers and other stakeholders during the design (see Table 4.1). These representations include instances of the executable code.

To understand cognitive iteration, it is important to explore how the minds of designers work. This task is not unproblematic due to the intangibility and nonobservability of cognitive activity. Representational artifacts, however, are tangible objects representing something about the design, and can be identified, discussed, and tracked in a relatively straightforward manner. Below, we analyze theoretical views of cognitive iteration in design, and then examine how cognitive processes are reflected in changes in representational artifacts.

COGNITIVE ITERATION IN DESIGN

In a sense, all systems analysis and design depends on what goes on in the heads of designers. It is a commonly held belief that this cognitive activity advances iteratively, where some forms of mental looping take place to guide the design. A substantiation of this simple observation, beyond a mere statement, demands, however, that we open ourselves to the vast cognitive science literature, as well as to the wide array of treatments of cognitive phenomena in psychology, design, computer science, and information systems research—complete with accompanying rival epistemologies and ontological assumptions. Rather than attempting in this chapter to establish any distinct ontological stance, we broadly review what we characterize as the "rationalistic" school of cognition. We also address an alternative tradition as represented in critiques of artificial intelligence and ethnographic analyses of design. We then offer examples of these two traditions in their treatment of cognitive iteration in software design. The goal of this section is thus to illustrate the common thread of cognitive iteration that permeates all perspectives on systems design, and to highlight the importance of representational artifacts in iteration from an individual designer's standpoint.

Views of Designer Cognition

The mainstream view of designer's cognition falls squarely within what computer scientists refer to as the "symbol system hypothesis" of cognition (Newell and Simon, 1976). This hypothesis claims that cognitive activity is essentially comprised of "patterns and processes, the latter being capable of producing, modifying, and destroying the former. The most important property of these patterns is that they designate objects, processes, or other patterns, and that, when they designate processes, they can be interpreted" (ibid., p. 125).

Two concepts that are associated with designer's cognition in this view are: abductive reasoning (Peirce, 1992) and mental models (Johnson-Laird, 1980). The reasoning process of a designer is described as abductive (or retroductive) inference, which is different from and should be contrasted with inductive and deductive inference, which are well-known modes of inference in scientific study (Peirce, 1992). Abduction generates a design hypothesis (a mapping between a problem space and a solutions space), often a "guess" by the designer in the face of an uncertain situation, to a given problem and then works with this hypothesis until it is no longer deemed workable—at which time another hypothesis is generated. Simon (1996) describes this form of cognitive activity as nested "generate-test cycles" and argues that they are fundamental to design. He conceives of design as problem solving, where designers engage in a "heuristic search" for alternatives and then choose a satisficing design to go forward. When the alternative is found not to be the proper course, a new cycle of heuristic search begins. During design activity, designers engage in iterative learning about both the problem space and the solution space (Cross, 1989; Simon, 1996).

Another critical aspect of a designer's cognition involves the mental models that represent both the problem spaces and the solutions spaces, which designers manipulate in order to connect the solution space with the problem space. "Mental model" here becomes a generic term that is used to describe (meta)concepts that organize representations of problems and solutions and their connections. This includes representational metamodels such as frames, schemas, causal models, situational models, and so on (Brewer, 1987). This notion was popularized by Johnson-Laird (1980) to refer to cognitive representations that are constructed as required to assist human cognition. Mental models are not images of problems or solutions, but can lead to such images. Specific, localized mental models are expected to both draw from and contribute to a global schema of "generic knowledge structures" within the individual that can later be expected to leverage a new "episodic" mental model during design (Brewer, 1987).

These ideas underpinning design cognition form the essence of the "rationalistic" tradition of cognition. Yet, alternatives exist that criticize some of the fundamental assumptions of rational models (Bruner, 1990; Hutchins, 1995; Suchman, 1987; Weick, 1979; Winograd and Flores, 1986; and others). Any attempt to reconcile these critiques with the rationalistic tradition would be problematic, as rationalist theories address issues such as "meaning" in a simplistic manner, whereas many of the other traditions view the meaning of "meaning" as highly nuanced and situated (Suchman, 1994). In the rationalistic tradition "the machinery of the mind has taken precedence in theory building, insofar as mental representations and logical operations are taken as the wellspring for cognition" (Suchman, 1994, p. 188). A family of alternatives that are particularly salient to research on design cognition can be called the "situated action" perspective, which calls attention to "the socially constructed nature of knowledge, meaning, and designs . . . no objective representations of reality are possible; indeed, intelligence is not based exclusively on manipulating representations" (Clancey, Smoliar, and Stefik, 1994, p. 170).

The situated action view does not focus exclusively on what happens within an individual's mind. Rather, it looks at the interactions between social and contextual phenomena within the ongoing activity of a designer (Suchman, 1987; Winograd and Flores, 1986). An example of an iterative cognitive activity in this tradition would be the idea of a hermeneutic circle of interpretation where the individual leverages his "pre-understanding" to understand something within its context and forms a new "pre-understanding" (Winograd and Flores, 1986). Each hermeneutic circle can be considered a cognitive iteration.

Although mainstream management and design research generally aligns with the rationalistic tradition, there is an increasing amount of research that emphasizes interpersonal negotiation and dialogue as a key to understanding design (Bucciarelli, 1994; Clark and Fujimoto, 1991). In this stream, the idea of cognitive iteration is not the neat, temporally ordered, and fully formed mental model of a design in an individual's mind. Rather, it is a messy, partially formed object and process of dialogue, laden with meaning and interests and evolving through hermeneutic cycles. In the situated action view, the notion of a discrete and individual cognitive iteration loses its vividness.

To summarize, we must first become aware of the assumptions of each tradition, as each tradition offers an alternative view of iteration. The rationalistic tradition assumes fully formed and well-organized mental models that emerge and are manipulated during design, whereas the situated action perspective assumes partial, evolving understandings of the design as realized in dialogue. Either way, both these cognitive iterations share three facets:

1. steps or stages within the design (e.g., generate-test cycles/hermeneutic circles);
2. the design process as a gradual movement of the "mental" object (mental model/understanding); and
3. the design object (the representation/the text).

The bulk of systems design research treats cognitive iteration in accordance with the rationalistic tradition and normally seeks to map a designer's mental operations into a set of corresponding operations on the artifacts. Since the mid-1990s, however, there has been a growing amount of research that draws upon the situated action perspective (Bergman, King, and Lyytinen, 2002; Boland and Tenkasi, 1995; Cockburn, 2002; Hazzan, 2002; and others). In this alternative tradition, design is an ongoing dialogue that is always open to reinterpretation. Next we review ways in which the information systems literature has addressed cognitive iteration and its three aspects of design activity, as well as prescriptive and descriptive accounts of systems design.

Cognitive Iterations Within Design

Surprisingly, cognitive iterations as such have gone largely unaddressed in the systems design literature. Although the design literature draws extensively upon the systems approach (Churchman, 1968), the mainstream of the systems design research rarely accounts for the iterating cognitive process inherent in design (Churchman, 1971). In contrast, systems development literature has focused mainly on the cognitive iterations in the form of operations associated with steps in the design process, and less so with the design process itself, or cognitive iterations about the design. Table 4.2 offers examples of each form of cognitive iteration as recognized in the literature. We emphasize that this is not an exhaustive list, but rather is intended as an illustration.

Cognitive Iterations of Stages in the Design Process

In the systems design tradition, cognitive activity is assumed to coincide with formal stages of the design—the moments at which a given aspect of the software crystallizes and becomes "frozen." The most common conceptual iteration observed in systems design is that of the step, stage, or phase. Stages are iterated as they are repeated during the design. Such iterations have traditionally been considered inevitable, necessary evils (Davis, 1974; Royce, 1970), but are now more commonly thought to enhance system quality (Basili and Turner, 1975; Beck, 2002; Boehm, 1981; Brooks, 1995; Cockburn, 2002; Floyd, 1984; Keen and Scott Morton, 1978; Larman and Basili, 2003; McCracken and Jackson, 1982). Such stages can be formal, such as the requirements determination phase that results in "frozen" requirements (Davis, 1982), or they can be fairly indeterminate, such as "time-boxed" steps in agile methods (Auer, Meade, and Reeves, 2003; Beck, 2002; Beynon-Davies, Tudhope, and Mackay, 1999). Stages, phases, rounds, or iterations of the process are prescribed by a methodology but are not directly related to the status of the design or the code (Beck, 2002; Boehm, 1988; Kruchten, 2000; Larman, 2004). The rationalistic tradition within systems design thus tends to equate cognitive iterations with the formal procedural iterations.

Cognitive Iterations About the Design Process

Cognitive iterations associated with system development are not necessarily limited to those within the process, but can also relate to the designer's conceptions about the process itself. If we follow the idea that a method is in itself a formal design model, this model can iterate during the design process much the same as conceptualizations of the design object itself. This idea is prominent in the concept of method engineering (Brinkkemper, 1996; Rossi et al., 2004; Tolvanen and Lyytinen, 1993). Method-engineering advocates claim that formal methodologies cannot specify a priori all design tasks to be completed, as problems and solutions spaces change. Therefore designers

Table 4.2

Cognitive Iterations

Cognitive iterations	Description	Method	Source
Stages in the design process			
Phase	Iteration between definition, design, and implementation processes	Life cycle	Davis (1974)
Round	Iterations of plans, prototypes, risk analyses together	Spiral model	Boehm (1988)
Iteration	Inception, elaboration, construction, and transition cycle	Rational	Kruchten (2000)
Time-box	Time period within which planned iteration of running, tested code	eXtreme Programming	Beck (2002)
Design process			
Model	Method engineering, method as model	n/a	Brinkkemper (1996)
Maturity	Formal assessment of the designer and design process maturity	Capability maturity model	Humphrey (1989)
Iteration	Reflection on methodology, cycle between artifact and representation	Soft systems	Checkland (1981)
Design			
Learning	Iteratively learning about the problem and the design together	n/a	Alavi (1984)
Object system	Conceptualization of the anticipated sociotechnical work system	n/a	Lyytinen (1987)
Hermeneutic	Cycle of comparison between artifact, context, and understanding	Soft systems	Checkland (1981)
Dialogue	Cycles of cooperation and conflict between developers and users	ETHICS	Mumford (2003)

must be reflective (Checkland, 1981; Hazzan, 2002). Through this reflection, designers learn and continuously revise their practices and iterate over the design objects and design processes they will engage in (Rossi et al., 2004). During design activity, designers thus learn by iterating over their cognitive models of the method (second loop learning), and they can also capture the rationale for these iterations in order to facilitate the continued evolution of methods and associated mental models (Rossi et al., 2004).

Cognitive Iterations of the Design

The situated action tradition frequently ventures beyond stages and models and draws attention to other forms of cognitive iteration. For example, systems design has been likened to a hermeneutic circle (Boland and Day, 1989), where a designer iteratively compares an artifact with its context to understand its meaning. Checkland (1981) recommends specific representations, such as rich pictures and holons, to guide a system developer in iterative hermeneutic cycles between the representations, personal judgments, and understandings of reality that will progressively refine his underlying design conception. To understand a given process, the analyst iterates cognitively between perceptions of the social world external to him, his internal ideas, various representations, and the methodology of the analysis (Checkland and Scholes, 1999).

Researchers have also likened forms of systems development to dialectic cycles (Churchman, 1971). Such cycles are evident in participatory approaches to design that encourage dialogues between system developers and the user community (Floyd et al., 1989; Mumford, 2003). These dialogues can result in a series of explicit agreements concerning system functionality, the anticipated environment, or appropriate methodologies (Mumford, 2003). They also typically involve iterations of cooperation and conflict that are intended to improve user-related outcomes such as user satisfaction or system use.

Other approaches consistent with the situated action perspective offer radically alternative iterations. For example, the early PIOCO methodology (Iivari and Koskela, 1987) goes beyond sequential stages and formulates iterative problem-solving processes within multiple levels of abstraction. Rather than freezing portions of the design into predetermined linear phases, development follows a nonlinear iterative (recursive) progression that is explicitly allowed throughout the design. The design can be frozen at specific levels of abstraction before tackling subsequent, lower levels of abstraction.

In all of these examples, the cognitive iteration does not stand on its own, but is intimately involved with the designer's interactions with representational artifacts, the social context, and managerial concerns. Cognitive iterations are not discrete, fully formed views of the information system and its design, but rather form incomplete perspectives about the design object and the design process. They instantiate representations of the system on three levels: technical (computer system, such as code), symbolic (data and inferences, such as data models), and the organizational level (tasks supported, such as anticipated sociotechnical work scenarios) (Iivari and Koskela, 1987; Lyytinen, 1987).

Little empirical research has been conducted on software developers' cognition (Boland and Day, 1989; Curtis, Krasner, and Iscoe, 1988; Jeffries et al., 1981). Most studies observe cognitive challenges related to designs that demand iteration, but do not test or compare iterative versus noniterative cognitive practices. Exceptions do exist, however. For example, an early study compared the traditional unidirectional flow of problem information from a user to a developer during requirements definition with an iterative dialogue, where both the user and developer prepared their suggestions and offered feedback in a "dance." The iterative method generated greater mutual understanding, better design quality, and enhanced system implementability (Boland, 1978). In another study, researchers found that novice developers benefited from sequential processes in database design, whereas experts leveraged iterative behaviors to improve design outcomes (Prietula and March, 1991).

ITERATIONS OVER REPRESENTATIONAL ARTIFACTS

Whatever the content of a designer's cognitive activity, it relies on representations that act as tools by which designers extend their cognition (Bucciarelli, 1994; Hutchins, 1995; Simon, 1996). A representation is a "way in which a human thought process can be amplified" (Churchman, 1968, p. 61). Designers represent their designs, the design process, and other associated information using symbolic and physical artifacts. In the making of these artifacts, in manipulating and navigating through them, and in reflecting on artifacts, design ideas crystallize and change, or new ideas emerge. Representational artifacts can take the form of documentation such as data models or system requirements documents, or the executable code itself (code, components, database schemata, etc). Table 4.3 describes a number of iterating representational artifacts identified in the literature. Again, this is intended as an illustration of the wide range of representational iterations that are prescribed in methodologies.

To appreciate the nature and role of representational artifacts in systems design, it is important to view an information system as a dynamic entity (Orlikowski and Iacono, 2001). Systems evolve, get revised, and behave differently in different contexts. In fact, there is no single entity or thing that is the system. Rather the system is a shared, ambiguous, and ambivalent conception about a slice of reality that can only be more or less accurately approximated through representations (Lyytinen, 1987). Yet throughout the process, individuals often discuss the information system as if it were a single, discrete entity, although all individuals have only partial views (Turner, 1987). Early in the design process, the information system may be little more than an idea invented by a handful of people whose only tangible artifact is a vague requirements memo or note. Later in the process, the system may become represented by lines of incomplete code, dozens of use cases, and a great number of varying rationales of the system's utility.

In the following sections we analyze how representational artifacts that are deemed pivotal in the information systems development and software engineering literature iterate. There are two broad categories of these artifacts: the descriptive documents associated with the design object and the executable code. We treat them differently because ultimately only the code inscribes new behaviors in the target system—the technical and sociotechnical system. The system descriptions are needed to make the code inscribe behaviors that are intended, acceptable, and correct. We then address the idea of "iterative development" as reflected in the ways in which artifacts iterate, as well as what we know about the impacts of "iterative development" on design outcomes.

Iterating Documents

Early representations of the system center on descriptions of system requirements. Over the course of the design, these representations change regularly and often evolve into other representations, such as "as built" software documentation. Because of this need for connecting requirements with downstream documentation and ultimately with the executable code, no development methodology can overlook iteration across documents entirely, although some, such as XP (Beck, 2002), aspire to remove a majority of documentation from the critical design path.

Traditional system development life-cycle and "heavy-weight" methodologies are thought to

Table 4.3

Iterating Representational Artifacts

Artifact	Description	Method	Source
Iterating document examples			
Requirements	Specify project purpose and customer needs	Waterfall	Royce (1970)
Project control list	Tasks that the system is expected to achieve	Iterative enhancement	Basili and Turner (1975)
Data model	Model to support inferences from anticipated use	n/a	Hirschheim, Klein, and Lyytinen (1995)
Agreements	Written contracts between users and developers	ETHICS	Mumford (2003)
Risk analysis	Simplify documentation to crucial requirements/specs	Spiral model	Boehm (1988)
Process assessments	Annual analysis of process and team to gauge maturity, and so on	CMM	Humphrey (1989)
Iteration plan	Plan for four-nested rational process phases	Rational	Kruchten (2000)
Inter-team specs	Specifications of interface between object-oriented teams	Crystal Orange	Cockburn (1998)
Iterating software code examples			
Pilot	First version of the code that is "thrown away"	Waterfall	Royce (1970)
Version	Output of a development process, followed by another	Life cycle	Davis (1974)
Refinement	Step-by-step elaboration on initial blunt "complete" code	Stepwise refinement	Wirth (1971)
Enhancement	Portion of the code evolves into "complete" code	Iterative enhancement	Basili and Turner (1975)
Prototype	Exploratory, experimental, and evolutionary types	n/a	Floyd (1984)
Refactored code	Iteration of entire code made to work on a daily basis	eXtreme Programming	Beck (2002)

focus on documentation and its iterations. They encourage "freezing" documentation upstream in order to move in a disciplined manner to the next steps in the design. This conceptualization is not, however, always the case, as most major methodologies allow for iteration of upstream documents at least to some extent (Boehm, 1981, 1988; Humphrey, 1989; Kruchten, 2000).

The waterfall model (Royce, 1970) is the best-known life-cycle methodology and is often characterized as top-down, unidirectional, and noniterative. Contrary to this claim, even in its earliest manifestation Royce suggested that unwanted changes and associated iterations are inevitable, and he recommended a number of practices to address such problems, including piloting any sizable software project with a "preliminary program design" (Royce, 1970, p. 331). This concept was later popularized by Brooks when he stressed "plan to throw one away; you will, anyhow" (Brooks, 1995, p. 116). Royce also suggested iterative maintenance of design documentation. He understood that requirements change as the developer learns, and therefore the requirements should evolve through a series of at least five classes of documents to the final documentation of the design "as built." Updates to design documentation occur for two primary reasons: to guide or to track development.

The extant literature addresses various forms of iterations related to upstream system representations —such as requirements determinations (Davis, 1982), data models (Hirschheim, Klein, and Lyytinen, 1995), and the wide array of technical and social documentations associated with formal methodologies (Boehm, 1981, 1988; Davis, 1974; Humphrey, 1989; Kruchten, 2000; Mumford, 2003; and others). Although most of the literature addresses changing documents throughout the design, the value of these changes is not elaborated beyond guiding and tracking. Even the more nuanced views of documentation that treat its creation as problematic and argue its content to be flawed (Parnas and Clements, 1986) have made no distinction between the value and cost of iterations across representations. There are some exceptions to this, however. For example, the "inquiry cycle model" (Potts, Takahashi, and Anton, 1994) describes iterative requirements refinement where stakeholders define, challenge, and change requirements. Using requirement goals to drive such practice is expected to be efficient, since many original goals can be eliminated, refined, or consolidated before entering the design step (Anton, 1996).

Iterating Software Code

The code evolves through multiple instantiations in many development approaches including "throw-away" prototypes (Baskerville and Stage, 1996), prototypes that evolve into a final system, or maintenance of different versions of a system. The common usage of "iterative development" normally refers to software design that proceeds through "self-contained mini-projects" where each produces partially complete software (Larman, 2004). This has traditionally been referred to as evolutionary prototyping (Alavi, 1984; Beynon-Davies et al., 1999; Floyd, 1984). Such "iterative development" practices emerged soon after waterfall was made the orthodox model. The idea of "stepwise refinement" involved a blunt, top-down design of the system, then a phased decomposition and modular improvement of the code—largely to increase system performance (Wirth, 1971). Stepwise refinement was criticized for requiring "the problem and solution to be well understood," and not taking into consideration that "design flaws often do not show up until the implementation is well under way so that correcting the problems can require major effort" (Basili and Turner, 1975, p. 390). To address these issues, Basili and Turner recommended an "iterative enhancement," where designers start small and simple, by coding a "skeletal sub-problem of the project." Then developers incrementally add functionality by iteratively extending and modifying the code, using a project control list as a guide, until all items on the list have been addressed. Each iteration involves design, implementation (coding and debugging), and analysis of the software.

This idea of iterative enhancement forms the foundation of evolutionary prototyping and recent agile methods. Agile methods are based on the assumption that design communication is necessarily imperfect (Cockburn, 2002), and that software design is a social activity among developers and users. A popular agile methodology—extreme programming (XP)—promotes a variety of iterative practices such as pair programming (cognitive iteration during each design step through dialogue), test-first development (generating test information that guides subsequent iteration), and refactoring (iterating the software artifact during each cycle) (Beck, 2002). The structure of XP is almost identical to the early evolutionary design, where limited functionality is first developed, and then incrementally expanded. However, XP can take advantage of a number of software tools that were not available to early software developers. Powerful toolsets are now available that enable unit testing, efficient refactoring, and immediate feedback, while object-oriented environments allow for modular assembly of significant portions of the system. Also, process innovations such as testing-first, time-boxing, collocation, story cards, pair programming, shared single code base, and daily deployment mitigate the communication problems found in earlier evolutionary processes.

The Promise of "Iterative Development"

The justification of evolutionary prototyping, or more commonly "iterative development," centers on trial-and-error learning about both the problem and solution. Users and developers do not know what they need until they see something—similar to Weick's (1979) illustration of organizational sensemaking: "how can I know what I think till I see what I say?" Thus generating prototypes assists communication better than traditional abstract upstream documentation and thereby supports mutual learning (Alavi, 1984; Basili and Turner, 1975; Beck, 2002; Boehm, 1981; Brooks, 1995; Cockburn, 2002; Floyd, 1984; Keen and Scott Morton, 1978; Larman and Basili, 2003; McCracken and Jackson, 1982; and others). We now review some of the anticipated outcomes associated with iterative development.

Anticipated benefits of evolutionary, or "iterative development", are many. By "growing" the design, software can be developed more quickly (Brooks, 1987). Beyond speed, evolutionary development enables a "more realistic validation of user requirements," the surfacing of "second-order impacts," and a greater possibility of comparing alternatives (Boehm, 1981, p. 656). Prototyping demonstrates technical feasibility, determines efficiency of part of the system, aids in design/specification communication, and structures implementation decisions (Floyd, 1984). Prototyping is thought to mitigate requirements uncertainty (Davis, 1982), aid in innovation, and increase participation (Hardgrave, Wilson, and Eastman, 1999), reduce project risk (Boehm, 1988; Lyytinen, Mathiassen, and Ropponen, 1998; Mathiassen, Seewaldt, and Stage, 1995), and lead to more successful outcomes (Larman and Basili, 2003). Because developers generate code rather than plan and document, they are expected to be more productive (Basili and Turner, 1975; Beck, 2002; Larman, 2004). Therefore, projects using evolutionary prototyping can be expected to cost less (Basili and Turner, 1975; Beck, 2002; Cockburn, 2002; Larman and Basili, 2003).

A problem often associated with strict evolutionary development, however, is the lack of maintaining "iterative" process plans. Starting with a poor initial prototype could turn users away; prototyping can contribute to a short-term, myopic focus, and "developing a suboptimal system" can necessitate rework in later phases (Boehm, 1981). Exhaustive design documentation will still be required even if prototyping forms the primary process (Humphrey, 1989). Also, the output of evolutionary development often resembles unmanageable "spaghetti code" that is difficult to maintain and integrate. These are similar to the "code and fix" problems that waterfall was originally intended to correct (Boehm, 1988). Many problems associated with evolutionary development include: "ad-hoc requirements management; ambiguous and imprecise communication; brittle architectures; overwhelming complexity; undetected inconsistencies in requirements, designs, and implementation; insufficient testing; subjective assessment of project status; failure to attack risk; uncontrolled change propagation; insufficient automation" (Kruchten, 2000, ch. 1).

Not surprisingly, many caution that evolutionary development is not suited to every situation, as the idea of continuous iteration makes unrealistic assumptions. Evolutionary methods assume that projects can be structured according to short-term iterations, face-to-face interaction is always tenable and superior to formal upstream documentation, and the cost of change remains constant over the project (Turk, France, and Rumpe, 2005). Issues such as scaling, criticality, and developer talent will often require hybrid methodologies—or a combination of evolutionary prototypes with formal and control-oriented methods (Boehm, 2002; Cockburn, 2002; Lindvall et al., 2002). Also, evolutionary development demands other complementary assets like smart designers or the availability of enlightened users in order to succeed (Beck, 2002; Boehm, 1981).

Empirical Impacts of "Iterative Development"

Empirical research on "iterative development" is as scarce as the prescriptive research is plentiful (Gordon and Biemen, 1995; Lindvall et al., 2002; Wynekoop and Russo, 1997). The empirical research that does exist focuses on the effects of prototyping on project success (e.g., Alavi, 1984; Boehm, Gray, and Seewaldt, 1984; and others), while neglecting the impact and role of other iterating representations. Nevertheless, in what follows, we assess the state of empirical research on iterations over representational artifacts.

Representational artifacts include the documents, data models, and other representations of the software, including artifacts such as user-interface mock-ups and "throw-away" prototypes. These representations are addressed quite extensively in the prescriptive literature, but the iteration of these representations and the effects of those iterations on design outcomes are notably absent. The primary exception is the research on "throw-away" prototypes. Although many researchers distinguish between prototypes that occur at different stages and are used for different purposes (Beynon-Davies et al., 1999; Floyd, 1984; Janson and Smith, 1985), the empirical literature does not underscore distinctions between these types of prototypes and their outcomes, and when they see a distinction, there is no significant difference in the outcomes (Gordon and Biemen, 1993, 1995).

As indicated earlier, the notion most commonly associated with "iterative development" is evolutionary prototyping. Table 4.4 summarizes the expected impacts of evolutionary prototyping and compares them with empirical findings. It is important to note that a good number of researchers have found empirical evidence to be inconclusive, and these data are not reported in our review. Furthermore, many expectations highlight the drawbacks of the evolutionary method, but these criticisms focus on design outcomes, which are addressed below.

The fundamental reason Basili and Turner advocated iterative enhancement is that problems and solutions are not well understood, and even if they were, "it is difficult to achieve a good design for a new system on a first try" (1975, p. 390). Subsequent empirical research found prototyping to be an excellent method for users and developers to learn about the requirements together (Alavi, 1984; Boehm, Gray, and Seewaldt, 1984; Naumann and Jenkins, 1982; Necco, Gordon, and Tsai, 1987). Prototyping has been found to support communication and problem solving between users and developers (Deephouse et al., 1995; Mahmood, 1987), and has led to greater user involvement (Alavi, 1984; Gordon and Bieman, 1995; Naumann and Jenkins, 1982). Improved user participa-

Table 4.4

Testing the Promise of "Iterative Development"

Promise of iterative development	Source	Conclusion	Source
1. Supports mutual learning between users and developers Learning about the problem and solution; addresses requirements uncertainty; more realistic validation of requirements; demonstrates technical feasibility	*Supported? Yes* Alavi (1984); Basili and Turner (1975); Beck (2002); Boehm (1981); Brooks (1995); Cockburn (2002); Davis (1982); Floyd (1984); Keen and Scott Morton (1978); Larman and Basili (2003); McCracken and Jackson (1982)	Learn about requirements; support communication and problem solving	Alavi (1984); Boehm, Gray, and Seewaldt (1984); Deephouse et al. (1995); Mahmood (1987); Naumann and Jenkins (1982); Necco, Gordon, and Tsai (1987)
2. Improves user-related outcomes Increase participation; more successful system use	*Supported? Yes* Hardgrave, Wilson, and Eastman (1999); Larman and Basili (2003)	Greater user involvement; better user satisfaction; ease of use; greater system use	Alavi (1984); Boehm, Gray, and Seewaldt (1984); Gordon and Bieman (1993, 1995); Mahmood (1987); Naumann and Jenkins (1982); Necco, Gordon, and Tsai (1987)
3. Improves design process Software developed more quickly; designers more productive; projects cost less; reduce risk	*Supported? Yes* Basili and Turner (1975); Beck (2002); Boehm (1988); Brooks (1987); Cockburn (2002); Larman (2004); Larman and Basili (2003); Lyytinen et al. (1998); Mathiassen, Seewaldt, and Stage (1995)	Shorten lead times for projects and/or less effort; designer satisfaction	Baskerville and Pries-Heje (2004); Boehm, Gray, and Seewaldt (1984); Gordon and Bieman (1995); Naumann and Jenkins (1982); Necco, Gordon, and Tsai (1987); Mahmood (1987); Subramanian and Zarnich (1996)
4. Improves design outcomes Better code with more successful outcomes; results in code that is easily modified and maintained; increased innovativeness	*Supported? Mixed* Basili and Turner (1975); Larman and Basili (2003); Hardgrave, Wilson, and Eastman (1999) *Supported*	Positively related to higher system performance; more maintainable code	Alavi (1984); Boehm, Gray, and Seewaldt (1984); Gordon and Bieman (1993); Larman (2004)
	Not supported	Less functional systems, with potentially less coherent designs; "negotiable" quality requirements	Baskerville and Pries-Heje (2004); Boehm, Gray, and Seewaldt (1984)
5. Requires complementary practices Requires complementary assets/practices; or more formal structure	*Supported? Yes* Beck (2002); Boehm (1981, 2002); Cockburn (2002); Lindvall et al. (2002)	Prototyping must be combined with other factors, such as tools, standards, expertise, and so on	Alavi (1984); Baskerville and Pries-Heje (2004); Beynon-Davies, Mackay, and Tudhope (2000); Gordon and Bieman (1995); Lichter et al. (1994); Naumann and Jenkins (1982)

tion is often credited with better user satisfaction (Naumann and Jenkins, 1982; Necco, Gordon, and Tsai, 1987), designer satisfaction (Mahmood, 1987), ease of use (Boehm, Gray, and Seewaldt, 1984; Gordon and Bieman, 1993), and greater use of the system (Alavi, 1984; Mahmood, 1987). Research on the effects of prototyping on system performance is generally mixed (Gordon and Bieman, 1993). Some found prototyping to be positively related to higher system performance (Alavi, 1984; Larman, 2004), but others found that prototyping might create less robust, less functional systems, with potentially less coherent designs (Boehm, Gray, and Seewaldt, 1984), and may call for "negotiable" quality requirements (Baskerville and Pries-Heje, 2004).

While Basili and Turner (1975) advocate iterative enhancement, they indicate that software created through evolutionary prototypes can require less "time and effort," and the "development of a final product which is easily modified is a by-product of the iterative way in which the product is developed" (1975, p. 395). A large number of subsequent studies indicate that prototyping can shorten lead times for projects and/or require less effort, typically measured by fewer man-hours (Baskerville and Pries-Heje, 2004; Boehm, Gray, and Seewaldt, 1984; Gordon and Bieman, 1995; Naumann and Jenkins, 1982; Necco, Gordon, and Tsai, 1987; Subramanian and Zarnich, 1996). A number of studies also support the claim that evolutionary prototyping results in more maintainable code (Boehm, Gray, and Seewaldt, 1984; Gordon and Bieman, 1993).

In most empirical studies, iteration is treated as an independent variable that affects outcomes. Additional moderators are sometimes introduced, but not in a systematic manner. For example, prototyping must be combined with other factors such as powerful development tools (Alavi, 1984; Naumann and Jenkins, 1982), a standardized architecture (Baskerville and Pries-Heje, 2004), greater developer expertise (Gordon and Bieman, 1995), a complementary culture (Beynon-Davies, Mackay, and Tudhope, 2000; Lindvall et al., 2002), and "low technology" artifacts and processes for scheduling and monitoring (Beynon-Davies, Mackay, and Tudhope, 2000). Also, if users are not involved, prototype-based outcomes can suffer (Lichter, Schneider-Hufschmidt, and Zullighoven, 1994). Prototyping can also be seen as a dependent variable. For example, researchers find that prototyping may pose challenges for management and planning (Alavi, 1984; Boehm, Gray, and Seewaldt, 1984; Mahmood, 1987).

In recent years there has been a dearth of rigorous research on the effects of prototyping on systems development. Most of the empirical literature on the impacts of agile methods is anecdotal (Lindvall et al., 2002). Although past studies have typically compared prototype-based processes with specification or plan-based processes, current empirical research will likely suggest combinations of iterative and specification-based processes (e.g., Mathiassen, Seewaldt, and Stage, 1995) or compare variations in agile practices. When pursuing either of these research avenues, it would make sense to adopt a more granular and refined view of iteration and define the dependent variables carefully.

DISCUSSION

"Iterative development" has been both advocated and contested as a systems analysis and design principle. Yet it has remained a fundamental building block of system analysis and design methodologies. In this chapter, we have consistently enclosed the term in quotation marks because literally all systems development is iterative. Both cognitive and, consequently, representational iterations are essential to every design practice. This begs the question: What is the difference, then, between "iterative" practices of today, and the traditional "noniterative" practices? The answer is not the presence or absence of iteration, as both types exhibit iteration.

One explanation of the difference can be the way in which the two types approach iteration.

Both modern and traditional practices focus on iteration as reactive fixes or improvements based on new information, or uncovered problems. Many modern methods, however, also anticipate the need for and inevitability of new information, and proactively seek it. Thus, the difference is not the presence of iteration, but, rather, the timing and visibility of it. With earlier visibility of iteration needs, designers invite user input and thus relinquish a certain amount of control over iteration decisions. Because this visibility is staged earlier, its granularity with regard to foundational details and assumptions of the system development is also greater. Fundamentally, "iterative development" is not necessarily more iterative. But it is likely to be more open, and the control over iterations is shared and at a much more detailed level.

Consider the code as an iterating artifact, for example. All application software iterates over its life even if its design methodology is the systems development life-cycle model (Davis, 1974). Each version of a software system can be considered an iteration. As bugs are fixed or enhancements added to code—even if consistent with the linear life-cycle method—any new instantiation of code can be considered an iteration. When all or some portions of the code are compiled, the result is an iteration of compiled code. Anytime a designer replaces or adds to any part of working code, he has iterated over that code.

In the traditional life-cycle method, however, the user is not highly involved beyond listing requirements. Management is not aware of each subsequent iteration, but sees only the code that is presented at key milestones. The bricolage of everyday workarounds, failures, and changes is neatly hidden from everyone except the designer himself—as are micro-level assumptions and decisions that can have disproportionately large impacts on path-dependent future designs. As systems development has become more "iterative," the veil hiding this practice has been progressively lifted. Prototyping invited other developers, users, and managers into discussions at a more granular level of detail sooner during development. When participating in this activity, those parties adopted more control over the process. Risk analysis (Boehm, 1988; Lyytinen, Mathiassen, and Ropponen, 1998) that focuses on continued risk mitigation—rather than overly detailed requirements that draw no real distinction of risks—exposes the key requirements of design to scrutiny outside of developers. Pair programming (Beck, 2002) opens ongoing moment-by-moment deliberations of an individual developer to observation and demands a dialogue with a fellow developer. This observation indicates that the key contingency for distinguishing the level of iteration between development practices is not whether one engages in evolutionary prototyping or not. Observations such as the following indicate that a focus on iteration as such may be misplaced:

- user involvement is a more important determinant of project outcomes than presence of iterative development (Lichter, Schneider-Hufschmidt, and Zullighoven, 1994);
- the success of any development, iterative or not, depends more on developer experience than anything else (Boehm, 2002); and
- for "iterative development" to succeed, the complementary practices such as co-location, pair programming, and so on are essential (Beck, 2002).

Therefore, it is not the presence of iteration that primarily determines the outcomes of systems analysis and design activity. Rather, these outcomes are determined by the activities that the types and forms of iterations can enable and constrain. The black box of iteration should be opened to understand structures and affordances of prescribed iterations and complementary processes, and their effect on design process and its outcomes. Rather than asking whether an organization should adopt "iterative development," it is more applicable for organizations to ask what level of granularity, visibility, and control over changes and decisions about design objects and processes is appropriate at different times, and for different purposes of the design.

Implications for Practice

We have indicated that the essential difference between what is widely considered to be "iterative development" and traditional software development is the audience for design activity. "Iterative development" allows visibility to other developers or some portion of the managerial and user community earlier in the process, and at a more granular level. With such activity, developers are also relinquishing a degree of control. Because of the dual nature of software code—acting as a representational artifact of the system as well as a fundamental physical structure within the task system—analysis of iterations solely on the basis of the presence of evolutionary prototyping may be a distraction from the issues that drive better results. The iterative processes by which key concerns arise throughout the development process are essential for understanding success. These processes can be facilitated by evolutionary prototyping, but also by the creative use of other representational artifacts, generative language and dialogue, or other collaborative mechanisms. Rather than attempting to implement new methodologies blindly, software developers would be better served in first determining who needs design input, at what level of granularity, and at what stage of the design process.

Implications for Research

In systems analysis and design literature, cognitive iterations are addressed (usually implicitly) through the iterative treatment of representational artifacts. The perspectives and meanings that designers ascribe to artifacts are rarely tackled. Instead the technical artifact itself is the central concern. Typically, the actual cognitive practices within development are not dealt with, but rather the formal steps and stages of the methodology as reflected in representational outcomes are treated at length. Genres of representations are typically advocated and designed to enable communication and human interaction at specific steps and junction points, and such artifacts are expected to change iteratively. This communication is not always seen as unproblematic, and the nature, content, and scope of these representations is seldom fully explicated in how they support the cognitive activities of design groups or their iterations (with some exceptions, of course; e.g., Checkland, 1981; Hirschheim, Klein, and Lyytinen, 1995).

This review of the literature related to iteration points to two broad areas of future research in systems analysis and design. First, cognitive iterations of software developers and other stakeholders need to be better understood. Perspectives of individuals associated with the design process do impact the design process, and understanding the evolution of these perspectives is imperative to improving outcomes. Second, future research should involve opening the black box of iteration over code and other representational artifacts to understand outcomes associated with particular design practices. By opening this black box, we encourage researchers not to treat the term "iteration" as an undifferentiated construct, but rather to look at the degrees of visibility, granularity, timing, and control associated with evolutionary changes of the code, various forms of documentation, and the perspectives of the various stakeholders.

CONCLUSION

The contribution of this chapter is to illustrate the multidimensional nature of the concept of iteration. Iteration is often characterized in the literature as a straightforward concept: either a development process is iterative or it is not. We have shown that this characterization is too simplistic, as all development practices contain significant levels of iteration. We also identified two fundamental dimensions of iteration: cognitive and representational. Cognitive processes of developers and others involved in a design are necessarily iterative, but this can mean different things depending on whether the rationalistic tradition or the situated action perspective of human cognition is adopted. In addition, cognitive iterations involve iterative engagement with representations acting as both extensions to cognition and mediation between individuals.

We identify two primary forms of representation: the descriptive documents associated with analysis and design activity, and the executable code itself. Although many representational artifacts for both types are prescribed by advocates of particular methodologies, the empirical literature is limited solely to examining iterations over the software code as evolutionary prototyping. Furthermore, recent "iterative development" identifies entirely with the centrality of the iterations associated with the code itself. In this chapter we provide a starting point for unpacking the notion of iteration to expand the discussion beyond iterating code to other artifacts and associated cognitive processes.

REFERENCES

Alavi, M. 1984. An assessment of the prototyping approach to information systems development. *Communications of the ACM,* 27, 6, 556–563.

Anton, A.I. 1996. Goal-based requirements analysis. In *Proceedings of the Second International Conference on Requirements Engineering.* Colorado Springs: IEEE Computer Society Press, 136–144.

Auer, K.; Meade, E.; and Reeves, G. 2003. The rules of the game. In F. Maurer and D. Wells (eds.), *Extreme Programming and Agile Methods—XP/Agile Universe 2002, Lecture Notes in Computer Science* 2753. Berlin-Heidelberg: Springer, 35–42.

Barrett, B.; Berry, M.; Chan, T.F.; Demmel, J.; Dongrra, J.; Eijkhout, V.; Pozo, R.; Romine, C.; and Van der Vorst, H. 1994. *Templates for the Solution of Linear Systems—Building Blocks for Iterative Methods.* Philadelphia, PA: SIAM. Available at www.netlib.org/templates/Templates.html (accessed on August 31, 2007).

Basili, V.R., and Turner, A.J. 1975. Iterative enhancement: a practical technique for software development. *IEEE Transactions on Software Engineering,* 1, 4, 390–396.

Baskerville, R., and Pries-Heje, J. 2004. Short cycle time systems development. *Information Systems Journal,* 14, 3, 237–264.

Baskerville, R.L., and Stage, J. 1996. Controlling prototype development through risk analysis. *MIS Quarterly,* 20, 4, 481–504.

Beck, K. 2002. *Extreme Programming Explained: Embrace Change.* Boston: Addison-Wesley.

Bergman, M.; King, J.L.; and Lyytinen, K. 2002. Large scale requirements analysis as heterogeneous engineering. *Scandinavian Journal of Information Systems,* 14, 1, 37–55.

Beynon-Davies, P.; Mackay, H.; and Tudhope, D. 2000. "It's lots of bits of paper and ticks and post-it notes and things . . .": a case study of a rapid application development project. *Journal of Information Systems,* 10, 3, 195–216.

Beynon-Davies, P.; Tudhope, D.; and Mackay, H. 1999. Information systems prototyping in practice. *Journal of Information Technology,* 14, 1, 107–120.

Beynon-Davies, P.; Carne, C.; Mackay, H.; and Tudhope, D. 1999. Rapid application development: an empirical review. *European Journal of Information Systems,* 8, 2, 211–223.

Blair, D.C. 2005. *Wittgenstein, Language, and Information: Back to the Rough Ground.* Berlin-Heidelberg: Springer.

Boehm, B. 1981. *Software Engineering Economics.* Upper Saddle River, NJ: Prentice Hall.

———. 1988. The spiral model of software development and enhancement. *Computer,* 21, 5, 14–24.

———. 2002. Get ready for agile methods, with care. *IEEE Computer,* 35, 1, 64–69.

Boehm, B.; Gray, T.E.; and Seewaldt, T. 1984. Prototyping vs. specification: a multi-project experiment. *IEEE Transactions on Software Engineering,* 10, 3, 290–303.

Boland, R.J. 1978. The process and product of system design. *Management Science,* 24, 9, 887–898.

Boland, R.J., and Day, W.F. 1989. The experience of system design: a hermeneutic of organizational action. *Scandinavian Journal of Management,* 5, 2, 87–104.

Boland, R.J., and Tenkasi, R.V. 1995. Perspective making and perspective taking in communities of knowing. *Organization Science,* 5, 4, 350–372.

Brewer, W.F. 1987. Schemas versus mental models in human memory. In I.P. Morris (ed.), *Modeling Cognition.* Chichester, UK: Wiley, 187–197.

Brinkkemper, S. 1996. Method engineering: engineering of information systems development methods and tools. *Information and Software Technology,* 38, 4, 275–280.

Brooks, F.P. 1987. No silver bullet: essence and accidents of software engineering. *IEEE Computer,* 20, 4, 1987, 10–19.

———. 1995. *The Mythical Man Month: Essays on Software Engineering,* anniversary ed. Boston: Addison-Wesley.

Bruner, J. 1990. *Acts of Meaning.* Cambridge, MA: Harvard University Press.

Bucciarelli, L.L. 1994. *Designing Engineers.* Cambridge, MA: MIT Press.

Checkland, P. 1981. *Systems Thinking, Systems Practice.* Chichester, UK: Wiley.

Checkland, P., and Scholes, J. 1999. *Soft Systems Methodology in Action.* Chichester, UK: Wiley.

Churchman, C.W. 1968. *The Systems Approach.* New York: Dell.

———. 1971. *The Design of Inquiring Systems.* New York: Basic Books.

Clancey, W.J.; Smoliar, S.W.; and Stefik, M.J. 1994. *Contemplating Minds: A Forum for Artificial Intelligence.* Cambridge, MA: MIT Press.

Clark, K., and Fujimoto, T. 1991. *Product Development Performance: Strategy, Organization, and Management in the World Auto Industry.* Cambridge, MA: Harvard Business School Press.

Cockburn, A. 1998. *Surviving Object-Oriented Projects.* Boston: Addison-Wesley.

———. 2002. *Agile Software Development.* Boston: Addison-Wesley.

Cross, N. 1989. *Engineering Design Methods.* Chichester, UK: Wiley.

Curtis, B.; Krasner, H.; and Iscoe, N. 1988. A field study of the software design process for large systems. *Communications of the ACM,* 31, 11, 1268–1287.

Davis, G.B. 1974. *Management Information Systems: Conceptual Foundations, Structure, and Development.* New York: McGraw-Hill.

———. 1982. Strategies for information requirements determination. *IBM Systems Journal,* 21, 1, 4–30.

Deephouse, C.; Mukhopadhyay, T.; Goldenson, D.; and Kellner, M. 1995. Software processes and project performance. *Journal of Management Information Systems,* 12, 3, 187–205.

Dowson, M. 1987. Iteration in the software process; review of the 3rd International Software Process Workshop. In *Proceedings of the Ninth International Conference on Software Engineering,* Monterey, CA, 36–41.

Floyd, C. 1984. A systematic look at prototyping. In Budde et al. (eds.), *Approaches to Prototyping.* Berlin-Heidelberg: Springer-Verlag.

Floyd, C.; Mel, W.M.; Reisin, F.M.; Schmidt, G.; and Wolf, G. 1989. Out of Scandinavia: alternative approaches to software design and system development. *Human-Computer Interaction,* 4, 4, 253–350.

Gordon, V.S., and Bieman, J.M. 1993. Reported effects of rapid prototyping on industrial software quality. *Software Quality Journal,* 2, 2, 93–108.

———. 1995. Rapid prototyping: lessons learned. *IEEE Software,* 12, 1, 85–95.

Hardgrave, B.C.; Wilson, R.L.; and Eastman, K. 1999. Toward a contingency model for selecting an information system prototyping strategy. *Journal of Management Information Systems,* 16, 2, 113–136.

Hazzan, O. 2002. The reflective practitioner perspective in software engineering education. *Journal of Systems and Software,* 63, 3, 161–171.

Hirschheim, R.; Klein, H.; and Lyytinen, K. 1995. *Information Systems Development and Data Modeling: Conceptual and Philosophical Foundations.* Cambridge: Cambridge University Press.

Humphrey, W.S. 1989. *Managing the Software Process.* Boston: Addison-Wesley.

Hutchins, E. 1995. *Cognition in the Wild.* Cambridge, MA: MIT Press.

Iivari, J., and Koskela, E. 1987. The PIOCO model for information systems design. *MIS Quarterly,* 11, 3, 401–419.

Janson, M.A., and Smith, L.D. 1985. Prototyping for systems development: a critical appraisal. *MIS Quarterly,* 9, 4, 305–316.

Jeffries, R.; Turner, A.A.; Polson, P.G.; and Atwood, M.E. 1981. *The Processes Involved in Designing Software.* Hillsdale, NJ: Erlbaum.

Johnson-Laird, P.N. 1980. Mental models in cognitive science. *Cognitive Science,* 4, 1, 71–115.

Keen, P.G.W., and Scott Morton, S. 1978. *Decision Support Systems: An Organizational Perspective.* Boston: Addison-Wesley.

Kruchten, P. 2000. *The Rational Unified Process: An Introduction,* 2nd ed. Boston: Addison-Wesley.

Larman, C. 2004. *Agile and Iterative Development, A Manager's Guide.* Boston: Addison-Wesley.

Larman, C., and Basili, V. 2003. Iterative and incremental development: a brief history. *Computer,* 36, 6, 47–56.

Lichter, H.; Schneider-Hufschmidt, M.; and Zullighoven, H. 1994. Prototyping in industrial software projects—bridging the gap between theory and practice. *IEEE Transactions on Software Engineering,* 20, 11, 825–832.

Lindvall, M.; Basili, V.; Boehm, B.; Costa, P.; Dongle, K.; Shull, F.; Tesoriero, R.; Williams, L.; and Zelkowitz, M. 2002. Empirical findings in agile methods. In F. Maurer and D. Wells (eds.), *Extreme Programming and Agile Methods—XP/Agile Universe 2002, Lecture Notes in Computer Science* 2753. Berlin-Heidelberg: Springer, 81–92.

Lyytinen, K. 1987. A taxonomic perspective of information systems development: theoretical constructs and recommendations. In R.J. Boland and R. Hirschheim (eds.), *Critical Issues in Information Systems Research.* Chichester, UK: Wiley, 3–41.

Lyytinen, K.; Mathiassen, L.; and Ropponen, J. 1998. Attention shaping and software risk—a categorical analysis of four classical risk management approaches. *Information Systems Research,* 9, 3, 233–255.

Mahmood, M.A. 1987. System development methods—a comparative investigation. *MIS Quarterly,* 11, 3, 293–311.

Mathiassen, L.; Seewaldt, T.; and Stage, J. 1995. Prototyping and specifying: principles and practices of a mixed approach. *Scandinavian Journal of Information Systems,* 7, 1, 55–72.

McCracken, D.D., and Jackson, M.A. 1982. Life cycle concept considered harmful. *ACM SIGSOFT Software Engineering Notes,* 7, 2, 29–32.

Mumford, E. 2003. *Redesigning Human Systems.* Hershey, PA: Idea Group.

Nauman, J.D., and Jenkins, M. 1982. Prototyping: the new paradigm for systems development. *MIS Quarterly,* 6, 3, 29–44.

Necco, C.R.; Gordon, C.L.; and Tsai, N.W. 1987. Systems analysis and design: current practices. *MIS Quarterly,* 11, 4, 461–476.

Newell, A., and Simon, H.A. 1976. Computer science as empirical inquiry: symbols and search. *Communications of the ACM,* 19, 3, 113–126.

Orlikowski, W.J., and Iacono, S. 2001. Desperately seeking the "IT" in IT research: a call to theorizing the IT artifact. *Information Systems Research,* 12, 2, 121–124.

Parnas, D.L., and Clements, P.C. 1986. A rational design process: how and why to fake it. *IEEE Transactions on Software Engineering,* 12, 2, 251–256.

Peirce, C.S. 1992. *Reasoning and the Logic of Things.* Cambridge, MA: Harvard University Press.

Potts, C.; Takahashi, K.; and Anton, A.I. 1994. Inquiry-based requirements analysis. *IEEE Software,* 11, 2, 21–32.

Prietula, M.J., and March, S.T. 1991. Form and substance in physical database design: an empirical study. *Information Systems Research,* 2, 4, 287–314.

Rossi, M.; Ramesh, B.; Lyytinen, K.; and Tolvanen, J.P. 2004. Managing evolutionary method engineering by method rationale. *Journal of the Association for Information Systems,* 5, 9, 356–391.

Royce, W.W. 1970. Managing the development of large-scale software systems. *Proceedings of IEEE WESCON,* Piscataway, NJ, August, 1–9.

Simon, H.A. 1996. *The Sciences of the Artificial,* 3rd ed. Cambridge, MA: MIT Press.

Subramanian, G.H., and Zarnich, G.E. 1996. An examination of some software development effort and productivity determinants in ICASE tool projects. *Journal of Management Information Systems,* 12, 4, 143–160.

Suchman, L.A. 1987. *Plans and Situated Actions: The Problem of Human-Machine Communication,* Cambridge: Cambridge University Press.

———. 1994. Review of Winograd and Flores, *Understanding Computers and Cognition.* In W.J. Clancey, S.W. Smoliar, and M.J. Stefik (eds.), *Contemplating Minds: A Forum for Artificial Intelligence.* Cambridge, MA: MIT Press.

Tolvanen, J.P., and Lyytinen, K. 1993. Flexible method adaptation in CASE. The metamodeling approach. *Scandinavian Journal of Information Systems,* 5, 51–77.

Turk, D.; France, R.; and Rumpe, B. 2005. Assumptions underlying agile software development processes. *Journal of Database Management,* 16, 4, 62–87.

Turner, J. 1987. Understanding the elements of system design. In R.J. Boland and R. Hirschheim (eds.), *Critical Issues in Information Systems Research.* Chichester, UK: Wiley, 97–111.

Weick, K. 1979. *The Social Psychology of Organizing.* Reading, MA: Addison-Wesley.

Wikipedia. 2007. Iteration. Available at http://en.wikipedia.org/wiki/Iteration (accessed on May 7, 2007).

Winograd, T., and Flores, F. 1986. *Understanding Computers and Cognition: A New Foundation for Design.* Reading, MA: Addison-Wesley.

Wirth, N. 1971. Program development by stepwise refinement. *Communications of the ACM,* 14, 4, 221–227.

Wynekoop, J.L., and Russo, N.L. 1997. Studying system development methodologies: an examination of research methods. *Information Systems Journal,* 7, 1, 47–65.

CHAPTER 5

A FRAMEWORK FOR IDENTIFYING THE DRIVERS OF INFORMATION SYSTEMS DEVELOPMENT METHOD EMERGENCE

SABINE MADSEN AND KARLHEINZ KAUTZ

Abstract: This chapter explores how unique and locally situated information systems development (ISD) methods unfold over time and why they emerge differently. The purpose is to identify the underlying process form and drivers of ISD method emergence. Based on a synthesis of literature about contextualism, structuration theory, and change processes, a theoretical framework is developed and used to perform a comparative analysis of two longitudinal case studies of method emergence in a Multimedia project and a Web project. The framework facilitates progression from narrative accounts, over systematic comparison, to generalization of findings to theory, thereby allowing for a movement from surface description to deep explanation. The analysis shows that while the two cases are very similar in some regards they can in fact be seen as two different sequences of change (dialectical versus teleological) driven by two different generative motors (conflict resolution versus social construction). We suggest that the demonstrated framework is relevant to both researchers and practitioners in reading a situation before project initiation, during development, and after project completion and in identifying and leveraging the dynamics inherent in or relevant to a particular situation and change process.

Keywords: ISD Methods, Emergence, Framework

INTRODUCTION

In the information systems development (ISD) literature, the concept of method is often used to refer to an orderly, predictable, and universally applicable process (Truex, Baskerville, and Travis, 2000, p. 54). Lyytinen (1987) defines a method as an organized collection of concepts, beliefs, values, and normative principles supported by material resources, while Andersen and colleagues (1990) and Mathiassen (1998) declare that a method consists of prescriptions for performing a certain type of work process with the help of principles, techniques, and computer-based tools and is characterized by its application area and its perspective—that is, a set of assumptions on the nature of the work processes and their environment. In line with these definitions, Fitzgerald, Russo, and Stolterman (2002, p. 13) put forward the term "formalized method" and define it as any formally documented in-house or commercially available method.

Most contributions within the field of ISD focus on formalized development methods: the prescriptive literature emphasizes how they *should* be used, while empirically grounded writings focus on how they actually *are* used. A number of method authors recommend that the development process should be tailored to fit the contingencies of the particular situation (Avison et al., 1998; Jacobsen, Booch, and Rumbaugh, 1999). In line with this, empirical studies show that in practice information systems (IS) developers rarely adopt methods in their entirety; instead they adapt and apply method elements in a pragmatic way (see, e.g., Bansler and Bødker, 1993; Fitzgerald, 1997, 1998; Fitzgerald, Russo, and Stolterman, 2002; Madsen and Kautz, 2002; Stolterman, 1991, 1992, 1994). Others argue that the formalized method is just one element among many that influence and shape the actual unfolding development process and situated use of methods—which has been referred to as the unique method (Truex, Baskerville, and Travis, 2000), the local methodology (Vidgen, 2002; Vidgen et al., 2002), or the method-in-action (Fitzgerald, Russo, and Stolterman, 2002). However, so far, little theoretical and empirical research has addressed the practical and temporal details of how and why the unique and local method emerges. To help overcome this deficiency, we have previously investigated and meticulously mapped the relationship between what influences and shapes the method and how it consequently emerges in a Multimedia project (Kautz, 2004) and a Web project (Madsen, Kautz, and Vidgen, 2006). In this chapter, we draw on and develop the research further and more conceptually by exploring how unique and locally situated ISD methods unfold over time and why they emerge differently. The purpose is to identify the underlying sequence and drivers of change in ISD method emergence.

As our object of study we focus on *the emergent method,* which we define as *the unfolding development process and the activities and the applied method elements that comprise this process.* This definition addresses the development process as a sequence of activities (Sambamurthy and Kirsch, 2000). The choice of the concepts of *emergent method,* when we describe and analyze concrete cases, and *method emergence,* when we relate to the phenomenon on a general level, is inspired by Pettigrew (1987). Studying change processes in firms, he argues that from a holistic and systemic perspective the language of process is characterized by verb forms such as emerging, elaborating, mobilizing, changing, dissolving, and transforming, whereas at the level of the individual actor the emphasis is on enacting, acting, reacting, interacting, and adapting (Pettigrew, 1987). While we take the individual actor into account, we are primarily interested in the unfolding of the development process as an outcome of a complex interplay of enacting and interacting actors and structures.

In the next sections, we describe our research approach and develop a theoretical framework for understanding method emergence in practice. Then we describe the emergent methods in two longitudinal case studies of a Multimedia project and a Web project. The chapter systematically compares the elements and interactions that contributed to the method emergence in the two cases with the aim of explaining why they unfolded differently. The results of the cross-case comparison are discussed in relation to process theory to identify the underlying process forms and drivers. The chapter ends with a summary of the main conclusions.

RESEARCH APPROACH

For the research presented in this chapter we draw on two empirical case studies of ISD projects in practice. The purpose of the first project was to develop a multimedia information system (MMIS) to spread knowledge about software process improvement (SPI) and quality management to information technology (IT) professionals. The project was undertaken for the European Union (EU) based on a joint bid by two software organizations: an IT consultancy and an academic organization. The Multimedia project lasted twenty-two months. The second project concerned the development of a Web based information system and was performed in-house in a small to medium-sized market research company. The Web project was conducted in contracted collaboration with academic researchers but for the benefit of the market research department. The purpose was to improve the department's internal work practices and support its online sales to customers by creating a research data repository (RDR) that would contain details of companies and production volumes in the drinks industry. The Web project lasted twenty-four months. The two cases have been selected for cross-case comparison because of their likeness as "the juxtaposition of seemingly similar cases by a researcher looking for differences can help break simplistic frames" (Eisenhardt, 1989, p. 541).

The roles and length of stay in the field have varied for the authors of this chapter. In the Multimedia project, one author was involved in the project as an action researcher throughout the twenty-two-month time period. This author participated on the development team as the overall project manager and documented the development process in several ways. Minutes were taken from all meetings and shared with all involved. In addition to product and process documentation, data were collected in the form of the researcher's personal diary as well as statements from e-mail and informal conversations. Finally, the project contract, the official project progress reports, and the final project report were available for this study. In the Web project, one author followed the RDR project closely during the two-year time period. A variety of documents such as the original project proposal, minutes of quarterly steering committee and monthly project team meetings, company documents, as well as project reports and deliverables were collected. Furthermore, the author participated actively in the project as an "action case" (Braa and Vidgen, 1999) or "involved" researcher (Walsham, 1995) for six months, contributing primarily to the requirements analysis activity. During these six months, as many details as possible were recorded in the researcher's personal diary. In addition, the study draws on seven semistructured interviews with employees of the case organization, the development team members, and the involved researcher. The interviews were conducted by the other chapter author acting in the role of an "outside observer" (Walsham, 1995). Individual case study accounts of both the Multimedia and Web cases have previously been peer-reviewed and published (Kautz, 2004; Madsen, Kautz, and Vidgen, 2006). These earlier published readings as well as unpublished write-ups have been included as relevant data material for this chapter, where our purpose, in line with Eisenhardt (1989), is to continue the work of theorizing from case study research by looking at and beyond the individual studies to identify patterns across the two cases.

In keeping with the research topic and interpretive approach, our data analysis and understanding of method emergence has come about through an iterative process of interpretation, comparison, and interlacing of prior research and empirical data. The framework presented below has been modified and refined over time according to the lessons learned from its use as a theoretical lens for understanding emerging change processes in practice (see, e.g., Kautz and Nielsen, 2004; Madsen, 2004; Madsen, Kautz, and Vidgen, 2005, 2006). For this chapter all data material have been reread and analyzed anew with an eye to the differences and similarities between the two cases, and single-case summary and cross-case comparison tables have been outlined. This chapter presents the findings relevant for understanding how and why the methods emerged differently in the Multimedia and Web cases.

THE THEORETICAL FRAMEWORK

The ISD literature reveals a lack of cumulative frameworks that integrate the theoretical and empirical findings from the many existing studies about ISD and ISD methods in practice. Notable exceptions are: the NIMSAD framework, which is based on both theory and practice and can be used to select and evaluate primarily formalized methods (Jayaratna, 1994); the social action model of situated information systems design derived from a case study of a practical design process (Gasson, 1999); an integrative framework of the information systems development process developed from a literature study (Sambamurthy and Kirsch, 2000); and the method-in-action framework that incorporates past and contemporary thinking and empirical findings about ISD methods into one conceptual frame (Fitzgerald, Russo, and Stolterman, 2002). Common to these frameworks is that they stress the importance of understanding the context, the formalized method(s), the developers' preconceptions and actions, and their interactions with other stakeholders, as well as the influence that these concepts have on the ISD process. Our work builds on the insight provided by these frameworks and models in that we draw on similar concepts and share similar assumptions about their relationship to the emergent method. However, our framework extends the line of thinking through a clear focus on the temporal dimension of the development process, and the emergent method is conceptualized as a sequence of activities that unfolds over time. To explain why emergent methods unfold differently, we draw on theoretical ideas as put forward in Pettigrew's contextualism (1985, 1987), and Giddens's structuration theory (1984), and subsequently synthesized by Walsham (1993) as well as Van de Ven and Poole's (1995) four process theories that specify four different process forms and drivers.

The framework constitutes an organizing structure for providing: first, a narrative account of how the emergent method unfolded in the individual cases; second, a systematic cross-case comparison to explain why the methods emerged differently; and third, a generalization of analysis results to process theory.

The object of study is the emergent method, which is defined as the unfolding development process and the activities, and the applied method elements that constitute this process. The narrative account of the emergent method describes what happened over time, because an event sequence with a clear beginning, middle, and end is the core of narrative structure (Pentland, 1999). However, the event sequence is only the first important step toward understanding why this particular pattern of activities occurred (Pentland, 1999). It is also necessary to focus on influential actors (their roles, perceptions, social relations, and demographics), power, culture, and broader context to generate meaningful explanations (Pentland, 1999). Thus, to explain why the processes unfolded as they did, we draw on the key concepts of *content of change, social process,* and *social context* (Walsham, 1993) as interlinked units of analysis that facilitate progression from surface description to explanation (Kautz, 2004; Kautz and Nielsen, 2004; Pentland, 1999; Pettigrew, 1987).

Content of change refers to the planned and actual process and product of the development endeavor (Kautz, 2004; Kautz and Nielsen, 2004); that is the planned and actual ISD process and information system under development. The planned is assumed to be an expression of expectation that shapes attention and action (Bruner, 2002), and we consider the gap between the expected and the actual important for an initial understanding of what characterizes the content and drives the process of change. After the initial narrative description of the emergent method, the concept of content is therefore applied to come to understand *what* characterizes the change (Pettigrew, 1987). Social process focuses on the political (i.e., the distribution of power and balance between autonomy and control) and the cultural (i.e., subcultures and the interaction between them) aspects of ISD and helps to explain *how,* that is, through which mechanisms, changes to the content take place (Pettigrew, 1987; Walsham, 1993). Social context addresses social relations, social infrastructure, and the history of previous procedures, structures, and commitments and helps to explain *why* the social process emerges as it does (Walsham, 1993). Previous application of the framework to empirical cases shows that the social context creates the social and structural landscape within which the social process can emerge and that the social process in turn both enables and constrains the content of change (Madsen, 2004; Madsen, Kautz, and Vidgen, 2005, 2006).

As the last step from empirical phenomena toward conceptual understanding, analysis results are generalized to Van de Ven and Poole's (1995) four process theories. Van de Ven and Poole

Table 5.1

The Theoretical Framework

Description	Object of study	*The emergent method*—the unfolding development process and the activities, and applied method elements that constitute this process
	Key concepts	Relations between concepts
	Content of change	What characterizes the planned and actual product and process of change?
	Social process	How do political and cultural aspects help explain the way changes to the content take place?
	Social context	How do social relations, infrastructure, and history help explain why the social process emerges as it does?
Explanation	Process forms and drivers	Which theoretical *process form(s)* does the emergent method resemble, if any? Which *generative motor(s)* drives the emergent method, if any?

(1995) suggest four different sequences of change driven by different generative motors: (1) *life cycle,* the change process follows a necessary and linear sequence of events driven forward by compliance to predefined rules regulated by nature, logic, or institutions; (2) *evolution,* the change process takes place as a recurrent and cumulative sequence of variation, selection, and retention driven forward by competitive survival; (3) *dialectical,* the change process takes the form of thesis–antithesis–synthesis and is generated by conflict among opposing forces; (4) *teleological,* the change process emerges as an ongoing sequence of goal setting, implementation, evaluation, and modification driven forward by consensus among cooperating actors. The four process theories constitute ideal types that individually or in combination help to explain how and why change unfolds (Van de Ven and Poole, 1995). The theoretical framework (see Table 5.1) will be used to organize and perform a comparative analysis of the two cases.

THE EMERGENT METHODS

This section presents narrative accounts of how the emergent methods unfolded first, in the Multimedia case and second, in the Web case.

The Multimedia Case

The Multimedia project concerned the development of a complex MMIS for dissemination of knowledge about SPI to practitioners. It was performed for the EU on a commercial fixed-price contract, which specified the project, the financial budget, the formal project organization, and the main building blocks and requirements for a phased development approach and project progress reporting. The formal project organization consisted of an overall project manager and predefined the distribution of work and responsibilities between a Norwegian IT consultancy and a Danish academic organization as well as bimonthly project meetings for all involved developers. The development was undertaken by a project team consisting of six to eight people, with three to four people from each of the two organizations. The overall project manager was located in Norway, while a local project manager was responsible for the Danish team members. All project team members had long formal educations in computer science, but varying degrees of practical experience in the relevant areas of SPI, ISD, and MMIS.

From the beginning, the application was envisioned as an MMIS consisting of components representing relevant themes of SPI in the form of hypermedia-linked textual and animated slide shows, a video film presenting a case company, a videotaped expert panel, and a large annotated bibliography. The planned development process covered a time period of eighteen months. It was outlined as an in-house developed method and formally included in the EU contract. The method specified (1) a number of sequential steps, (2) milestones and deliverables, (3) development activities, (4) the application of MMIS analysis and design techniques for information content modeling as well as functional, interface, and technical design (such as treatment writing, storyboards, flowcharts, and scripting languages), and (5) the use of supporting software tools for multimedia development. The in-house developed method was inspired by a waterfall model approach to MMIS development and multimedia development techniques recommended in available books and papers (e.g., Bergman and Moore, 1990; Sørensen, 1997).

The actual ISD process lasted twenty-two months and only partially followed the path outlined in the method description. Two months into the project, communication problems between the IT consultancy and the academic team led to adaptation and standardization of information-content templates and the accompanying storyboards. Moreover, after four months, it became apparent that the planned sequential process could not appropriately deal with a number of complex tasks. It proved difficult to develop storyboards for the individual information elements without specifying the overall information architecture. In addition, attempts to define the relationships between the different interlinked hypermedia elements were difficult. This made the related task of determining the user's access to the features describing the navigational possibilities equally problematic. Thus, from month four, the overall information architecture, the hyperlink navigation structure, and user interface modeling activities were performed in parallel. Furthermore, in month six, these activities were officially assigned to and performed by one subteam (i.e., the Danish academic team), which was geographically located in the same place. From that period on, the other subteam (i.e., the IT consultancy team) largely provided input for the modeling and design tasks in the form of literature reviews. This specialization of tasks and the resulting reallocation of resources in favor of the academic team had not been anticipated in the original project plan. Thus, even though an elaborate in-house–developed method that incorporated the unique requirements of the particular situation had been outlined, it was necessary to devote much time during the project to negotiating, revising, and revisiting the way of (co)working.

The Web Case

The Web project was performed in a UK-based market research company. It concerned the development of a technically complex Web-based research data repository for collection, storage, processing, and formatting of a large volume of market data about companies in the drinks industry, such as manufacturers, packagers, and distributors. The RDR project was undertaken as in-house development, but was performed collaboratively by the market research company and academic staff within a government-funded program, the Teaching Company Scheme (TCS), which promotes collaboration between industry and university. TCS specified the project duration (two years) and the formal project organization, which comprised a steering committee (quarterly meetings), a project team (monthly meetings), and the involvement of support from academic researchers (weekly). The steering committee consisted of six to eight people, including the project team, which was made up of three to four people with one full-time developer who did most of the actual hands-on work. All of the project team members had long formal educations in computer science and from zero to fifteen years of practical experience, with the full-time developer being a newly graduated master's student with no prior industry experience. For this reason, the developer was formally supported by a university-employed academic supervisor and an industry supervisor, who was part of the company management and the daily leader of the market research department.

From the outset, the application was envisioned as an RDR to be implemented based on a commercial Web content management system, which would support the market research department's internal work practices (i.e., the report production process) and external sale to customers through storage and online analysis and reporting of data at a high granularity. Before project initiation, the contingency approach Multiview/WISDM (Vidgen et al., 2002) was chosen as the formalized method and used to inform the construction of a situation-specific method outlined in the form of a detailed project plan, which was included in the original TCS project proposal and formally approved by the TCS program. The development process was planned as a prototype driven approach where two of the department's core products, paper-based market reports on the bottled water and watercooler markets, would be used as the point of departure for implementing the first working prototype. As the application was expected to be based on a Web content management system, the development approach was planned with an emphasis on the Web-based front-end, organizational change and implementation.

However, when the project commenced, the two paper-based market reports quickly led the project team to discover that the amount of data and data relationships was extensive and an initial market scan of available content management systems revealed that they were not sophisticated enough to support that kind of data complexity. Thus, a few months into the project, the project team decided that the RDR application would be custom-made and a software tool was adopted to support the now more technically complex development task. Furthermore, the RDR application was not developed with an equal eye to internal process improvement and external sale as planned, but with an emphasis on the internal report production process. This was due to a performed requirements analysis, which showed that the current report production process could be greatly improved by automation of mundane tasks (e.g., data collection, data entry, and report formatting). The project team and company management therefore decided to give priority to the internal process. Eight months into the project, company management also decided that the RDR application should be able to produce what they perceived as the market research department's main product, namely, paper-based reports. In contrast, the project team had expected all data analysis and reporting to be online. The technical complexity of the system was ever-increasing, and after ten months the project team decided that the planned three-layer architecture would have to be expanded with an additional layer of prespecified data queries and report-formatting scripts. The first working prototype was released for use by market researchers after approximately a year and a half, but work to enhance and extend functionality continued throughout and well beyond the project's two-year time frame. The vision remained constant throughout the project, namely to "create an enterprise repository for [the market research company's] research data" (TCS project proposal), but the practicalities of what (product) and how (process) to implement were continuously reconceived and scoped.

CROSS-CASE COMPARISON OF THE EMERGENT METHODS

On first inspection the Multimedia and Web cases seem very similar. Both cases concerned technically complex information systems, were performed by relatively small project organizations

Table 5.2

Content of Change

	Multimedia case	Web case
Similarities	Stable vision of product purpose Product and process subject to ongoing reinvention and configuration	Stable vision of product purpose Product and process subject to ongoing reinvention and configuration
Differences	Reinventions and configurations of content driven by perceived gap between the planned and the actual *process*	Reinventions and configurations of content driven by perceived gap between the planned and the actual *product*

consisting of IS developers with long formal educations, were undertaken as joint university–company collaborations on EU and TCS contracts, respectively, and in both cases, the formal contacts contained situation-specific formalized methods. However, already the different outlines of the planned methods viewed as the involved actors' expressions of the expected indicate that the emergent methods would unfold differently: in the Multimedia case the formalized method was a phased and sequential process, while in the Web case a prototype-driven development process was chosen.

In this section, we analyze the elements and interactions that contributed to method emergence in the Multimedia and Web projects. The aim is to explain why the emergent methods unfolded differently. In the following, a systematic cross-case comparison is provided, structured according to the key concepts of *content, process,* and *context.*

Content

What characterized the planned and the actual product and process of change in the two cases? In both projects the initial vision of the information systems' purpose as stated in the formal EU and TCS contracts remained relatively stable throughout the development process. Nevertheless, in both cases the application and the process did not emerge as planned. Instead, the narrative descriptions of the two unfolding methods show that in both cases the product and process were subject to ongoing reinventions and reconfigurations (see Table 5.2).

However, the two projects differ in terms of the events that the involved actors considered "unexpected" and either problematic or opportune as compared with the expectations manifested as the planned product and process. Thus, with regard to the Multimedia case we propose that the perceived problems and applied solutions primarily concerned the gap between the planned and the actual *process,* that is, process deviations, iterations, methodical breaches, organization, and specialization. In contrast, we suggest that the involved actors' conceptualization of challenges and coping mechanisms in the Web case largely concerned the gap between the envisioned and the actual *product,* that is, technical obstacles, and continuous definition and revision of systems architecture and prototype content.

Process

How do political and cultural aspects help to explain how changes to the content took place in the two cases? In both the Multimedia and Web cases, the social process was facilitated by a

Table 5.3

Social Process

	Multimedia case	Web case
Similarities	Power distribution in favor of the two project managers and the principal designer	Power distribution in favor of company management and academic supervisor
	Subteams and cultures exist (IT consultants, academic personnel)	Subteams and cultures exist (company management, academic researchers, TCS representative)
	Subculture interaction facilitated by formal project organization specified in EU contract	Subculture interaction facilitated by formal project organization specified in TCS contract
Differences	*Two* subteams and cultures within project team	Project team a homogeneous group led by academic supervisor
	Altered power distribution, manifested in academic team achieving a dominant position	*Unaltered* power distribution throughout the process
	Subculture interaction mediated by *written documents*	Subculture interaction mediated by *working code*

few influential actors who wrote the initial EU and TCS project proposals, suggested the major changes, and approved all intermediate results during the process; a number of subteams and cultures were involved and influenced the continuous reinventions and configurations of the content of change (both product and process); and the interaction between these subcultures was mediated by the formal project organizations as specified in the EU and TCS contracts, respectively (see Table 5.3).

However, there are also important differences between the two cases. In the Multimedia case, the power distribution between the project team's two subgroups was altered during the course of the project, with the result that the Danish academic team achieved a dominant position due to their greater knowledge about multimedia development and different work values. The Danish academic team was, for example, willing to work overtime and deliver beyond specification, while the Norwegian IT consultants were used to strive to meet customer demands with minimum resources. In comparison, the Web project team was a more homogeneous group led by the academic supervisor, and the power distribution within the project team and between the project team and company management remained unaltered over time. Another significant difference relates to subculture interaction. While in both cases the formal project organization was an important mechanism in ensuring that there was interaction between subgroups, the difference concerns the main boundary objects that were used to mediate the interaction, namely, written documents and working code, respectively. We suggest that the two cases can be seen as representing two different perspectives on systems development: one in favor of and with a strong focus on methods, plans, and written documents (i.e., method as overarching approach and important means) and one in favor of working code produced through pragmatic application of select methods and techniques (i.e., method as helpful tools). The distinction between method as overarching approach and/or tool is inspired by Stolterman and Russo (1997) and also relates to the process and product orientations identified in the section on content of change.

Context

How do social relations, social infrastructure, and the history of previous structures, commitments, and procedures help to explain why the social processes emerged as they did? In the Multimedia project, the social context was shaped by long-term social relations between the overall project manager, the local project manager, and the principal designer, a former student of the local project manager, and the social infrastructure was characterized by the involvement and easy accessibility of these three influential actors. However, already from project initiation there was some rivalry between the two project managers, which led to a slightly competitive atmosphere and ultimately to the shift in task and power distribution. The overall project manager explains:

> In the early stages of the project, the two project managers based on a certain personal rivalry had, despite the defined information strategy and the existing treatment document, different, but not clearly, articulated levels of ambitions with regard to the MMIS. (Kautz, 2004)

Historically, the overall project manager and the IT consultancy team members in general had experience with EU projects, ISD, and SPI, but not with multimedia development. The local Danish project manager had previously developed and tested his own methodical approach in a number of educational projects, was an expert in SPI and an experienced teacher in the fields of ISD and multimedia. The principal designer had experience with MMIS development and knowledge about ISD, but little acquaintance with SPI. The local project manager and the principal designer advocated and facilitated the introduction of additional templates and standards as a means for coping with differences in the project team members' knowledge, work practices, levels of detail, expectations, and ambitions, while the overall project manager was attentive toward the monitoring and reporting of project plans, progress, finances, and resources. Together, the three influential actors' different backgrounds and different emphasis during development (i.e., EU reporting requirements, formalized method development, multimedia development) as well as their relationship to each other help to explain why the development process was driven by *conflicts, power issues,* and a strong methodical *process orientation* manifested in a focus on *written documents.*

In the Web case, the social context was shaped by long-term trust-based social relations between company management and the academic supervisor due to, among other things, a previous two-year project within the TCS program. This meant that there was a shared understanding of the project vision, the appropriate development approach, the information technology to be used, and the required project organization specified by the TSC. The social atmosphere is illustrated in the following citations.

> Between management and project team: "Once a month is a technical meeting, which I receive the minutes of . . . I can contribute at the broader level and just reassure myself that the project is going well, but because they are a particularly good team, they are getting on with it and I'm happy with that." (The Web case, company chairman, interview, November 2002)

> Within project team: "The tone and atmosphere was very friendly and cozy. It is a small team and there seems to be close collaboration, even though there is a physical distance between [the market research company] and the University." (The Web case, involved researcher's personal project diary, entry: March 5, 2002)

Table 5.4

Social Context

	Multimedia case	Web case
Similarities	Long-term social relations between the three influential actors (the overall project manager, the local project manager, and the principal designer)	Long-term social relations between company management and academic supervisor
	Social infrastructure characterized by involved and easily accessible overall and local project manager	Social infrastructure characterized by involved and easily accessible management and academic supervisor
Differences	Close relations, but also a certain *rivalry* between the two project managers	Influential actors' long-term *trust*-based relation and collaboration within TCS program, academic supervisor as boundary spanner
	The three influential actors had *different* backgrounds and emphasized different aspects during development (i.e., EU reporting requirements, formalized method development, multimedia development)	*Shared* understanding of company, project vision, and established work practices passed on from management and academic supervisor to newly employed developer

The strong relations and shared assumptions cemented the distribution of power in favor of company management and the academic supervisor and meant that the shared understanding was passed on from these actors to the newly employed developer. The academic supervisor's background and his preference for data modeling, technology, and prototyping were especially influential (Madsen, 2004; Madsen, Kautz, and Vidgen, 2006), as was his role as a "boundary spanner" (Curtis, Krasner, and Iscoe, 1988), linking the steering committee and project team as well as the past, present, and future. Together, management's and the academic supervisor's history and long-term trust-based collaboration help to explain that even though the content of change was continuously reconceived, the development process was driven by a set of *shared underlying assumptions, stable power relations,* and an agreed-upon *product orientation* manifested in a focus on *working code.*

In both the Multimedia and Web cases, the social context was characterized by long-term social relations between, and a high degree of involvement of, the influential actors. However, the analysis of social context shows that the two cases are distinctively different in that the emergent method in the Multimedia project to a large extent can be explained by *conflict,* while the unfolding of the method in the Web case is best understood in terms of *consensus* (see Table 5.4).

THE EMERGENT METHODS' FORMS AND DRIVERS

In the Multimedia case, the project was initially planned to follow a phased and sequential in-house-developed method. However, the emergent method took the form of a dialectical process (Van de Ven and Poole, 1995), where the two subgroups in the project team engaged in a power struggle leading to a sequence of events that roughly followed a thesis–antithesis–synthesis pattern. In this dialectical process, *conflict regarding how to perform the development process* was the major driver of change, and the outcome was an altered power balance, reallocation of tasks, and standardization of documentation templates. In the Web case, the project was initially outlined in a detailed plan for a prototyping approach. In practice, the emergent method unfolded as a teleological process (Van de Ven and Poole, 1995), where the project team and company management acted from a shared understanding resulting in a process of continuous social construction of goals according to new decisions and discoveries. In this teleological process, *consensus regarding the (re)formulation of goals for the product under development* was the main generative motor of change and the outcome was a custom-built information system aimed at the company's internal report production process. We conclude that the answers to the questions of how the two methods emerged and why they emerged differently can be understood with reference to *conflict* versus *consensus.*

This is not to say that the Multimedia case was not also a teleological process at times, that there was not a single conflict or dialectical aspect in the Web case, or that, if closely scrutinized, the empirical data would not also reveal life-cycle elements. Moreover, by advocating a conceptual understanding of method emergence we do not aim to simplify the complexity of practice. The application of the theoretical framework to the two empirical cases shows clearly that in practice there are numerous factors, actors, and interactions that all influence and shape the emergent methods. As such, it is easy to conclude that emergent methods come about in a largely unpredictable and unmanageable (i.e., uncontrollable) way. This may be so. However, we propose, based on the research presented in this chapter, that theories and frameworks are needed to help practitioners and researchers go beyond the immediate and "messy" surface phenomena of the empirical world to a deeper, more conceptual understanding of the form(s) and driver(s) of method emergence. From theories of method emergence it may in turn be possible to identify and proactively exploit or avoid the generative motor(s) of a change process (Van de Ven and Poole, 1995). We suggest that our theoretical framework or similar work can be applied by both practitioners and researchers to read the situation before project initiation, during development, and after project completion in order to proactively identify the dynamics inherent in or relevant to a particular change process, to leverage these dynamics, and to be attentive to their potential pitfalls. In line with this, Walz, Elam, and Curtis (1993) state that conflict is a powerful mechanism for facilitating learning, and not a debilitating factor that should be suppressed. To spark creativity through conflict management, these authors recommend the use of, for example, the devil's advocate approach, dialectical methods, and techniques for surfacing and resolving the project team's underlying differences and similarities. However, there is no guarantee that conflicts produce the desired creative syntheses that drive the process forward in a dynamic way. Without facilitation, conflict may well lead to unresolved power struggles or one subgroup's unproductive domination. Facilitated social construction of goals is also a powerful vehicle for change, which can be leveraged through, for example, formal organization (meetings, staffing, etc.) and more or less formally appointed boundary spanners (Curtis, Krasner, and Iscoe, 1988; Walz, Elam, and Curtis, 1993). However, teleological processes where goals are reformulated on an ongoing basis are inherently unpredictable and risk discontinuity. Moreover, there may be underlying and undiscovered conflicts and differences of opinion, even when such processes are facilitated.

CONCLUSION

This chapter aims to explain how and why emergent methods unfold differently. Based on literature about contextualism, structuration theory, and change processes, a theoretical framework is developed and used to provide narrative accounts, systematic comparisons, and generalization of findings to theory for two longitudinal case studies of method emergence in a Multimedia project and a Web project.

The application of the theoretical framework shows that the Multimedia and Web cases are very similar with regard to structural characteristics (such as system complexity, team size, contract type, etc.), the emergent nature of the development process and product, and the long-term social relations between, and high involvement of, a few influential actors. However, despite these similarities, the emergent methods unfolded as two fundamentally different sequences of change. In the Multimedia case, the emergent method unfolded as a dialectical process, where conflict regarding how to perform the development process was the major driver of change. In the Web case, the emergent method took the form of a teleological process, where shared assumptions and ongoing (re)formulation of goals for the information system under development were the main generative motor of change. We conclude that how the two methods emerged and why they emerged differently can be explained with reference to *power struggles and conflict resolution* in the Multimedia case versus *consensus and social construction of goals* in the Web case.

The research presented in this chapter points to the need for theories and frameworks that go beyond the "messy" surface phenomena of method emergence in practice. The demonstrated theoretical framework is a step toward a more conceptual understanding and can be applied by both researchers and practitioners to read a situation before, during, and after an ISD project and to identify and leverage the drivers of emergent methods.

In this chapter and at this stage of theory development, the two empirical cases were selected and analyzed due to their apparent likeness, in particular, that both projects concerned contract-regulated university–company collaborations. However, more research is needed to overcome this deliberately imposed limitation. Future work will therefore involve the analysis and comparison of more and more purely industry-based cases to refine the theoretical ideas and to identify patterns in the underlying forms and drivers of ISD method emergence that can be avoided or exploited depending on situational factors, actors, and their interactions.

REFERENCES

Andersen, N.E.; Kensing, F.; Lunding, J.; Mathiassen, L.; Munk-Madsen, A.; Rabech, M.; and Sørgaard, P. 1990. *Professional Systems Development: Experience, Ideas, and Action.* Upper Saddle River, NJ: Prentice Hall.

Avison, D.E.; Wood-Harper, A.T.; Vidgen, R.T.; and Wood, J.R.G. 1998. A further exploration into information systems development: the evolution of Multiview2. *Information Technology & People,* 11, 2, 124–139.

Bansler, J., and Bødker, K. 1993. A reappraisal of structured analysis: design in an organizational context. *ACM Transactions on Information Systems,* 11, 2, 165–193.

Bergman, R.E., and Moore, T.V. 1990. *Managing Interactive Video/Multimedia Projects.* Englewood Cliffs, NJ: Educational Technology Publications.

Braa, K., and Vidgen, R.T. 1999. Interpretation, intervention and reduction in the organizational laboratory: a framework for in-context information systems research. *Accounting, Management and Information Technologies,* 9, 25–47.

Bruner, J. 2002. *Making Stories: Law, Literature, Life.* Cambridge, MA: Harvard University Press.

Curtis, B.; Krasner, H.; and Iscoe, N. 1988. A field study of the software design process for large systems. *Communications of the ACM,* 31, 11, 1268–1287.

Eisenhardt, K.M. 1989. Building theories from case study research. *Academy of Management Review,* 14, 4, 532–550.

Fitzgerald, B. 1997. The use of systems development methodologies in practice: a field study. *Information Systems Journal,* 7, 3, 201–212.

———. 1998. An empirical investigation into the adoption of systems development methodologies. *Information & Management,* 34, 317–328.

Fitzgerald, B.; Russo, N.L.; and Stolterman, E. 2002. *Information Systems Development, Methods in Action.* London: McGraw-Hill.

Gasson, S. 1999. A social action model of situated information systems design. *DATA BASE,* 30, 2, 82–97.

Giddens, A. 1984. *The Constitution of Society.* Cambridge, UK: Polity Press.

Jacobsen, I.; Booch, G.; and Rumbaugh, J. 1999. *The Unified Software Development Process.* Reading, PA: Addison-Wesley.

Jayaratna, N. 1994. *Understanding and Evaluating Methodologies, NIMSAD: A Systemic Framework.* London: McGraw-Hill.

Kautz, K. 2004. The enactment of methodology—the case of developing a multimedia information system. In *Proceedings of the International Conference on Information Systems,* Washington, DC, December 12–15.

Kautz, K., and Nielsen, P.A. 2004. Understanding the implementation of software process improvement innovations in software organisations. *Information Systems Journal,* 14, 1, 3–22.

Lyytinen, K. 1987. A taxonomic perspective of information systems development, theoretical constructs and recommendations. In R.J. Boland et al. (eds.), *Critical Issues in Information System Research.* Chichester, UK: Wiley, 3–41.

Madsen, S. 2004. Emerging methods—an interpretive study of ISD methods in practice. Ph.D. diss. København: Samfundslitteratur.

Madsen, S., and Kautz, K. 2002. Applying systems development methods in practice—the RUP example. In J. Grundspenkis et al. (eds.), *Information Systems Development: Advances in Methodologies, Components and Management.* New York: Kluwer, 267–278.

Madsen, S.; Kautz, K.; and Vidgen, R.T. 2005. Method emergence—influences and consequences. In *Proceedings of the Thirteenth European Conference on Information Systems,* Regensburg, Germany, May 26–28.

———. 2006. A framework for understanding how a unique and local IS development method emerges in practice. *European Journal of Information Systems,* 15, 225–238.

Mathiassen, L. 1998. Reflective systems development. Dissertation. Aalborg University.

Pentland, B.T. 1999. Building process theory with narrative: from description to explanation. *Academy of Management Review,* 24, 4, 711–724.

Pettigrew, A.M. 1985. Contextualist research and the study of organisational change processes. In E. Mumford et al. (eds.), *Research Methods in Information Systems.* Amsterdam: North-Holland, Elsevier, 53–78.

———. 1987. Context and action in the transformation of the firm. *Journal of Management Studies,* 24, 6, 649–670.

Sambamurthy, V., and Kirsch, L.J. 2000. An integrative framework of the information systems development process. *Decision Sciences* (ABI/INFORM Global), 31, 2, 391–411.

Stolterman, E. 1991. The hidden rationality of design work—a study in the methodology and practice of system development. Ph.D. diss. Institute of Information Processing, University of Umeå, Sweden.

———. 1992. How system designers think about design and methods—some reflections based on an interview study. *Scandinavian Journal of Information Systems,* 4, 137–150.

———. 1994. The transfer of rationality, acceptability, adaptability and transparency of methods. In *Proceedings of the Second European Conference on Information Systems.* Breukeln: Nijehrode University Press, 533–540.

Stolterman, E., and Russo, N.L. 1997. The paradox of information systems methods: public and private rationality. In *Proceedings of the British Computer Society's Fifth Annual Conference on Information System Methodologies,* Lancaster, England.

Sørensen, M.H. 1997. Development of development methodologies. In B. Fibinger (ed.), *Design of Multimedia.* Aalborg: Aalborg University, 61–84.

Truex, D.; Baskerville, R.; and Travis, J. 2000. Amethodical systems development: the deferred meaning of systems development methods. *Accounting Management & Information Technologies,* 10, 1, 53–79.

Van de Ven, A., and Poole, M.S. 1995. Explaining development and change in organizations. *Academy of Management Review,* 20, 3, 510–540.

Vidgen, R.T. 2002. WISDM: constructing a Web information system development methodology. *Information Systems Journal,* 12, 3, 247–261.

Vidgen, R.T.; Avison, D.E.; Wood, J.R.G.; and Wood-Harper, T.A. 2002. *Developing Web Information Systems.* Oxford: Elsevier.

Walsham, G. 1993. *Interpreting Information Systems in Organisations.* Chichester, UK: Wiley, Wiley Series on Information Systems.

———. 1995. Interpretive case studies in IS research: nature and method. *European Journal of Information Systems,* 4, 74–81.

Walz, D.B.; Elam, J.J.; and Curtis, B. 1993. Inside a software design team: knowledge acquisition, sharing, and integration. *Communications of the ACM,* 36, 10 (October), 63–77.

CHAPTER 6

TRANSITION TO AGILE SOFTWARE DEVELOPMENT IN A LARGE-SCALE PROJECT

A Systems Analysis and Design Perspective

YAEL DUBINSKY, ORIT HAZZAN, DAVID TALBY, AND ARIE KEREN

Abstract: *In this chapter we focus on the implementation of Extreme Programming, one of the agile software development methods, in a large-scale software project in the Israeli Air Force, and describe the transition from a plan-driven process to an agile one as it is perceived from the systems analysis and design perspective. Specifically, during the first eight months of transition, the project specifications and acceptance tests of the agile team are compared with those of a team that continues working according to the previous plan-driven method. Size and complexity measures are used as the basis of the comparison. In addition, the role of the systems analysts during the transition process is examined and different development models with respect to systems analysis and design are discussed.*

Keywords: *Software Engineering, Agile Software Development, Systems Analysis and Design, Systems Analyst Role*

INTRODUCTION

Agile software development methods mainly aim at increasing software quality by fostering customer collaboration and performing exhaustive testing (Cockburn, 2002; Highsmith, 2002). The introduction of agile software development in general and of a specific agile method, for example, Extreme Programming (Beck, 2000; Beck and Andres, 2005) into an organization is accompanied with conceptual and organizational changes. For example, with Extreme Programming all teammates listen to the customer stories, contribute to high-level design, and maintain detailed designs during each iteration of development. Another example is the concept of whole team, which means that all role holders are part of the development team, in contrast to an organizational structure composed of separate groups such as systems analysts, developers, and quality assurance people.

The role of systems analysts, as well as other roles, receives a different meaning in the agile software development environment. The change might pass smoothly in a one-team project in a small company; however, the change becomes significant when agile-oriented software development process is introduced into a large-scale project in a large organization in which many software teams work for many years according to a traditional plan-driven software development process.

Review of the most recent literature on agile software development reveals that the research that deals specifically with the design-related activities carried out in agile software development environments is very limited. The existing literature that does address design-related aspects of agile software development deals mainly with the incorporation of a specific design method in an agile project and with the effectiveness of the agile approach with respect to the design activity. For example, Patton (2002) describes how user-centered design in agile software development increases success, helps to meet end-user expectations sooner and supports the development of a usable software; Feldman (2003) describes how design by contract is synergistic with several practices of Extreme Programming; Macias, Holcombe, and Gheorghe (2003) illustrate how Extreme Programming reduces the time dedicated to specification and design—7 percent in an Extreme Programming project vs. 14 percent in a plan-driven project. In addition, literature exists on refactoring, test-driven development, agile modeling, and other agile practices that are closely attached to design in agile software development processes.

This chapter presents one aspect of a research project we conducted for the past three years. Specifically, it examines the transition from a plan-driven process to an agile one in a large-scale software project using the perspective of systems analysis and design. The project is conducted in the army, which can be characterized as a large and hard-to-change organization with respect to fixed regulations, project approval, management methods, organizational structure, and culture. In previous works we presented results with respect to the specifications and testing artifacts (Dubinsky et al., 2005, 2006; Talby et al., 2006). In this chapter, we enrich with further research data and elaborate with data analysis about the role of the systems analyst.

The main contribution of this research is expressed in the field-based evidence that it provides with respect to the role and the functionality of systems analysis and design in an agile large-scale software project in a large organization. Thus, we address the need for increasing the body of knowledge that deals with agile practices (Erickson, Lyytinen, and Siau, 2005) by adding the topic from the systems analysis and design perspective.

THE TRANSITION PROCESS

The in-transition software project on which this chapter focuses has been developed by a dozen small teams of skilled systems engineers, systems analysts, developers, and testers, organized in a hierarchical structure of small teams. The project develops large-scale, enterprise-critical software, intended to be used by a large and varied user population.

As aforementioned, from an organizational perspective, the army is known as a large and hard-to-change organization. However, in our case of software development, when the project leadership decided to change the software development method to cope with the challenges that the project set, the unit leadership supported the decided-upon transition as a means to improve software process and quality.

After several months during which the fitness of different development methods to the project had been investigated, Extreme Programming was selected to be implemented and a pilot team of fifteen people was established and started working according to this agile method. All of the other teams on the project continued working according to the previous plan-driven method.

It is important to note that prior to the transition, tools and procedures were developed and used by the people in this software unit for years. Though it was accepted that agile development can improve the process, it was also agreed that there are tools and procedures that will not be changed at the current stage, either because they are good practices or because of time constraints.

The software project is built based on a large-scale in-house object-oriented framework (Fayad, Schmidt, and Johnson, 1999), which handles many of the underlying technical aspects of the system. One aspect is *formal detailed specifications*. This framework relies on a metadata repository (Talby et al., 2002), which contains most of the system's specifications: data entities, data types, actions, transactions, user types and privileges, messages, external interfaces, and so forth. These data are edited in the repository, in formal forms—in contrast to free-text documents—and much of it is used to automatically generate code and other files.

As a result of working with this framework, the process of development starts with functional analysis, continues with writing the formal detailed specifications in the metadata repository, and then coding those parts of the specifications that are not automatically generated. In such a process, the specification writers should adopt a formal and precise style, and as the formality increases, the cost of communication increases since team members should communicate later for clarifications.

During the transition process all teams in the project, including the agile team, continue working with formal detailed specifications and with the tools that support them.

The roles involved with the systems analysis and design in this project are architects, operational systems analysts, functional systems analysts, and systems engineers. In this work we focus on the operational and functional systems analysts. The operational systems analysts are practitioners in the operational aspects of the project subject matter and are part of an operational analysis group. They define the system to be developed and they represent the customer and the end users. The functional systems analysts process the operational specifications, converting them into engineered technical specifications. They are part of the development group.

The change in the role definitions stems mainly from the change in development process. As part of the transition process, prior to the development work of the agile team, systems analysts make *only* preliminary analysis and deliver the knowledge to the agile team by face-to-face conversations, presentations, and/or high-level documents. The agile team then, together with the customer and systems analysts, produces the detailed project specifications.

THE RESEARCH FRAMEWORK

The exploration of this transition process started two years ago when it was decided to change the traditional plan-driven software development method that had been used in this organization for many years. In previous work, we presented the way agile software development was introduced into this project (Dubinsky, Hazzan, and Keren, 2005) as well as the set of product and process metrics evolved in the first release of the pilot team, which guided in practice the development process (Dubinsky et al., 2005).

Two approaches were used in this research of the transition process: a quantitative comparative approach and a qualitative approach, as is elaborated in what follows.

Quantitative Comparative Approach

The first approach is a quantitative comparative one, by which we aimed at measuring the implications of the transition to the agile method on the systems analysis and design. Accordingly, we examined and compared two sets of specifications and tests produced by both kinds of teams. The first set belongs to the team that worked according to the plan-driven method and during the examined period was in the phase of development and fault corrections before delivery. The second set belongs to the team that worked according to the agile method and during the examined period developed four releases that were each two months long and composed of four two-week-long iterations.

We use several measures to compare specifications and tests. One measure is the *size* of the specifications and tests, which is used for comparison alignment. Another measure of the specifications is composed of two measures that are used to assess the complexity of the specifications, one of which is inspired by the measure of code cyclomatic complexity (McCabe, 1976; Watson and McCabe, 1996). In the data analysis section the measures are elaborated and illustrated. These measures were selected because we wanted the quantitative data to represent ongoing real work rather than one or a few checkpoints of an artificial setting. Using the specifications and test data enables us to examine continuous fieldwork over eight months.

Though the compared specifications and tests are taken from two different products of two different teams, we suggest that when a comparison between two development methods is made, it is more important that the two teams work in the same organization, with the same infrastructure and tools, and with people of similar experience and expertise. Furthermore, in order to eliminate as much as possible the differences in the two products, we searched for trends and relative-to-size technical measures rather than absolute numbers.

Qualitative Approach

The second research approach is a qualitative approach in which we sought to understand the process from the systems analysts' and designers' point of view. Accordingly, we interviewed systems analysts and asked them questions such as "Do you feel that your role has changed? If no, please describe your role before and after the transition. If yes, please describe how your role has changed." "Compare the traditional method of software development and the agile Extreme Programming one."

In addition, we used two questionnaires. The first one is a software development culture questionnaire (Hazzan and Dubinsky, 2005) that maps the perspective of our interviewees with respect to software development processes (see Appendix 6.1). The second questionnaire is related to the role of the systems analyst (see Appendix 6.2).

DATA ANALYSIS

In this section, the project specifications and acceptance tests are compared, and the change in the role of the systems analysts is examined.

Specifications Comparison

As stated earlier, some of the specification measures consider modularity and relative complexity. To define such measures, we define a module of specifications—in contrast to a module of code, such as a class or a package. As described above, the specifications of the analyzed projects were written in a semiformal metadata repository, which enabled the systems analysts and architects to define specifications modules.

The chosen method of specifications was data-centered; that is, a module in this system completely specifies one data entity and its related processes. Each module specifies—for one entity and its subentities—the database layout and properties, application server services, user interface forms, queries, input and output to external interfaces, permissions, and other specified features. This comprises the entire business logic that must be implemented. Part of this business logic is

Figure 6.1 **Number of Entities**

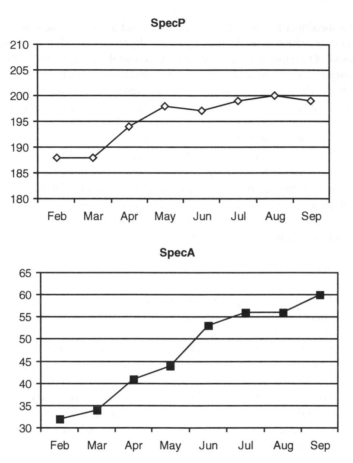

specified formally, and later, code was generated based on this specification; other parts of the business logic are expressed in free text. Naturally, free-text logic entails more complexity in the system, since it specifies nonstandard logic. This will be a key issue when we define the measures.

We denote the specifications of the team that worked according to the plan-driven method by *SpecP* and the specifications of the team that worked according to the agile method by *SpecA*. During four releases, continuing eight months, we took monthly measurements. During the examined period, the number of entities nearly doubled in the agile project (87.5 percent growth), in comparison with about 6 percent in the plan-driven project (see Figure 6.1). These numbers closely match the growth in size and complexity of both projects. The difference in growth levels reflects the different stages of these two projects. This fact is also reflected in the difference between the absolute sizes of the two projects: the agile project grew from 32 to 60 modules in an intense development stage, while the plan-driven project, which was in a fault correction phase before delivery phase, grew from 188 to 199 modules during the same period.

As stated before, part of the specifications is written formally in order to enable automatic code generation. Figure 6.2 shows an example of a specification fragment. The first measure we use, size, intuitively represents the number of decisions made in the specifications. Therefore, a size

Figure 6.2 **Specifications Sample**

Field Name:	Name
Field Type:	String
Description:	The customer's full name
Minimal Length:	1
Maximal Length:	40
Field Editor:	Text Box
Is Required:	only *if* the ID field is empty
Do on Change:	*If* the ID field is non-empty,
	check that it matches the new name.
	If match,
	enable the "OK" button,
	else display the "Name/ID Mismatch" error message.

of 1 is given to each simple specified value (such as minimal value and maximal value) and to each line of free-text specifications. Therefore, the size of the fragment in Figure 6.2 is 12 since it has 6 simple values, 1 for the one line of the "Is Required" specification, and 5 for the five lines of the "Do on Change" specification.

Since the simple values in a specification result in generated code, and hence do not require any coding, the size measure does not reflect the complexity of a given specification for the development team.

Therefore, complexity is created only by the free-text specifications. To represent this, we derived two complexity measures. The first one is the *Logic-Based Complexity* calculated by counting the number of lines of nontrivial specifications. For the specification shown in Figure 6.2, this measure would be 6 (the six last lines). The second is the *Keyword-Based Complexity* that is inspired by the cyclomatic complexity measure (McCabe, 1976; Watson and McCabe, 1996), in which a sequential method has a complexity of 1, and each decision that causes a binary split raises the complexity by 1. This definition is equivalent to the definition of complexity as the number of paths in the method's decision graph. Accordingly, we emulate the cyclomatic complexity measure by defining the complexity of free-text specifications paragraphs to be 1 and add the number of appearances of the following popular keywords: if, else, for-every, for-each. For the specification in Figure 6.2, this measure would be 6, since we count 2 from the "Is Required" specification (1 + 1 occurrences of "if"), and 4 from the "Do on Change" specification (1 + 2 "if" + 1 "else"). Validating with the specifications, this emulation was found as an appropriate and sensible approximation for the actual number of paths in the specification. Although these specifications are free text, the analysts writing the specifications normally use only these words. They are often manually marked by bold font, as shown in Figure 6.2. This is a project-wide practice, ensuring the quality of data.

Figure 6.3 presents the averaged keyword-based complexity of *SpecP* and *SpecA*. Note that the scale range in the two graphs has different values; still it is the same scale size so the view is comparative. The first evident difference between the graphs, depicting the average (per-module) keyword-based complexity of the plan-driven versus the agile project, is the absolute values. The per-module keyword-based complexity of the agile project is considerably smaller—about 3.5 times smaller— than that of the plan-driven project. This does not mean that the agile project is simpler, but rather that its specification uses more modules to convey the same amount of specifications, and thus the average is lower. In other words, the graphs indicate that the agile project is more modular, a fact that has implications for software life cycle.

Figure 6.3   **Averaged Keyword-Based Complexity in Eight Monthly Checkpoints**

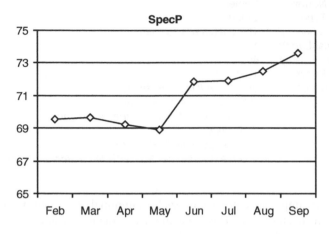

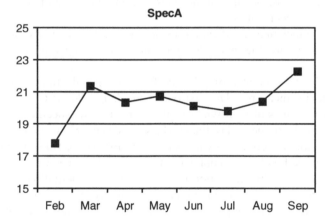

Several complementing explanations for this outcome follow.

- First, the plan-driven project is three years older than the agile one and is at a much later development stage. Although the plan-driven project is still being developed, a large existing code base sometimes enforces the enhancement of existing modules rather than the creation of new ones.
- Second, in the agile project, continuous refactoring is performed in order to break down large modules and reduce dependencies. When a module gets too complex, it is refactored into (possibly several) simpler modules. The goal is to keep the design simple over a long period of time, rather than assuming the "right" design in advance. In contrast, in traditional software projects, the design of modules is usually set in advance. Further, the high absolute complexity of the plan-driven project, achieved over time (recall that it is in a more mature state than the agile project), makes refactoring at this stage more expensive and risky.
- Third, some of the business analysts who worked in the agile project had previous analysis experience in the plan-driven project. Thus, they corrected past mistakes and produced a more modular design this time.

- Fourth, in the agile project, all team members may potentially work on the specifications—all have been trained to do so—a fact that promotes the separation of specifications into more modules, so that more people can edit them in parallel. This tends to make modularity and refactoring a practical necessity, ensuring their ongoing realization and consideration in practice.
- And finally, the complexity measures may be higher for the plan-driven project because most of its specifications are not standard features in the framework, and accordingly are specified via free-text business logic, which implies higher complexity. This hypothesis is referred to in the sequel by examining the ratios of complexity to size (in contrast to number of modules) in the two projects.

Further observation of the two graphs shows that the agile project managed to keep modules simple over time. This is true even though the agile project grew faster than the plan-driven project during the examined period. Putting aside the agile project's first month, which included major one-time setup work, it can be observed that from February to September the number of modules and the overall size of the specifications grew by 65 percent and 70 percent, respectively, while keyword-based complexity grew by 4.3 percent. In contrast, while the plan-driven project's number of entities and total size grew by 6 percent and 8 percent, respectively, its keyword-based complexity grew at a larger rate—by 5.7 percent.

This means not only that the agile project is more modular, but also, in addition, it is developed in a manner that maintains its modularity better than that of the plan-driven project. Again, this can be attributed to the same factors mentioned above: the project's stage and the analysts' experience, in addition to the agile practices of *refactoring* and *collective ownership,* which in this project were applied to the specifications as well.

Figure 6.4 presents the logic-based complexity of *SpecP* and *SpecA,* averaged over all modules of each project. The graphs show a very similar picture to that shown by the average keyword-based complexity graphs. Once again, the complexity values of the plan-driven project are four to five times greater than those for the agile project. The results, and hence the possible explanations, are consistent with those given for keyword-based complexity.

The difference in absolute complexity can be explained by several factors that do not stem from the development method. For example, the agile project could be inherently simpler than the plan-driven one. However, developers' evidence in both projects revealed that this is definitely not the case. As an explanation, it was suggested that the agile project reuses more features built into the framework and therefore can be specified in a way that enables automatic code generation. By presenting the ratio of logic-based and keyword-based complexity to the size measure, thereby measuring the proportion of complexity to specification size, Figure 6.5 supports the above explanation.

In both the "logic-based and the keyword-based complexity versus size" graphs, the project values are relatively constant over time, and are 20–50 percent higher for the plan-driven project. This means that in general, the specifications of the plan-driven project use more free-text business logic and fewer framework-ready features in order to convey the same size of specifications.

A combination of setting and process can explain this phenomenon. From the setting point of view, the agile project started after experience in specification had been gained in the plan-driven project, and therefore business analysts knew more about how to utilize the framework. From the process perspective, the agile project's focus on simplicity and ongoing refactoring drives toward the writing and maintaining of specifications that are as simple as possible. We do not have quantitative data to assess the relative contribution of each of these factors to the results, but interviews with the project team members indicate that both factors influence them.

Figure 6.4 **Averaged Logic-Based Complexity in Eight Monthly Checkpoints**

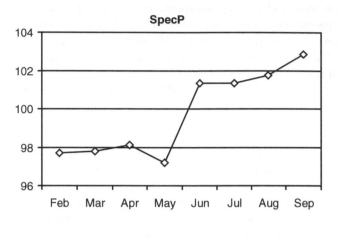

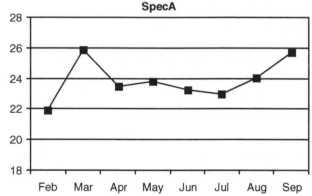

Test Comparisons

In this section, we analyze the comparative data dealing with acceptance tests created according to the specifications. Figure 6.6 shows the number of test suites (separate test files) of the agile versus the plan-driven projects. As can be observed, although the agile project is three years younger and several times smaller than the plan-driven project, within the examined period it produced more test suites than the plan-driven project developed.

However, this does not mean that the agile project is tested more thoroughly, but, rather, that it is tested differently. In the plan-driven project, the development team and the quality assurance (QA) team are separate, working in two separate rooms, while only the QA team members write tests. Each QA team member is usually responsible for testing several modules, and the team's method is to keep each module's tests within one large test suite. Since different people normally do not test the same module in parallel, this does not pose a configuration control problem. On the agile team, on the other hand, all team members write and execute tests on an ongoing basis. Therefore, a small number of large test suites would create a serious practical problem, since two people would not be able to work on the same test suite in parallel, at least not without requiring advance work to enable them to merge their work later on. Therefore, there are two methodologies

Figure 6.5 **Complexities per Size in Eight Monthly Checkpoints**

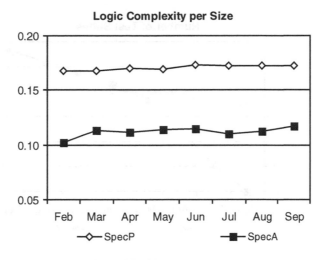

for the division of tests into test suites: by modules in the plan-driven project and by tasks in the agile project. This gives the plan-driven project the advantage of matching the structure of test suites to the structure of the specifications, and gives the agile project the advantage of parallel development and a larger available testing force.

Accordingly, as has been explained above, the absolute number of test suites in each project is not an appropriate indicator of the actual complexity of the tests in each project. The number of tests steps, however, is a sound factor for assessing test complexity, since, by nature, it does not depend on how tests are packaged. The number of test scenarios (a list of test steps) is also a reasonable indicator, since scenarios are usually written in the same way in both projects.

In order to compare the two projects, some form of normalization is required. It is possible to normalize in different ways: by the number of modules in each project, the total size, the keyword-based complexity, or the logic-based complexity. Table 6.1 summarizes, according to these four factors in the last checkpoint, the ratio of the plan-driven project to the agile project.

Figure 6.6   **Absolute and per-Module Number of Test Suites**

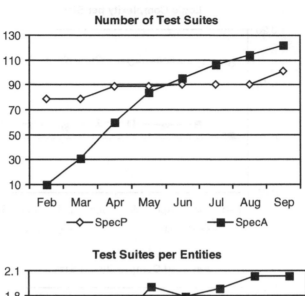

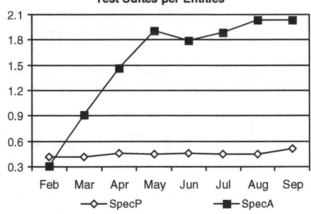

As the numbers indicate, any choice of normalization will produce biased results. For example, on the one hand, normalization by the number of modules points "against" the agile project, since it is more modular and therefore, it seems to have fewer tests per module. On the other hand, normalization by the complexity metrics points "against" the plan-driven project, since it has a higher complexity-to-size ratio, due to its higher ratio of free-text specifications.

Table 6.1

Ratio of Plan-Driven Versus Agile Project Measures (September 2005)

Number of modules	3.3
Size	9.0
Keyword-based complexity	11.0
Logic-based complexity	13.3

Figure 6.7 **Test Steps and Scenarios per Size**

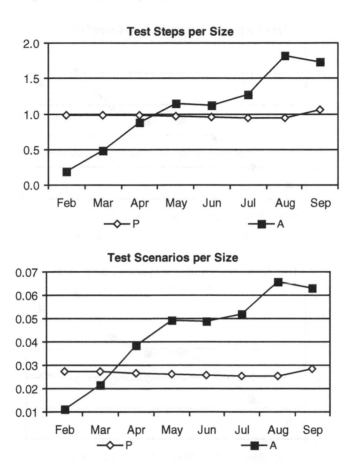

Therefore, the most appropriate normalization method seems to be by total size. However, according to the projects' QA personnel, complexity is a more accurate choice, since it is higher complexity that requires thorough testing, and not size per se. The rationale for this is that a large specification that relies mainly on the existing framework leaves little to be tested, since the use of the framework features does not require testing—that would be redundant. At the same time, free-text specifications require testing of each business logic. The way we defined complexity is highly correlated to the size and complexity of the required tests. The higher the specification's McCabe-like complexity, the more test steps and scenarios are required to cover all of its possible paths of execution.

In order to provide a complete picture, we review the testing measures with respect to all four normalizations. Starting with size, as shown in Figure 6.7 (top), the plan-driven (denoted by P) project's test steps to size ratio remains relatively constant during this period and is 0.98 on average. The ratio of the agile project (denoted by A) changes significantly during this period, starting at 0.29 after the first setup month of the project, passing the plan-driven project's ratio after four months with a value of 1.14, and reaching 1.74 at the last measurement point.

Figure 6.8 **Test Steps and Scenarios per Logic- and Keyword-based Complexity**

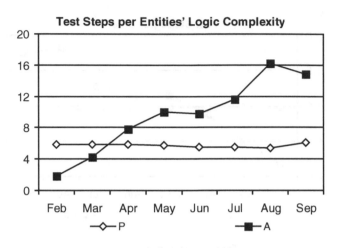

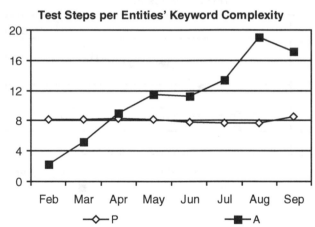

The number of test scenarios versus size in Figure 6.7 (bottom) indicates a similar picture. The plan-driven project is stable over time, while the agile project changes considerably during the examined period, stabilizing in the last three measured months at a value that is on average 2.3 times higher than that of the plan-driven project.

According to these results, the agile project is more thoroughly tested than the plan-driven project. This can be attributed mainly to the development process. In the agile project, a task is not considered complete until its tests are written and have been passed; further, it is the responsibility of the developer who coded a task to write and run the tests. This ensures that tests are written for all tasks, and not just for high-priority tasks, as has happened during high-pressure periods in the plan-driven project. In the plan-driven project, if the QA team lags behind the development team for any reason (insufficient personnel, new features that take more time to test than to code, other urgent work, etc.), the developers keep coding features and the lag increases further. This quickly leads to prioritizing test writing and focusing on high-risk features. In contrast, in an agile project, the QA personnel are part of the development team, and developers are responsible for writing tests as well. In this way, the team does not move on with development before testing is completed.

Figure 6.8 *(continued)*

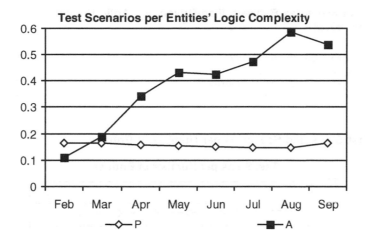

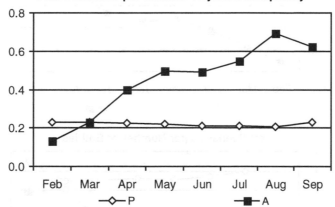

The four graphs presented in Figure 6.8 show test steps and scenarios versus logic- and keyword-based complexity; as can be clearly observed, the pattern repeats. The values of the plan-driven project are stable, while those of the agile project grow mostly over time, and when the agile project's values seem to stabilize, they are higher than those of the plan-driven project.

Table 6.2 summarizes the average ratio for the last three measured months of the four normalized metrics in the plan-driven project versus the agile project. As can be observed again, these consistent results suggest that the overall coverage and level of testing in the agile project are higher than those of the plan-driven project.

Further, the results indicate that it took about four months for the agile project to achieve the plan-driven project's level of testing, and that its measures changed greatly during the examined period. This can be explained by the fact that in contrast to the plan-driven project, the examined period starts with the very beginning of the agile project's development, and it took several months for the development process and environment to stabilize. In contrast, in the plan-driven project, tests were not written at all during the first year of the project, and only then did the QA team start working. This is a common distinction between agile and plan-driven projects. Agile projects start

Table 6.2

Average Ratio of Measures Between Plan-Driven and Agile Project
(July–September 2005)

Test steps per keyword-based complexity	2.1
Test steps per logic-based complexity	2.5
Test scenarios per keyword-based complexity	2.9
Test scenarios per logic-based complexity	3.5

Figure 6.9   **Test Steps and Scenarios per Number of Entities**

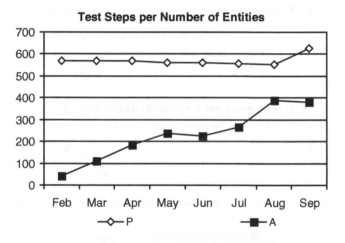

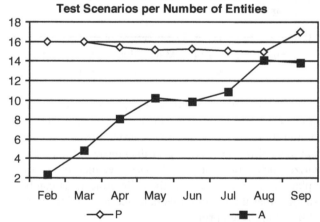

testing at day one, from the very first task, while traditional projects start testing only after some infrastructure exists and some features are stable enough so that tests can be written for them without planning major refactoring of these tests as the project evolves.

The last comparison is presented in Figure 6.9, in which the number of test steps and scenarios are normalized by the number of entities. As can be seen, this is the only measure in which the plan-driven project shows higher values.

Considering our previous analysis, this makes sense. Although the plan-driven project is nine times larger than the agile project in terms of the size measure, it has only six times more modules at the beginning of the examined period, and three times more modules toward its end. This means that each module in the plan-driven project contains many more specifications than in the agile one, and this in turn implies that even though the tests-per-size ratio in the agile project is higher, its overall tests-per-module ratio is lower.

The Role of the Systems Analysts

In this subsection, we focus on the systems analyst role and the changes in its characteristics during the transition period. Since everyone on both the plan-driven and the agile teams has been exposed to the agile notions, we compare the responses of the systems analysts who work in the examined project, with those of systems analysts from a major Israeli software company, who do not work according to the agile concepts.

The data analysis reveals three working models that may clarify the transition process in the examined project as well as its future management.

The first development model is a *pipeline-distributed* model, according to which a specific software project consists of three different groups—the systems analysts group, the developers group, and the QA testers group. During the development process each group refers to the output of the previous group as its input. This description is simplified and therefore does not refer to the feedback loops between the groups, assuming that in an ideal pipeline process feedback is not needed. In general, this model fits the development process of the plan-driven project team.

The agile movement, and specifically Extreme Programming, refers to a working model that is more *concentrated* in terms of space. The Extreme Programming notions of *Sit Together* and *Whole Team,* along with the practice of *Weekly Cycle,* require the groups of analysts, developers, and testers to share one space, to collaborate on a daily basis, and to produce common artifacts on a weekly basis. In general terms, this model fits the way shaped by the agile team during the transition period.

We suggest that on a small software team the *concentrated* model may work also for the entire systems analysts group. However, this model did not work for the transition-to-agile team that we examined. As has been mentioned before, during the transition process, one functional systems analyst worked together with the agile development team and another systems analyst stayed a part of the external functional analysts group. The group of operational systems analysts did not change at all. We refer to this model as a *hybrid,* in which its hybridism level depends on project size and complexity as well as on the perspectives and cooperation of the people involved.

In what follows we describe how systems analysts conceive of their role and what effect the transition to agile development has on their perceptions. As mentioned previously, to learn about these conceptions, we used two questionnaires. The first one is a Software Development Culture Questionnaire (SDCQ) (presented in Hazzan and Dubinsky, 2005) and is shown in Appendix 6.1. The second questionnaire is a Systems Analysts Questionnaire (SAQ), and is shown in Appendix 6.2.

Below we compare answers to the SDCQ given, after a few months of the transition period, by fifteen systems analysts of one of the major software companies in Israel with those of five systems analysts of the examined project. Several illustrative examples of the differences are identified.[1]

Figure 6.10 **The Position of the System Analyst: The System Analyst's Perspective**

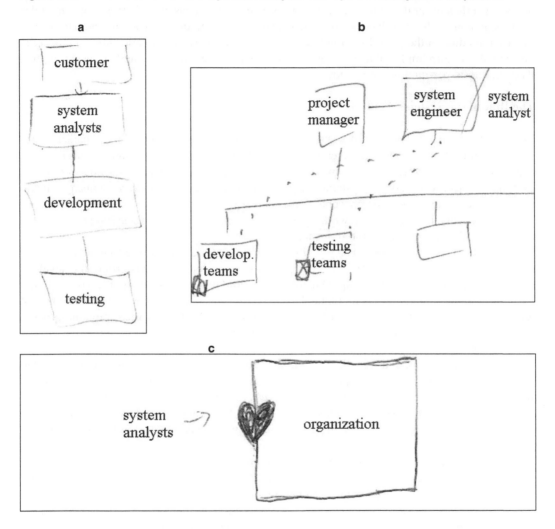

- The SDCQ statement: "It is important to me that development tasks are allocated equally among team members." Four from the industry sample (26 percent) disagree, while the rest agree. All five from the examined project agree (none disagree).
- The SDCQ statement: "The Israeli hi-tech industry is characterized by unplanned software development." Seven from the industry sample (46 percent) agree, while the rest disagree. All five from the examined project disagree (none agree).
- The SDCQ statement: "It is important to enable software developers to work flexible hours ("come when you want, leave when you want")." Six from the industry sample (40 percent) agree, while the rest disagree. Four out of five from the examined project disagree.

In the SAQ (Appendix 6.2), the interviewees were asked to draw the position of the systems analyst in the organization as they perceive it. Figure 6.10 shows the common perspectives of the

Figure 6.11   **The Position of the System Analyst According to the Examined-Project System Analysts**

a

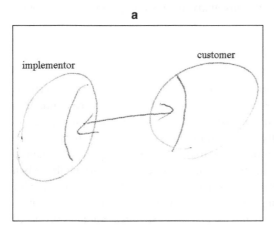

b

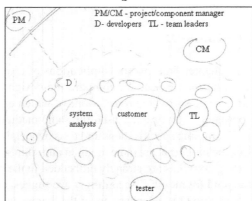

fifteen interviewees from the Israeli software industry. We note that this is field material that is used for the analysis. The text was translated to English for the purpose of presentation.

As can be observed, some of the systems analysts conceive of their position as part of project management (Figure 6.10b) or even as the heart of the entire organization (Figure 6.10c). Most of them, however, draw pictures similar to Figure 6.10a, which means that they receive input from the customer and deliver their product to the developers, who, in turn, work with the testers. We referred to this model earlier as the *pipeline-distributed* model.

In contrast, and as has been illustrated in our previous work (Dubinsky et al., 2006), the drawings of the systems analysts of the examined project reflect that their role is mainly conceived as a *bridge* between the customer and the developers. In an additional interview, three months later, the systems analysts of the examined project still perceived their position as a bridge, which is part of both sides—the customer side as well as the implementation side, which is composed of functional analysts, developers, and testers (see Figure 6.11a).

Figure 6.11b reflects that the strict lines of hierarchy (presented in Figure 6.10) are replaced with circles, which reflect joint work. The dashed line in the top left corner is directed to the project manager and indicates a common goal for all people involved, who, as the figure shows, are systems analysts, developers, team leaders, testers, the customer, and the component managers. The placement of the customer ellipse in the middle of the picture is not a coincidence; rather, it emphasizes the intensive collaboration between the customer and the other parties involved.

The second and third questions in the SAQ refer to the main skills and difficulties of the systems analysts. Most of the systems analysts from both research samples indicated the following main skills: global perspective, creativity, capability of high-level of abstraction, and openness. Most of the systems analysts from both populations indicated the following main difficulties: understanding the customer, technical and performance limitations of the development group, tight schedules, and continuous changes in requirements.

The forth SAQ question, again, reveals a difference between the general systems analysts and those of the agile team. In the industry sample, ten out of fifteen systems analysts mentioned only systems analysis tasks like requirements analysis and design. Only five systems analysts mentioned tasks such as knowledge transfer and communication with the development team;

still, these tasks that involve communication with the developers consume only about 20 percent of their time. In contrast, on the agile team (the examined project), the five systems analysts allocated 10, 20, 25, 40, and 50 percent of the systems analysis tasks to communication with development.

CONCLUSION

This chapter presents the implications of transition to agile software development on systems analysis and design. We compare the design and testing products of two software teams in a large-scale software project—one of which used a plan-driven approach and the other, an agile approach. Both projects used the same methodology and tools for systems analysis.

Examining specifications and tests over eight months, we found that the agile process produces specifications that are more modular and simpler than the plan-driven one. We also found that when testing activities are strongly embedded in the process, more tests are provided and this behavior can hold for months. Accordingly, we suggest emphasizing the testing practice by creating whole teams with QA testers as part of the teams, and writing acceptance test suites that are correlated with the specifications to strengthen the systems analysis and design.

We further examined the role of systems analysts in the agile environment and found that for large-scale projects the suggested hybrid development model fits better, meaning that the project analysts' group is in charge of preliminary analysis and then the agile team together with the customer and the team's systems analysts produce the detailed specifications.

NOTE

1. For simplicity, we merged the "tend to disagree" and "disagree" answers with "disagree," and "tend to agree" and "agree" answers with "agree."

REFERENCES

Beck, K. 2000. *Extreme Programming Explained: Embrace Change.* Reading, MA: Addison-Wesley.
Beck, K., and Andres, C. 2005. *Extreme Programming Explained: Embrace Change,* 2nd ed. Boston: Addison-Wesley.
Cockburn, A. 2002. *Agile Software Development.* Boston, MA: Addison-Wesley.
Dubinsky, Y.; Hazzan, O.; and Keren, A. 2005. Introducing extreme programming into a software project at the Israeli air force. In *Proceedings of the Sixth International Conference on Extreme Programming and Agile Processes in Software Engineering.* Springer LNCS, Sheffield, UK, 19–27.
Dubinsky, Y.; Hazzan, O.; Talby, D.; and Keren, A. 2006. System analysis and design in a large-scale software project: the case of transition to agile development. In *Proceedings of the Eighth International Conference on Enterprise Information Systems (ICEIS),* 11–18.
Dubinsky, Y.; Talby, D.; Hazzan, O.; and Keren, A. 2005. Agile metrics at the Israeli air force. In *Proceedings of the Agile Conference,* Denver, CO, 12–19.
Erickson, J.; Lyytinen, K.; and Siau, K. 2005. Agile modeling, agile software development, and Extreme Programming: the state of research. *Journal of Database Management,* 16, 4, 88–100.
Fayad, M.E.; Schmidt, D.C.; and Johnson, R.E. (eds.). 1999. *Building Application Frameworks: Object-Oriented Foundations of Framework Design.* New York: Wiley.
Feldman, Y.A. 2003. Extreme design by contract. In *Proceedings of the Fourth International Extreme Programming Conference,* Genova, Italy, 261–270.
Hazzan, O., and Dubinsky, Y. 2005. Clashes between culture and software development methods: the case of the Israeli hi-tech industry and extreme programming. In *Proceedings of the Agile Conference,* Denver, CO, 59–69.
Highsmith, J. 2002. *Agile Software Development Ecosystems.* Boston: Addison-Wesley.

Macias, F.; Holcombe, M.; and Gheorghe, M. 2003. Design-led and design-less: one experiment and two approaches. In *Proceedings of the Fourth International Extreme Programming Conference,* Genova, Italy, 394–401.

McCabe, T. 1976. A complexity measure. *IEEE Transactions on Software Engineering,* 2, 4, 308–320.

Patton, J. 2002. Designing requirements: incorporating user-centered design into an agile SW development process. In *Proceedings of the Second Extreme Programming Universe and First Agile Universe Conference,* Chicago, IL, 1–12.

Talby, D.; Hazzan, O.; Dubinsky, Y.; and Keren, A. 2006. Agile software testing in a large-scale project. *IEEE Software,* Special Issue on Software Testing, vol. 23, no. 4, 30–37.

Talby, D.; Adler, D.; Kedem, Y.; Nakar, O.; Danon, N.; and Keren, A. 2002. The design and implementation of a metadata repository. In *Proceedings of the International Council on Systems Engineering Israeli Chapter Conference,* available at http://www.cs.huji.ac.il/~davidt/papers/Metadata_Repository_INCOSE02.pdf.

Tomayko, J., and Hazzan, O. 2004. *Human Aspects of Software Engineering.* Hingham, MA: Charles River Media.

Watson, A.H., and McCabe, T.J. 1996. Structured testing: a testing methodology using the cyclomatic complexity metric. *NIST Special Publication,* 235–500, available at http://www.mccabe.com/iq_research_nist.htm.

APPENDIX 6.1. SOFTWARE DEVELOPMENT CULTURE QUESTIONNAIRE

For each of the following, please mark + in the appropriate column according to your agreement with the statement.

Statement	Agree	Tend to agree	Tend to disagree	Disagree
It is important to me that development tasks are allocated equally among team members.				
It is preferable to develop software by planning at the design level, not at the development task level.				
It is accepted in the software industry that developers who frequently go home at 5 p.m. do not invest enough effort at work.				
It is preferable to minimize, as much as possible, the dependency level among software team members.				
Customers expect that software development will not be completed on time, thus, it is reasonable to commit to an unreasonable timetable.				
The Israeli hi-tech industry is characterized by unplanned software development.				
It is preferable to work in small teams in order to foster decision-making processes as much as possible.				
Single-release software development is preferable to a gradual development process consisting of several releases.				
It is important to enable software developers to work flexible hours ("come when you want, leave when you want").				
If a software project does not proceed as planned, the team must work nights and weekends to catch up.				
No one on my team cares about how the software is written as long as it works.				
A team should extend the development period if it ensures improvement of software quality.				
When I chose a profession, I took into consideration that I would have to devote many hours every day to work and give up my personal life.				
It is better not to estimate development periods a priori since software development is characterized by unexpected problems.				
During software development, it is preferable to invest in code readability in order to help future developers whose job will be to maintain the software.				
If software development does not proceed according to the planned schedule, the schedule should be replanned.				
Intuition and improvisation are important in software development processes.				
It is not important to integrate a reflective process (analysis of the past and learning of lessons) into the software development process.				
When it is difficult to check software, it is okay to move forward and not to insist on testing.				
There is a tendency on my team not to take personal responsibility.				
My team tends to adhere to the timetable.				
Even if I see an opportunity to shorten the development period by skipping tests, I will not take it.				
My team tends to build tight timetables (sometimes by compromising the software quality).				

APPENDIX 6.2. SYSTEMS ANALYSTS QUESTIONNAIRE

1. Please draw the position of systems analysts in software development organizations.

2. Please indicate at least three main skills required from systems analysts.

3. Please indicate at least three difficulties that systems analysts deal with.

4. In the following table, please describe how the time of systems analysts is allocated to their different professional activities.

Activity	Percentage (%) of time
Total	100%

PART III

AGENT-ORIENTED SYSTEMS ANALYSIS AND DESIGN METHODOLOGIES

CHAPTER 7

AGENT-ORIENTED INFORMATION SYSTEMS ANALYSIS AND DESIGN

Why and How

PAOLO GIORGINI, MANUEL KOLP, AND JOHN MYLOPOULOS

Abstract: We argue that emerging application areas such as e-business, peer-to-peer and ubiquitous computing require new software development paradigms that support open, distributed, and evolving architectures, such as agent-oriented software. We then sketch the Tropos methodology for agent-oriented software development and compare it with other proposals.

Keywords: Agent-Oriented Software Engineering, Agents and Multi-Agent Systems

INTRODUCTION

Information systems (hereafter IS) analysis and design techniques have been taught and practiced since the 1970s to support the development of IS around the globe. These techniques were founded on seminal proposals for expressive languages that model the content of databases and the requirements for software systems. For databases, Peter Chen's entity-relationship model (Chen, 1976) stood out among many proposals for semantic data models, and became a de facto standard for designing databases in research and practice. For software, Douglas Ross's structured analysis and design technique (SADT) (Ross, 1977) founded the research area known as requirements engineering and influenced software development practice through a number of follow-up proposals for modeling languages, including data flow diagrams (DFDs). The growing influence of object-oriented software development techniques in the 1980s led to a wide range of new proposals for modeling languages founded on the primitive notions of object, class, inheritance, and method (e.g., Rumbaugh et al. 1991). These techniques were consolidated by Rational Inc. and the Three Amigos (Booch, Rumbaugh, and Jacobson, 1999) in the mid-1990s into the Unified Modeling Language (UML). UML is the first-ever modeling language standard for software development. Its arrival has meant ever-wider recognition and use for analysis and design techniques in both academia and industry.

But not only IS analysis and design techniques have evolved over the past thirty years. The nature of the information systems we build has changed profoundly as well. Information systems in the 1970s were monolithic software towers (running on monolithic *hardware* towers) operating in isolation to serve a whole organization. For the past fifteen years, IS have become distributed, based on client-server and web-driven architectures. Moreover, these architectures are open, thanks to Web service and agent technologies, so that their components are no longer determined at design-time, and can instead be discovered and composed at run-time to fulfill a system's mandate. IS are also multiply interconnected to many other information systems running within and outside an organization, so that they can share data and support business processes that are geographically and organizationally distributed. Most important, these interconnections continuously evolve along with the organization in which they were conceived and its strategic alliances. "Service orientation," "peer-to-peer," and "virtual organizations" are the buzzwords of the day. Welcome to the Age of the Internet!

Within such a context, the components of IS need to support mechanisms for *discovering* external components that can help them fulfill their mission, for *negotiating* with these components, and for *composing* selected ones dynamically. In addition, they need *monitoring* and *diagnostic* mechanisms that supervise the operation of relevant software pieces and ensure that everything is in order. Moreover, they need ways of *self-repairing* and *self-tuning* to ensure that the overall system will be robust, reliable, and effective—despite the fact that it operates in open, dynamic environments. None of these mechanisms is intrinsic to the object-oriented software paradigm. But they all are intrinsic to the agent-oriented software paradigm (Jennings, 2000).

Not surprisingly, there has been growing interest in agent-oriented software development during the past few years, including several projects aimed at the development of a comprehensive methodology for building agent-oriented software. Many of these projects approached the problem by proposing extensions to object-oriented software development techniques (e.g., Odell, Van Dyke Parunak, and Bauer, 2000). Others adopted agent-oriented programming platforms as a baseline and sought to extend these by introducing agent-oriented analysis and design techniques (e.g., Wooldridge, Jennings, and Kinny, 2000). An excellent overview of the whole field can be found in Bergenti, Gleizes, and Zambonelli (2004). A brief summary is also included in this chapter.

This chapter introduces the Tropos methodology for agent-oriented software development and compares it with other proposals in the same family. The following sections present the Tropos methodology and its development phases, a brief introduction of the Media Shop case study used in later sections to show the Tropos phases, a discussion of related work, and a concluding section.

TROPOS

Tropos rests on the idea of using requirements modeling concepts to build a model of the system-to-be within its operational environment. This model is incrementally refined and extended, providing a common interface to the various software development activities. The model also serves as a basis for documentation and evolution of the software system.

In the following, we describe and illustrate the four development phases of the Tropos methodology: *requirements analysis* (early and late), *architectural design,* and *detailed design.*

Requirements Analysis

Requirements analysis represents the initial phase in most software engineering methodologies. Requirements analysis in Tropos consists of two phases: *early requirements* and *late requirements* analysis. The early requirements phase is concerned with understanding the organizational context within which the system-to-be will eventually function. Late requirements analysis, on the other hand, is concerned with a definition of the functional and nonfunctional requirements of the system-to-be.

Tropos adopts the *i** (Yu, 1995) modeling framework for analyzing requirements. In *i** (which stands for "distributed intentionality"), stakeholders are represented as (social) actors who depend on each other for goals to be achieved, tasks to be performed, and resources to be furnished. The *i** framework includes the *strategic dependency model* (actor diagram in Tropos) for describing the network of interdependencies among actors, as well as the *strategic rationale model* (rationale diagram in Tropos) for describing and supporting the reasoning that each actor goes through concerning relationships with other actors. These models have been formalized using intentional concepts from artificial intelligence, such as goal, belief, ability, and commitment (e.g., Cohen and Levesque, 1990). The framework has been presented in detail (Yu, 1995) and has been related to different application areas, including requirements engineering (Yu, 1993), software processes (Yu, 1994), and business process reengineering (Yu and Mylopoulos, 1996).

During early requirements analysis, the requirements engineer identifies the domain stakeholders and models them as social actors who depend on one another for goals to be fulfilled, tasks to be performed, and resources to be furnished. Through these dependencies, one can answer *why* questions, besides *what* and *how*, regarding system functionality. Answers to *why* questions ultimately link system functionality to stakeholder needs, preferences, and objectives. Actor diagrams and rationale diagrams are used in this phase.

An actor diagram is a graph involving *actors* who have *strategic dependencies* on each other. A dependency represents an "agreement" (called *dependum*) between two actors: the *depender* and the *dependee*. The *depender* depends on the *dependee*, to deliver on the dependum. The dependum can be a *goal* to be fulfilled, a *task* to be performed, or a *resource* to be delivered. In addition, the depender may depend on the dependee for a *softgoal* to be fulfilled. Softgoals represent vaguely defined goals, with no clear-cut criteria for their fulfillment. Graphically, actors are represented as circles; dependums—goals, softgoals, tasks, and resources—are respectively represented as ovals, clouds, hexagons, and rectangles; and dependencies have the form *depender* → *dependum* → *dependee*.

Actor diagrams are extended during early requirements analysis by incrementally adding more specific actor dependencies, discovered by a means–ends analysis of each goal. This analysis is specified using rationale diagrams. A rationale diagram appears as a balloon within which goals of a specific actor are analyzed and dependencies with other actors are established. Goals are decomposed into subgoals, and positive/negative contributions of subgoals to goals are specified.

During *late requirements* analysis, the conceptual model developed during early requirements is extended to include the system-to-be as a new actor, along with dependencies between this actor and others in its environment. These dependencies define functional and nonfunctional requirements for the system-to-be. Actor diagrams and rationale diagrams are also used in this phase.

Architectural Design

System architectural design has been the focus of considerable research during the past fifteen years that has produced well-established architectural styles and frameworks for evaluating their effectiveness with respect to particular software qualities. Examples of styles are pipes-and-filters, event-based, layered, control loops, and the like (Shaw and Garlan, 1996). In Tropos, we are interested in developing a suitable set of architectural styles for multi-agent software systems. Since the fundamental concepts of a multi-agent system (MAS) are intentional and social, rather than implementation-oriented, we turn to theories that study social structures resulting from a design process, namely, *organization theory and strategic alliances.* Organization theory (e.g., Scott, 1998) describes the structure and design of an organization; strategic alliances (e.g., Morabito, Sack, and Bhate, 1999) model the strategic collaborations of independent organizational stakeholders who have agreed to pursue a set of business goals.

We define an organizational style as a metaclass of organizational structures offering a set of design parameters to coordinate the assignment of organizational objectives and processes, thereby affecting how the organization itself functions (Kolp, Giorgini, and Mylopoulos, 2003). Design parameters include, among others, goal and task assignments, standardization, supervision and control dependencies, and strategy definitions.

For instance, *structure-in-5* (Mintzberg, 1992) specifies that an organization is an aggregate of five substructures. At the base level sits the *operational core,* which carries out the basic tasks and procedures directly linked to the production of products and services (acquisition of inputs, transformation of inputs into outputs, distribution of outputs). At the top lies the *strategic apex,* which makes executive decisions ensuring that the organization fulfills its mission in an effective way and defines the overall strategy of the organization in its environment. The *middle line* establishes a hierarchy of authority between the strategic apex and the operational core. It consists of managers responsible for supervising and coordinating the activities of the operational core. The *technostructure* and the *support* are separated from the main line of authority and influence the operating core only indirectly. The technostructure serves the organization by making the work of others more effective, typically by standardizing work processes, outputs, and skills. It is also in charge of applying analytical procedures to adapt the organization to its operational environment. The support provides specialized services, at various levels of the hierarchy, outside the basic operating workflow (e.g., legal counsel, research and development, payroll, cafeteria). (For further details about architectural styles in Tropos, see Do, Faulkner, and Kolp, 2003; Kolp, Giorgini, and Mylopoulos, 2003.)

Styles can be compared and evaluated with quality attributes (Shaw and Garlan, 1996), also called nonfunctional requirements (Chung et al., 2000) such as predictability, security, adaptability, coordinability, availability, fallibility tolerance, or modularity.

To cope with nonfunctional requirements and select the style for the organizational setting, we go through a means–ends analysis using the nonfunctional requirement (NFR) framework (Chung et al., 2000). We refine the identified requirements to subrequirements that are more precise and evaluate alternative organizational styles against them.

The analysis for selecting an organizational setting that meets the requirements of the system to be built is based on propagation algorithms. Basically, the idea is to assign a set of initial labels for some requirements of the graph, about their satisfiability and deniability, and to see how this assignment leads to the labels propagation for other requirements. In particular, we adopt both a qualitative and a numerical axiomatization (Giorgini et al., 2003) for goal (requirements) modeling primitives and label propagation algorithms that are shown to be sound and complete with respect to their respective axiomatization.

Detailed Design

The detailed design phase is intended to introduce additional detail for each architectural component of a system. It consists of defining how the goals assigned to each actor are fulfilled by agents with respect to social patterns.

For this step, designers can be guided by a catalogue of multi-agent patterns that offer a set of standard solutions. Considerable work has been done in software engineering for defining software patterns (see, e.g., Gamma et al., 1995). Unfortunately, little emphasis has been placed on social and intentional aspects. Moreover, proposals for agent patterns that do address these aspects (see, e.g., Aridor and Lange, 1998) are not intended for use at a design level. Instead, such proposals seem to aim at the implementation phase, when issues such as agent communication, information gathering, or connection setup are addressed.

Social patterns in Tropos (Do, Kolp, and Pirotte, 2003) are design patterns focusing on social and intentional aspects that are recurrent in multi-agent and cooperative systems. In particular, the structures are inspired by the federated patterns introduced in Hayden, Carrick, and Yang, (1999) and Kolp, Giorgini, and Mylopoulos (2001). We have classified them into two categories: *pair* and *mediation*.

The pair patterns—such as booking, call-for-proposal, subscription, or bidding—describe direct interactions between negotiating agents. For instance, the bidding pattern involves an initiator and a number of participants. The initiator organizes and leads the bidding process, publishes the bid to the participants, and receives various proposals. At every iteration, the initiator can accept an offer, raise the bid, or cancel the process.

The mediation patterns—such as monitor, broker, matchmaker, mediator, embassy, or wrapper —feature intermediary agents that help other agents to reach an agreement on an exchange of services. For instance, in the broker pattern, the broker agent is an arbiter and intermediary that requests services from a provider to satisfy the request of a consumer.

Detailed design also includes actor communication and actor behavior. To support it, we propose the adoption of existing agent communication languages like FIPA-ACL (Labrou, Finin, and Peng, 1999) or KQML (Finin, Labrou, and Mayfield, 1997), message transportation mechanisms and other concepts and tools. One possibility is to adopt extensions to UML (OMG, 1999), such as Agent Unified Modeling Language (AUML) (Bauer, Muller, and Odell, 2001; Odell, Van Dyke Parunak, and Bauer, 2000) proposed by the Foundation for Physical Intelligent Agents (FIPA, 2001) and the OMG Agent Work group.

We have also proposed and defined a set of stereotypes, tagged values, and constraints to accommodate Tropos concepts within UML (Mylopoulos, Kolp, and Castro, 2001) for users who wish to use UML as the notation in Tropos.

CASE STUDY

Media Shop is a store selling and shipping different kinds of media items such as books, newspapers, magazines, audio CDs, videotapes, and the like. Media Shop customers (on-site or remote) can use a periodically updated catalogue describing available media items to specify their order. Media Shop is supplied with the latest releases from *Media Producer* and in-catalogue items by Media Supplier. To increase market share, Media Shop has decided to open up a B2C (business to consumer) retail sales front on the Internet. With the new setup, a customer can order *Media Shop* items in person, by phone, or through the Internet. The system has been *Medi@* and is available on the World Wide Web using communication facilities provided by Telecom Cpy. It also uses financial services supplied by Bank Cpy, which specializes in online transactions. The basic objective for the new system is to allow an online customer to examine the items in the Medi@ Internet catalogue and place orders. The main interface of the system is shown in Figure 7.1.

There are no registration restrictions or identification procedures for *Medi@* users. Potential customers can search the online store by either browsing the catalogue or querying the item database. The catalogue groups media items of the same type into (sub)hierarchies and genres (e.g., audio CDs are classified into pop, rock, jazz, opera, world, classical music, soundtrack, etc.) so that customers can browse only (sub)categories of interest. An online search engine allows customers with particular items in mind to search title, author/artist, and description fields through keywords

Figure 7.1   **Interface of the System**

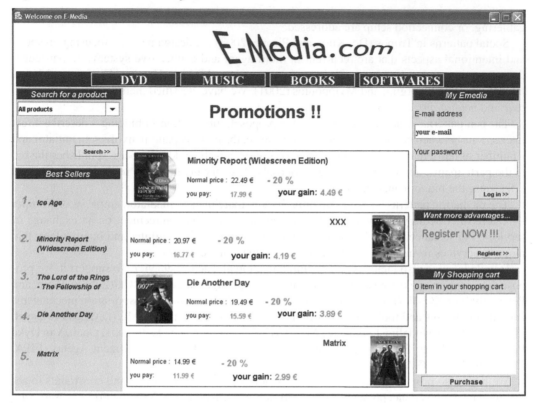

or full-text search. If the item is not available in the catalogue, the customer has the option of asking Media Shop to order it, provided the customer has editor/publisher references (e.g., ISBN, ISSN), and identifies him/herself (in terms of name and credit card number). Details about media items include title, media category (e.g., book) and genre (e.g., science-fiction), author/artist, short description, editor/publisher international references and information, date, cost, and sometimes pictures (when available).

EARLY REQUIREMENTS ANALYSIS

The elements described in the previous section are sufficient for producing a first model of an organizational environment. For instance, Figure 7.2 depicts the actor diagram of our *Medi@* example. The main actors are *Customer*, *Media Shop*, *Media Supplier*, and *Media Producer*. Customer depends on Media Shop to fulfill his/her goal: Buy Media Items. Conversely, Media Shop depends on Customer to *increase market share* and make." Since the dependum *Happy Customers* cannot be defined precisely, it is represented as a softgoal. The Customer also depends on Media Shop to *consult the catalogue* (task dependency). Furthermore, Media Shop depends on Media Supplier to supply media items in a continuous way and get a *Media Item* (resource dependency). The items are expected to be of good quality because, otherwise, the *Continuing Business* dependency would not be fulfilled. Finally, Media Producer is expected to provide Media Supplier with *Quality Packages*.

Figure 7.2 **Actor Diagram for a Media Shop**

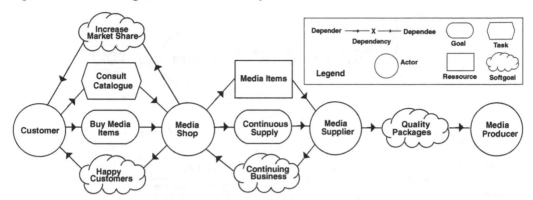

Figure 7.3 focuses on one of the (soft)goal dependencies identified for Media Shop, namely, *Increase Market Share*. To achieve that softgoal, the analysis postulates a goal *Run Shop* that can be fulfilled by means of a task *Run Shop*. Tasks are partially ordered sequences of steps intended to accomplish some (soft)goal. In Tropos, tasks can be decomposed into subtasks but also goals, whose collective fulfillment completes the task. In Figure 7.3, *Run Shop* is decomposed into goals *Handle Billing* and *Handle Customer Orders*, tasks *Manage Staff* and *Manage Inventory*, and softgoal *Improve Service,* which together accomplish the top-level task. Subgoals and subtasks can be specified more precisely through refinement. For instance, the goal *Handle Customer Orders* is fulfilled either through tasks *Order By Phone*, *Order In Person,* or *Order By Internet*, while the task *Manage Inventory* would be collectively accomplished by tasks *Sell Stock* and *Enhance Catalogue*. These decompositions eventually allow us to identify actors who can accomplish a goal, carry out a task, or deliver some needed resource for Media Shop. Such dependencies in Figure 7.3 are, among others, the goal and resource dependencies on *Media Supplier* for supplying, in a continuous way, media items to enhance the catalogue and sell products, the softgoal dependencies on *Customer* for increasing market share (by running the shop) and making customers happy (by improving service), and the task dependency *Accounting* on *Bank Cpy* to keep track of business transactions.

LATE REQUIREMENTS ANALYSIS

For our example, the *Medi@* system is viewed as a fully fledged actor in the actor diagram depicted in Figure 7.4. With respect to the actors previously identified, *Customer* depends on Media Shop to buy media items while Media Shop depends on *Customer* to increase market share and make customers happy (with Media Shop service). *Media Supplier* is expected to supply *Media Shop* with media items in a continuous way since it depends on the latter for continuing business. It can also use *Medi@* to determine new needs from customers, such as media items not available in the catalogue, while expecting *Media Producer* to provide him/her with *quality packages*. As indicated earlier, Media Shop depends on *Medi@* to process Internet orders and on *Bank Cpy* to process business transactions. *Customer*, in turn, depends on *Medi@* to place orders through the Internet, to search the database for keywords, or simply to browse the online catalogue. With respect to relevant qualities, *Customer* requires that transaction services be secure and available, while Media

Figure 7.3   **Means–Ends Analysis for the Softgoal Increase Market Share**

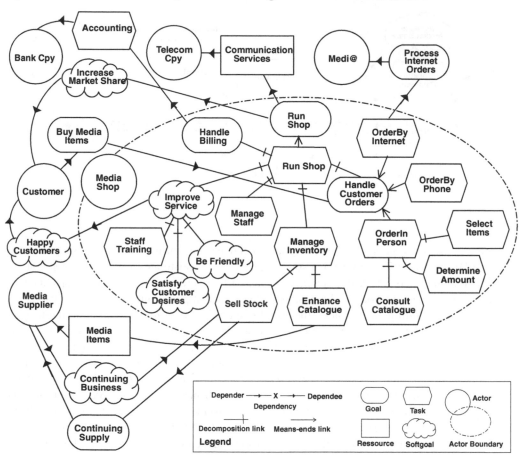

Shop expects *Medi@* to be easily adaptable (e.g., catalogue enhancing, item database evolution, user interface update, etc.). Finally, *Medi@* relies on Internet services provided by *Telecom Cpy* and on secure online financial transactions handled by *Bank Cpy*.

Although an actor diagram provides hints about why processes are structured in a certain way, it does not sufficiently support the process of suggesting, exploring, and evaluating alternative solutions. As late requirements analysis proceeds, *Medi@* is given additional responsibilities and ends up as the dependee of several dependencies. Moreover, the system is decomposed into several subactors, which take on some of these responsibilities. This decomposition and responsibility assignment is realized using the same kind of means–ends analysis as that illustrated in Figure 7.3. Hence, the analysis in Figure 7.5 focuses on the system itself, instead of an external stakeholder.

Figure 7.5 postulates a root task *Internet Shop Managed* providing sufficient support (++) (Chung et al., 2000) to the softgoal *Increase Market Share*. That task is first refined into goals *Internet Orders Handled* and *Item Searching Handled*, softgoals *Attract New Customer, Secure,* and *Available,* and tasks *Produce Statistics* and *Adaptation.* To manage Internet orders, *Internet Orders Handled* is achieved through the task *Shopping Cart,* which is decomposed into subtasks

Figure 7.4   **Refined Actor Diagram for Media Shop**

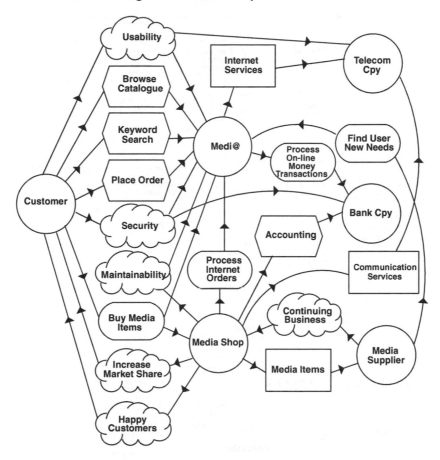

Select Item, Add Item, Check Out, and *Get Identification Detail.* These are the main process activities required to design an operational online shopping cart (Conallen, 1999). The latter task is achieved either through subgoal *Classic Communication Handled,* dealing with phone and fax orders, or *Internet Handled,* managing secure or standard form orderings. To allow for the ordering of new items not listed in the catalogue, *Select Item* is also further refined into two alternative subtasks, one dedicated to the selection of catalogued items, the other to backordering unavailable products. To provide sufficient support (++) to the *Adaptable* softgoal, *Adaptation* is refined into four subtasks dealing with catalogue updates, system evolution, interface updates, and system monitoring. The goal *Item Searching Handled* might alternatively be fulfilled through the tasks *Database Querying* or *Catalogue Consulting* with respect to customers' navigating desiderata, that is, searching with particular items in mind by using search functions or simply browsing the catalogued products.

In addition, as already pointed out, Figure 7.5 introduces softgoal contributions to model sufficient/ partial positive (respectively ++ and +) or sufficient/partial negative (respectively – – and –) support to softgoals *Secure, Available, Adaptable, Attract New Customers,* and *Increase Market Share.* The result of this means–ends analysis is a set of (system and human) actors who are dependees for some of the dependencies that have been postulated.

Figure 7.5   **Rationale Diagram for Medi@**

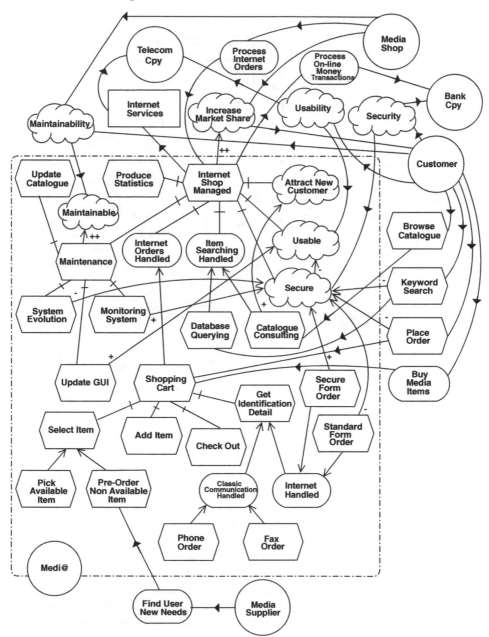

Resource, task, and softgoal dependencies correspond naturally to functional and nonfunctional requirements. Leaving (some) goal dependencies between system actors and other actors is a novelty. Traditionally, functional goals are "operationalized" during late requirements (Dardenne, van Lamsweerde, and Fickas, 1993), while quality softgoals are either operationalized or "metricized" (Davis, 1993). For example, Billing Processor may be operationalized during late requirements analysis into particular business processes for processing bills and orders. Likewise, a security softgoal might be operationalized by defining interfaces that minimize input/output between the system and its environment, or by limiting access to sensitive information. Alternatively, the security requirement may be metricized into something such as "No more than X unauthorized operations in the system-to-be per year."

Leaving goal dependencies with system actors as dependees makes sense whenever there is a foreseeable need for flexibility in the performance of a task on the part of the system. For example, consider a communication goal "communicate X to Y." According to conventional development techniques, such a goal needs to be operationalized before the end of late requirements analysis, perhaps into some sort of a user interface through which user Y will receive message X from the system. The problem with this approach is that the steps through which this goal is to be fulfilled (along with a host of background assumptions) are frozen into the requirements of the system-to-be. This early translation of goals into concrete plans for their fulfillment makes systems fragile and less reusable.

In our example, we have left three (soft)goals (*Availability, Security, Adaptability*) in the late requirements model. The first goal is *Availability* because we propose to allow system agents to automatically decide at run-time which catalogue browser, shopping cart, and order processor architecture best fit customer needs or navigator/platform specifications. Moreover, we would like to include different search engines, reflecting different search techniques, and let the system dynamically choose the most appropriate. The second key softgoal in the late requirements specification is *Security*. To fulfill this, we propose to support a number of security strategies in the system's architecture and let the system decide at run-time which one is the most appropriate, taking into account environment configurations, Web browser specifications, and network protocols used. The third goal is *Adaptability,* meaning that catalogue content, database schema, and architectural model can be dynamically extended or modified to integrate new and future Web-related technologies.

ARCHITECTURAL DESIGN

Figure 7.6 suggests a possible assignment of system responsibilities for *Medi@* following the *structure-in-5* style (Do, Faulkner, and Kolp, 2003). It is decomposed into five principal actors: *Store Front, Coordinator, Billing Processor, Back Store,* and *Decision Maker. Store Front* serves as the *Operational Core*. It interacts primarily with Customer and provides him/her with a usable front-end Web application for consulting and shopping media items. *Back Store* constitutes the *Support* component. It manages the product database and communicates to the *Store Front* information on products selected by the user. It *stores* and *backs up* all Web information from the *Store Front* about customers, products, sales, orders, and bills to produce *statistical information* to the *Coordinator*. It provides the *Decision Maker* with *strategic information* (analyses, historical charts, and sales reports).

The *Billing Processor* is in charge of handling orders and bills for the *Coordinator* and implementing the corresponding procedures for the *Store Front*. It also ensures the secure management of financial transactions for the *Decision Maker*. As the *Middle Line,* the *Coordinator* assumes the central position of the architecture. It ensures the coordination of *e-shopping* services provided by the *Operational Core,* including the management of conflicts between itself, the *Billing Processor,* the *Back Store,* and the *Store Front*. To this end, it also handles and implements strategies to manage and prevent *security* gaps and *adaptability* issues. The *Decision Maker* assumes the *Strategic Apex* role. To this end, it defines the *Strategic Behavior* of the architecture ensuring that

Figure 7.6   **The Medi@ Architecture in Structure-in-5**

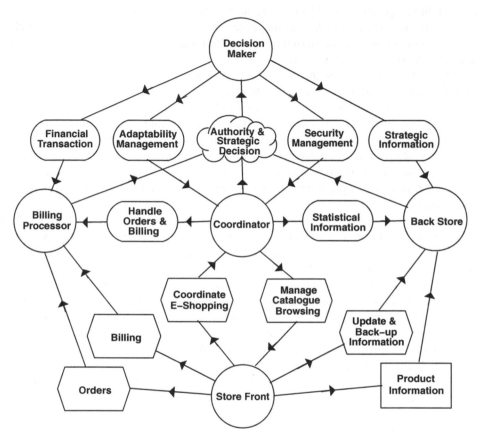

objectives and responsibilities delegated to the *Billing Processor, Coordinator,* and *Back Store* are consistent with that global functionality.

Three software quality attributes have been identified as being particularly strategic for e-business systems (Do, Faulkner, and Kolp, 2003).

Adaptability

Adaptability deals with the way the system can be designed using generic mechanisms to allow Web pages to be dynamically changed. It also concerns the catalogue update for inventory consistency.

The *structure-in-5* separates each typical component of the *Medi@* architecture, isolating one from the other and allowing dynamic manipulation.

Security

Clients, exposed to the Internet are, like servers, at risk in Web applications. It is possible for Web browsers and application servers to download or upload content and programs that could open up the client system to crackers and automated agents. JavaScript, Java applets, ActiveX controls, and

Figure 7.7   **Decomposing the Store Front with Social Patterns**

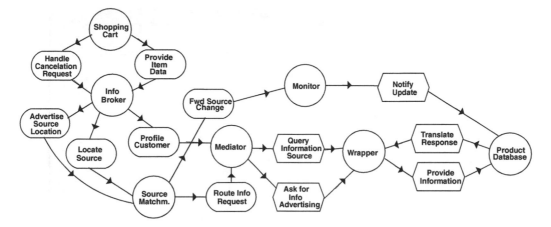

plug-ins represent a certain risk to the system and the information it manages. Equally important are the procedures checking the consistency of data transactions.

In the *structure-in-5*, checks and control mechanisms can be integrated at different levels assuming redundancy from different perspectives. Contrary to the classical layered architecture (Shaw and Garlan, 1996), checks and controls are not restricted to adjacent levels. Besides, since the *structure-in-5* permits the separation of process (*Store Front, Billing Processor,* and *Back Store*) from control (*Decision Maker* and *Monitor*), security and consistency of these two hierarchies can also be verified independently.

Availability

Network communication may not be very reliable, which can cause sporadic loss of the server. There are data integrity concerns about the capability of the e-business system to do what needs to be done, as quickly and efficiently as possible, in particular about the ability of the system to respond in time to client requests for its services.

The *structure-in-5* architecture prevents availability problems by differentiating process from control. Besides, contrary to the classical layered architecture (Shaw and Garlan, 1996), higher levels are more abstract than lower levels: lower levels only involve resources and task dependencies while higher ones propose intentional (goals and softgoals) relationships.

DETAILED DESIGN

Figure 7.7 shows a possible use of the patterns for the *Store Front* component of the e-business system of Figure 7.6. In particular, it shows how to realize the dependencies *Manage Catalogue Browsing, Update Information,* and *Product Information* from the point of view of the *Store Front.* The *Store Front* and the dependencies are decomposed into a combination of social patterns (Do, Kolp, and Pirotte, 2003) involving agents, pattern agents, subgoals, and subtasks.

The booking pattern is applied between the *Shopping Cart* and the *Information Broker* to reserve available items. The broker pattern is applied to the *Information Broker,* which satisfies the *Shopping Cart*'s requests for information by accessing the *Product Database.* The *Source Match-*

Figure 7.8   **The Information Broker of Medi@**

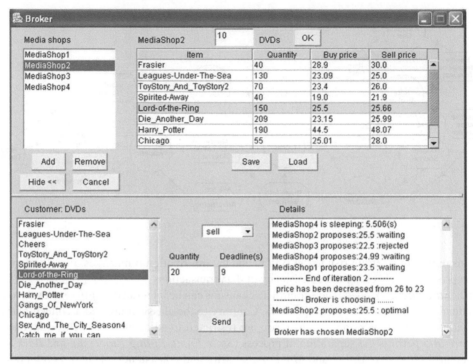

maker applies the matchmaker pattern to locate the appropriate source for the *Information Broker,* and the monitor pattern is used to check any possible change in the *Product Database*. Finally, the mediator pattern is applied to dispatch the interactions between the *Information Broker,* the *Source Matchmaker,* and the *Wrapper*, while the wrapper pattern forms the interaction between the *Information Broker* and the *Product Database*.

Figure 7.8 shows the remote administrative tool for the information broker of Figure 7.7. The customer sends a service request to the broker requesting the buying or selling of DVDs. He/she chooses which DVDs to sell or buy, selects the corresponding DVD titles, the quantity and the deadline (the timeout before which the broker has to realize the requested service). When receiving the customer's request, the broker interacts with the media shops. The interactions between the broker and the media shops are shown in the bottom-right corner of the figure.

To go deeper into the details, the rest of the section concentrates only on the *Store Front* actor. Figure 7.9 depicts a partial, extended UML class diagram (Castro, Kolp, and Mylopoulos, 2002) focusing on the actor that will be implemented as an aggregation of several *CartForm*s and *ItemLine*s.

To specify the *checkout* operation identified in Figure 7.9, extensions of interaction diagrams (Castro, Kolp, and Mylopoulos, 2002) allow us to use templates and packages to represent *checkout* as an object, as well as in terms of sequence and collaborations diagrams.

Figure 7.10 focuses on the protocol between *Customer* and *Shopping Cart,* which consists of a customization of the FIPA Contract Net Protocol (Odell, Van Dyke Parunak, and Bauer, 2000). Such a protocol describes a communication pattern among actors as well as constraints on the contents of the messages they exchange. When a *Customer* wants to check out, a request-for-proposal message

Figure 7.9 **Partial Class Diagram for Store Front**

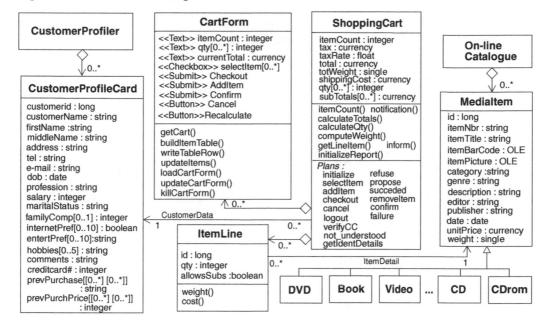

is sent to *Shopping Cart*, which must respond before a given timeout (for network security and integrity reasons). The response may refuse to provide a proposal, submit a proposal, or express miscomprehension. The diamond symbol with an "X" indicates an "exclusive or" decision. If a proposal is offered, *Customer* has a choice of either accepting or canceling the proposal.

At the lowest level, we use plan diagrams (Kinny and Georgeff, 1996) to specify the internal processing of atomic actors. Each identified plan is specified as a plan diagram, which is denoted by a rectangular box. The lower section, the plan graph, is a state transition diagram. However, plan graphs are not just descriptions of system behavior developed during design. Rather, they are directly executable prescriptions of how a BDI (belief-desire-intention) agent should behave (execute identified plans) in order to achieve a goal or respond to an event.

The initial transition of the plan diagram is labeled with an activation event (*Press checkout button*) and activation condition (*[checkout button activated]*), which determine when and in what context the plan should be activated. Transitions from a state automatically occur when exiting the state and no event is associated (e.g., when exiting *Fields Checking*) or when the associated event occurs (e.g., *Press cancel button*), provided in all cases that the associated condition is true (e.g., *[Mandatory fields filled]*). When the transition occurs, any associated action is performed (e.g., *verifyCC()*).

The elements of the plan graph are three types of node: start states, end states, and internal states; and one type of directed edge: transitions. Start states are denoted by small filled circles. End states may be pass-or-fail states, denoted respectively by a small target or a small no-entry sign. Internal states may be passive or active. Passive states have no substructure and are denoted by a small open circle. Active states have an associated activity and are denoted by rectangular boxes with rounded corners. An important feature of plan diagrams is their notion of failure. Failure can occur when an action upon a transition fails, when an explicit transition

Figure 7.10 **Agent Interaction Protocol Focusing on a Checkout Dialogue**

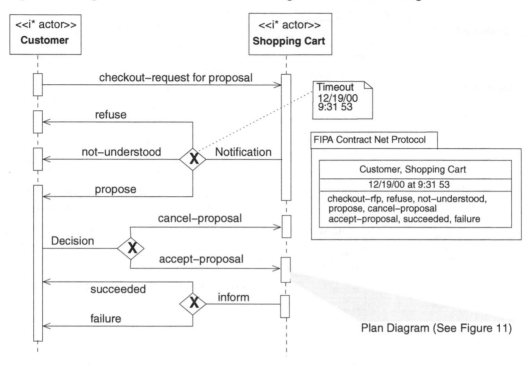

to a fail state occurs, or when the activity of an active state terminates in failure and no outgoing transition is enabled.

Figure 7.11 depicts the plan diagram for *Checkout*, triggered by pushing the checkout button. Mandatory fields are first checked. If any mandatory fields are not filled, an iteration allows the customer to update them. For security reasons, the loop exits after five tries ([I<5]) and causes the plan to fail. Credit Card (CC) validity is then checked. Again for security reasons, when not valid, the CC# can be corrected only three times. Otherwise, the plan terminates in failure. The customer is then asked to confirm the CC# to allow item registration. If the CC# is not confirmed, the plan fails. Otherwise, the plan continues: each item is iteratively registered, final amounts are calculated, stock records and customer profiles are updated, and a report is displayed. When finally the whole plan succeeds, the *Shopping Cart* automatically logs out and asks the *Order Processor* to initialize the order. When, for any reason, the plan fails, the *Shopping Cart* automatically logs out. At any time, if the cancel button is pressed, or the timeout is more than ninety seconds (e.g., due to a network bottleneck), the plan fails and the *Shopping Cart* is reinitialized.

From the above case study, we understand that Tropos insists on requirements phases, especially early requirements analysis through goals and social dependencies elicitation. While Tropos focuses on organizational and intentional modeling, useful when analyzing agent-oriented information systems, it does not really focus on the process and workflow modeling usually needed for developing business systems such as enterprise resource planning packages. Moreover, Tropos does not propose specific models for detailed design. Instead, the methodology reuses UML-based agent design models. The methodology is so far not really usable for project software management since it does not include cost estimation models or iterative process.

Figure 7.11   **A Plan Diagram for Checkout**

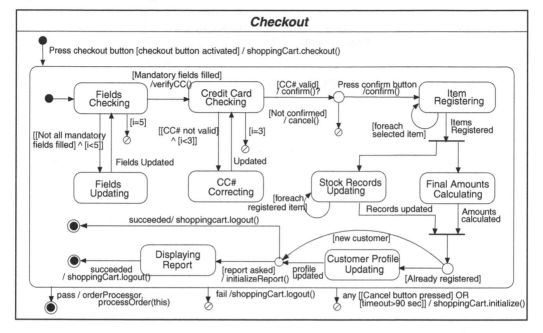

RELATED WORK

The most important feature of the Tropos methodology is that it aspires to span the overall software development process, from early requirements to implementation. Figure 7.12 shows graphically the relative coverage of the software development process by Tropos and other methodologies, including KAOS (Dardenne, van Lamsweerde, and Fickas, 1993), Gaia (Wooldridge, Jennings, and Kinny, 2000), AAII (Kinny, Georgeff, and Rao, 1996), MaSE (Deloach, Wood, and Sparkman 2001), and AUML (Bauer, Muller, and Odell, 2001). Other agent-oriented software development methodologies have been proposed as well (see, e.g., Brazier et al., 1997; Ciancarini and Wooldridge, 2001; Wooldridge, Ciancarini, and Weiss, 2002).

While Tropos covers all software development phases, at the same time it is well integrated with other existing work. Thus, for early and late requirements analysis, it adapts ideas from requirements engineering, and in particular Eric Yu's *i** methodology (Yu, 1995). During design phases, UML (Booch, Rumbaugh, and Jacobson, 1999) and AUML (Bauer, Muller, and Odell, 2001) concepts are used to model and analyze static and dynamic aspects of a software system design.

The Tropos metamodel presented in Bresciani and colleagues (2004) has been developed in the same spirit as the UML metamodel for class diagrams. A comparison between the two metamodels readily points out fundamental differences between the primitive concepts adopted by the two modeling frameworks. This contrast also defines the key difference between object-oriented and agent-oriented development methodologies. Agents (and actor diagrams) cannot be thought of as specializations of objects (and class diagrams), as argued elsewhere. The Tropos modeling framework supports the process of modeling and analyzing social and intentional settings. UML was designed to support modeling and analysis of static and dynamic settings. In that sense, the two approaches (a) give designers very different concepts

Figure 7.12 **Comparison of Different Software Development Methodologies**

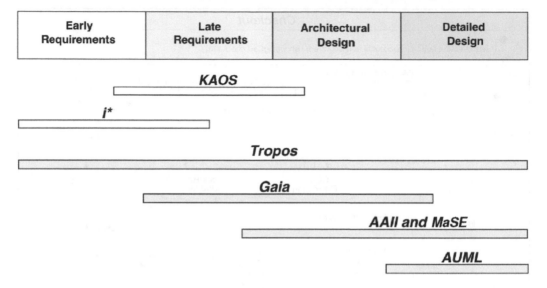

for conceptualizing an application; (b) offer different sets of questions to be asked in building models for that application; and (c) offer different tools to support various forms of analysis for these models.

CONCLUSIONS

We have presented the Tropos methodology for developing agent-oriented information systems. The methodology is particularly appropriate for generic, component-based software for e-business applications that can be downloaded and used in a variety of operating environments and computing platforms. The methodology is currently supported by a range of formal analysis tools (www.troposproject.org), and its application is being explored along a number of fronts: design of Web services and business processes (Lau and Mylopoulos, 2004), design of autonomic software (Lapouchnian et al., 2005), and also design of Web sites and user interfaces (Bolchini and Mylopoulos, 2003).

Tropos is founded on intentional and social concepts inspired by early requirements analysis. The modeling framework views software from five complementary perspectives:

- Social—who are the relevant actors and what do they want? What are their obligations? What are their capabilities?
- Intentional—what are the relevant goals and how do they interact? How are they being fulfilled, and by whom?
- Communicational—how do actors communicate with each other to fulfill their goals?
- Process-oriented—what are the relevant business/computer processes? Who is responsible for what?
- Object-oriented—what are the relevant objects and classes, along with their interrelationships?

The requirements-driven approach, on which Tropos is based, suggests that the methodology favorably complements proposals for agent-oriented programming environments (Castro, Kolp, and Mylopoulos, 2002; Bresciani et al., 2004) given that—according to Tropos—software is conceived in terms of (system) actors, goals, and social dependencies among them. Moreover, it does not force the developer to operationalize these intentional and social structures early on during the development process, thereby avoiding the hardwiring of solutions into software requirements.

Clearly, Tropos is not the right methodology for developing any kind of software. For system software (such as compilers and operating systems) or embedded software, the operating environment of the system-to-be is an engineering artifact, with no identifiable stakeholders. In such cases, traditional software development techniques may be most appropriate. However, a large and growing percentage of software systems today operate within open, dynamic organizational environments. For such software, the Tropos methodology and others in the same family apply and promise to deliver more robust, reliable, and usable software systems. The Tropos methodology in its current form is also not suitable for sophisticated software agents requiring advanced reasoning mechanisms for plans, goals, and negotiations. Further extensions will be required, mostly at the detailed design phase, to address this class of software applications.

Much remains to be done to further refine the proposed design framework and validate its usefulness with large case studies. We are currently working on the development of additional formal analysis techniques for Tropos, including goal and social network analysis. We are also developing tools that support different phases of the methodology.

ACKNOWLEDGMENTS

This work has been partially funded by PAT-STAMPS and PRIN-MEnSA projects.

REFERENCES

Aridor, Y., and Lange, D. 1998. Agent design patterns: elements of agent application design. In *Proceedings of the Second International Conference on Autonomous Agents*, Agents '98, St. Paul, MI, 108–115.

Bauer, B.; Muller, J.; and Odell, J. 2001. Agent UML: a formalism for specifying multiagent interaction. In Paolo Ciancarini and Michael Wooldridge (eds.), *Agent-Oriented Software Engineering*, Berlin: Springer, 91–103.

Bergenti, F.; Gleizes, M.-P.; and Zambonelli, F. 2004. *Methodologies and Software Engineering for Agent Systems*. Norwell, MA and Dordrecht, Netherlands: Kluwer Academic.

Bolchini, D., and Mylopoulos, J. 2003. From task-oriented to goal-oriented web requirements analysis. In *Proceedings of the Fourth International Conference on Web Information Systems Engineering* (WISE '03), Rome. 166–175.

Booch, G.; Rumbaugh, J.; and Jacobson, I. 1999. *The Unified Modeling Language: User Guide*. Reading, MA: Addison-Wesley.

Brazier, F.M.T.; Dunin Keplicz, B.M.; Jennings, N.R.; and Treur, J. 1997. DESIRE: modelling multi-agent systems in a compositional formal framework. *International Journal on Cooperative Information Systems*, 6, 1, 67–94.

Bresciani, P.; Giorgini, P.; Giunchiglia, F.; Mylopoulos, J.; and Perini, A. 2004. Tropos: an agent-oriented software development methodology. *Journal of Autonomous Agents and Multi-Agent Systems*, 8, 3, 203–236.

Castro, J.; Kolp, M.; and Mylopoulos, J. 2002. Towards requirements-driven information systems engineering: the Tropos project. *Information Systems*, 27, 6 (September), 365–389.

Chen, P.P. 1976. The entity-relationship model—toward a unified view of data. *ACM Transactions on Database Systems*, 1, 1 (March), 9–36.

Chung, L.; Nixon, B.; Yu, E.; and Mylopoulos, J. 2000. *Non-Functional Requirements in Software Engineering*. Boston: Kluwer Academic.

Ciancarini, P., and Wooldridge, M. (eds.) 2001. Agent-oriented software engineering. In *Lecture Notes in AI*, vol. 1957. Springer-Verlag.

Cohen, P., and Levesque, H. 1990. Intention is choice with commitment. *Artificial Intelligence*, 32, 3, 213–261.

Conallen, J. 1999. *Building Web Applications with UML*. Reading, MA: Addison-Wesley.

Dardenne, A.; van Lamsweerde, A.; and Fickas, S. 1993. Goal-directed requirements acquisition. *Science of Computer Programming*, 20, 1–2, 3–50.

Davis, A. 1993. *Software Requirements: Objects, Functions, and States*. Englewood Cliffs, NJ: Prentice Hall.

Deloach, S.A.; Wood, M. F.; Sparkman, C. H. 2001. Multiagent systems engineering. *International Journal of Software Engineering and Knowledge Engineering*, 11(3), 231–258.

Do, T.T.; Faulkner, S.; and Kolp, M. 2003. Organizational multi-agent architectures for information systems. In *Proceedings of the Fifth International Conference on Enterprise Information Systems*, ICEIS '03, Angers, France. Available at http://www.isys.ucl.ac.be/descartes/.

Do, T.T.; Kolp, M.; and Pirotte, A. 2003. Social patterns for designing multi-agent systems. In *Proceedings of the Fifteenth International Conference on Software Engineering and Knowledge Engineering*, SEKE '03, San Francisco, CA, 103–110.

Finin, T.; Labrou, Y.; and Mayfield, J. 1997. KQML as an agent communication language. In J. Bradshaw (ed.), *Software Agents*. Cambridge, MA: MIT Press, 291–316.

Foundation for Intelligent Physical Agents (FIPA). 2001. Available at www.fipa.org.

Gamma, E.; Helm, R.; Johnson, J.; and Vlissides, J. 1995. *Design Patterns: Elements of Reusable Object-Oriented Software*. Reading, MA: Addison-Wesley.

Giorgini, P.; Mylopoulos, J.; Nicchiarelli, E.; and Sebastiani, R. 2003. Formal reasoning techniques for goal models. *Journal of Data Semantics 1*, 1–20.

Hayden, S.; Carrick, C.; and Yang, Q. 1999. Architectural design patterns for multiagent coordination. In *Proceedings of the Third International Conference on Autonomous Agents*, Agents '99, Seattle, WA. Available at http://citeseerx.ist.psu.edu/.

Jennings, N.R. 2000. On agent-based software engineering. *Artificial Intelligence*, 117, 2, 277–296.

Kinny, D., and Georgeff, M. 1996. Modelling and design of multi-agent systems. In *Proceedings of the Third International Workshop on Intelligent Agents: Agent Theories, Architectures, and Languages*, ATAL '96, Budapest, Hungary, 1–20.

Kinny, D.; Georgeff, M.; and Rao, A. 1996. A methodology and modelling technique for systems of BDI agents. In W. Van de Velde and J. W. Perram (eds.), *Agents Breaking Away: Proceedings of the Seventh European Workshop on Modelling Autonomous Agents in a Multi-Agent World*. Berlin: Springer-Verlag, 56–71.

Kolp, M.; Giorgini, P.; and Mylopoulos, J. 2001. A goal-based organizational perspective on multi-agents architectures. In *Proceedings of the Eighth International Workshop on Intelligent Agents: Agent Theories, Architectures, and Languages*, ATAL '01, Seattle, WA. Springer Berlin, Heidelberg, 128–140.

———. 2003. Organizational patterns for early requirements analysis. In *Proceedings of the Fifteenth International Conference on Advanced Information Systems*, CAiSE '03, Velden, Austria. Lecture Notes in Computer Science #2681, Springer, 617–632.

Labrou, Y.; Finin, T.; and Peng, Y. 1999. The current landscape of agent communication languages. *Intelligent Systems*, 14, 2, 45–52.

Lapouchnian, A.; Liaskos, S.; Mylopoulos, J.; and Yu, Y. 2005. Design of autonomic software through requirements models. In *Proceedings of the DEAS Workshop, Twenty-seventh International Conference on Software Engineering (ICSE '05)*, St. Louis, MO. ACM Press, 1–7.

Lau, D., and Mylopoulos, J. 2004. Designing Web services with Tropos. In *Proceedings of the IEEE International Conference on Web Services* (ICWS '04), San Diego, CA, 306–314.

Mintzberg, H. 1992. *Structure in Fives: Designing Effective Organizations*. Reprint ed. Englewood Cliffs, NJ: Prentice Hall.

Morabito, J.; Sack, I.; and Bhate, A. 1999. *Organization Modeling: Innovative Architectures for the 21st Century*. Upper Saddle River, NJ: Prentice Hall.

Mylopoulos, J.; Kolp, M.; and Castro, J. 2001. UML for agent-oriented software development: the Tropos proposal. In *Proceedings of the Fourth International Conference on the Unified Modeling Language*, UML '01, Toronto, Canada. Lecture Notes in Computer Science #2185, Springer, 422–441.

Object Management Group (OMG). 1999. OMG Unified Modeling Specification. Available at www.omg.org.

Odell, J.; Van Dyke Parunak, H.; and Bauer, B. 2000. Extending UML for agents. In *Proceedings of the Second International Bi-Conference Workshop on Agent-Oriented Information Systems*, Austin, TX. Available at http://scholar.google.ca/schhp?hl=en&tab=ws.

Ross, D. 1977. Structured analysis (SA): a language for communicating ideas. *IEEE Transactions on Software Engineering,* SE-3, 1, 16–34.

Rumbaugh, J.; Blaha, M.; Premerlani, W.; Eddy, F.; and Lorensen, W. 1991. *Object-Oriented Modeling and Design*. Englewood Cliffs, NJ: Prentice Hall.

Sabater, J.; Sierra, C.; Parsons, S.; and Jenning N.R. 1999. Using multi-context systems to engineer executable agent. In N. R. Jennings and L. Lesperance (eds.), *Proceedings of the Sixth International Workshop on Agent Theories Architectures, and Languages* (ATAL-99), LNCS #1757. Springer-Verlag, 277–294.

Scott, W.R. 1998. *Organizations: Rational, Natural, and Open Systems*, 4th ed. Upper Saddle River, NJ: Prentice Hall.

Shaw, M., and Garlan, D. 1996. *Software Architecture: Perspectives on an Emerging Discipline*. Upper Saddle River, NJ: Prentice Hall.

Wooldridge, M.; Ciancarini, P.; and Weiss, G. (eds.). 2002. *Agent-Oriented Software Engineering: Second International Workshop*, AOSE 2001, Montreal, Canada. Lecture Notes in Computer Science, number 2222, Springer.

Wooldridge, M.; Jennings, N.R.; and Kinny, D. 2000. The Gaia methodology for agent-oriented analysis and design. *Journal of Autonomous Agents and Multi-Agent Systems,* 3, 285–312.

Yu, E. 1993. Modeling organizations for information systems requirements engineering. In *Proceedings of the First International Symposium on Requirements Engineering*, RE '93, San Jose, CA, 34–41.

———. 1995. Modelling strategic relationships for process reengineering. Ph.D. dissertation, University of Toronto, Department of Computer Science.

Yu, E., and Mylopoulos, J. 1994. Understanding "why" in software process modeling, analysis and design. In *Proceedings of the Sixteenth International Conference on Software Engineering*, ICSE '94, Sorrento, Italy, 159–168.

———. 1996. Using goals, rules, and methods to support reasoning in business process reengineering. *International Journal of Intelligent Systems in Accounting, Finance and Management,* 5, 1, 1–13.

CHAPTER 8

AGENT-ORIENTED METHODS AND METHOD ENGINEERING

BRIAN HENDERSON-SELLERS

Abstract: Agent-oriented (AO) methodologies vary in style and, particularly, in heritage and often with a specific focus (either in terms of domain, application style, or life-cycle coverage). For industry adoption it is essential that full life-cycle coverage is achieved in a "standardized" way. One way of achieving some degree of standardization yet maintaining full flexibility is through the application of situational method engineering to the creation of agent-oriented methodologies. With this approach, method fragments are created and stored in a repository. Whenever a methodology is needed, a subset of these is then selected from the repository and a project-specific (or sometimes organization-specific) AO methodology is constructed. Here, we demonstrate how this might work by using the OPEN Process Framework (OPF) approach.

Keywords: Agents, Situational Method Engineering, Software Engineering, OPEN Process Framework (OPF), Methodologies

INTRODUCTION

To support the development of agent-oriented (AO) software systems, an appropriate method(ology)[1] is needed. Of the many AO methodologies in existence today, many show influences from earlier object-oriented methodological approaches and methodological thinking.

In this chapter, we describe briefly a number of contemporary AO methodological approaches and examine their evolution from and their relationship to earlier object-oriented (OO) methodologies. We then introduce the suggestion that a better approach than attempting to create a "one-size-fits-all" AO methodology is based on the ideas of situational method engineering (SME) and then illustrate this proposal with a brief case study.

It should be noted in passing that, while in most cases the meaning of "AO" in the term "agent-oriented methodology" means a methodology to be used for building agent-oriented software systems, some authors (e.g., Bresciani et al., 2004) use the term to mean that agent-related concepts are used in the conceptual underpinning of the methodology itself. Furthermore, although we use the term "methodology" in this chapter to mean a full description of process, people, social structures, project management, modeling language, products, and so on (e.g., Henderson-Sellers, 1995; Rolland and Prakash, 1996), some of the (so-called) methodologies referred to here provide only partial support—perhaps only in terms of addressing analysis and design (as does Gaia—e.g., Wooldridge, Jennings, and Kinny, 2000) or omitting any discussion of the "people element," for instance, MaSE (DeLoach, 1999) or AOR (Wagner, 2004), the latter being primarily a modeling language.

AGENT-ORIENTED METHODOLOGIES

A Genealogy of Agent-Oriented Methodologies

The development of AO methodologies has taken many routes. Some methodologists have based their methodological approach on Artificial Intelligence (AI) or Knowledge Representation ideas; others have commenced with basic definitions of objects and then asked what modifications are necessary to support agents; others have commenced with an established OO methodology and asked how agent support can be grafted on.

Figure 8.1 graphically depicts some of these linkages and influences. OO methodologies such as the Rational Unified Process (RUP) (Kruchten, 1999), the Object Modeling Technique (OMT) (Rumbaugh et al., 1991), and Fusion (Coleman et al., 1994) have all been used by various AO methodology groups as the basis for agent-oriented extensions. RUP has formed the basis for Adelfe (Bernon et al., 2002) and also for MESSAGE (Caire et al., 2001), which, in turn, is the basis for INGENIAS (Pavón, Gomez-Sanz, and Fuentes, 2005), and, more recently, RUP has been a useful input to the Radical Agent-oriented Process (RAP) (Wagner and Taveter, 2005), a direct descendant of Agent-Object-Relationship (AOR) (Wagner, 2003). OMT is said to have directly influenced MAS-CommonKADS (Iglesias et al., 1996, 1998), which merges these OO ideas with concepts from AI and Knowledge Engineering, as well as the AAII approach (Kinny, Georgeff, and Rao, 1996), which, in turn, is said to have been a major influence on MaSE (DeLoach, 1999; Wood and DeLoach, 2000). Fusion has strongly influenced Gaia, which, in turn, has influenced SODA (Omicini, 2000). ROADMAP (Juan, Pearce, and Sterling, 2002) is an extension of Gaian ideas. Prometheus (Padgham and Winikoff, 2002a, 2002b) is a fully AO methodology but states that one should use UML-style diagrams when appropriate rather than "reinvent the wheel." All of these AO methodologies are "standalone"—effectively "one size fits all"—approaches, although some mergers are currently being initiated (e.g., between ROADMAP and Prometheus). Care must, however, be taken when merging methodologies, since this can lead to an excessively large (sometimes implicit) and partially redundant metamodel.

Other methodologies in Figure 8.1 do not acknowledge any influence from any OO approach—although clearly some have had an implicit influence. Tropos is said to be based on i^* (Yu, 1995) and has a distinct strength in early requirements modeling. Its use of the i^* modeling language gives it a different look and feel from those that use Agent UML (AUML); (Odell, Van Dyke Parunak, and Bauer, 2000) as a notation. It also means that the non-OO mindset permits users of Tropos to take a unique approach to the modeling of agents in the methodological context.

There is no obvious, explicit evidence of an OO influence in the published versions of Cassiopeia (Collinot and Drogoul, 1998; Collinot, Drogoul, and Benhamou, 1996), the earlier versions of PASSI (Burrafato and Cossentino, 2002; Cossentino and Potts, 2002),[2] and the work of Kendall, Malkoun, and Jiang (1996). CAMLE (Shan and Zhu, 2004) does, however, draw some parallels, particularly between a CAMLE caste and an OO class and with respect to UML's composition and aggregation relationships.

Synopsis of Specific Agent-Oriented Methodologies

As noted above, many individualistic methodologies have been formulated and published. Here, we briefly review a small selection. Each description below emphasizes the *agent*-oriented aspects of that methodology, which are needed to go beyond the basic object-oriented concepts that many of them utilize.

Figure 8.1   **Genealogy of Various Agent-Oriented Methodologies and Their Relationships to Object-Oriented Methodologies**

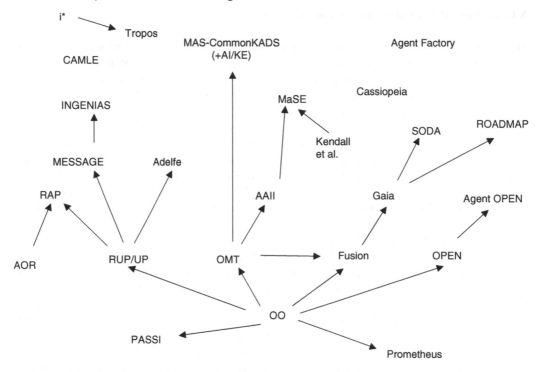

Source: Modified from Henderson-Sellers (2005).

There are several AO methods acknowledging an OO influence, either from OMG, RUP, or OPEN (the last of these is discussed in more detail below).

MaSE (DeLoach, 1999; Wood and DeLoach, 2000) is drawn from the legacy of object-oriented methodologies such as OMT together with influences from the more recent UML as well as pre-existing work in the realm of agents and multi-agent systems (e.g., Kinny, Georgeff, and Rao, 1996; Kendall and Zhao, 1998). It aims to guide the designer through the multi-agent system development process from an initial system specification to a set of formal design documents. It has two phases: analysis and design. The former deals with the specification of system goals, use cases, sequence diagrams, roles, and tasks, while the latter uses the analysis phase's outputs to design agent classes, agent interactions, and agents' internal components. It is also well supported by a software tool. Another input to MaSE (Figure 8.1) is the work of Zhang, Kendall, and Jiang (2002) (referred to hereafter as the ZKJ methodology). The ZKJ methodology focuses on the identification of goals and roles. It represents the process by a set of ten "activities," each having an input, an output, a control, and a mechanism. Four of these activities (Identify actors, Identify use cases, Identify objects, and Determine business objects) are grouped as "object-oriented analysis activities," the rest being focused on agent goals and roles. There are six activities focused on roles and goals (Identify goals, Develop goal cases, and Identify beliefs, Identify roles, Assign goals to responsibilities, Assign and compose roles, and Identify composite roles). Indeed, role identification is an important activity in the ZKJ methodology. Roles are seen as able to execute a set of activities in order to fulfill one or more responsibilities.

Although influenced by OMT, *MAS-CommonKADS* (Iglesias et al., 1998) also has strong AI/knowledge engineering influences (CommonKADS: Schreiber et al., 1994). It is an agent-oriented methodology that supports the development of MAS from the conceptualization phase through to a detailed design that can be directly implemented. The main modeling concepts in MAS-CommonKADS are agent, knowledge, organization, and coordination.

Being based to some degree on ideas in the OO Fusion methodology, itself based in part on OMT, *Gaia* (Wooldridge, Jennings, and Kinny, 2000) views the process of multi-agent system (MAS) development as a process of *organizational design*, where the MAS is modeled as an organized society with agents playing different roles. The methodology allows a developer to move systematically from a statement of requirements to a design detailed enough to be implemented directly. It supports both macro (societal) and micro (agent) aspects of MAS design, and is also neutral to both application domain and agent architecture. The newest version of Gaia (Zambonelli, Jennings, and Wooldridge, 2003) extends the original version with various organizational abstractions, enabling it to be used for the design of an open MAS (which was not achievable previously). Another AO methodology said to extend Gaia is Societies in Open and Distributed Agent spaces (SODA; Omicini, 2000). As its name implies, it focuses on societal descriptions of multi-agent systems, especially Internet-based applications. SODA concentrates on interagent issues and leaves the developer to choose his/her own internal agent model. Also initially influenced strongly by Gaia is Role-Oriented Analysis and Design for Multi-Agent Programming (ROADMAP; Juan, Pearce, and Sterling, 2002; Juan and Sterling, 2003). It introduces into Gaia UML-style use cases for requirements gathering, explicit models of the agent environment, and agent knowledge together with an interaction model based on AUML (Odell, Van Dyke Parunak, and Bauer, 2000). ROADMAP draws a clear distinction between analysis and design with a focus on roles and goals (as do many other AO methodologies).

A group of AO methods have been influenced by RUP (Kruchten, 1999) rather than the older OMT. These include MESSAGE, INGENIAS, Adelfe, and AOR/RAP. *MESSAGE* (e.g., Garijo, Gomez-Sanz, and Fuentes, 2005) arose from the needs of the telecommunications industry. It is said to extend UML to cover analysis and design considerations, adding agent-specific concepts to describe organizations, roles, goals, and tasks. *INGENIAS* (Pavón, Gomez-Sanz, and Fuentes, 2005) builds on the ideas of MESSAGE, focusing on five views: organization, agent, goals/tasks, interactions, and environment. These viewpoints are then complemented by the use of extensions of OO notations such as UML. The process elements in *INGENIAS* are based on those in the UDP (Jacobson, Booch, and Rumbaugh, 1999). A set of interrelated activities (approximately 100) are then defined, which assist the developer in creating the final MAS specification. Also using RUP as a basic input, RAP (Taveter and Wagner, 2005) uses the AOR notation of Wagner (2003). Its focus is business processes that emerge as social interactions from the behavior of the participating agents.

Although also using many RUP-like ideas, *Adelfe* (e.g., Bernon et al., 2002, 2005; Piquemal-Baluard et al., 1996) is aimed at a very different kind of AO system than most other AO methodologies. Adelfe is primarily intended to be used for the development of *adaptive* multi-agent software applications. It tailors RUP and introduces its phases as either WorkDefinitions (WDi), Activities (Aj) or Steps (Sk) following the vocabulary of the OMG's Software Processing Engineering Metamodel (SPEM) (OMG, 2002), which has been used to underpin Adelfe.

There are a number of AO methods that offer only a passing acknowledgment to OO. These include PASSI and Prometheus. *PASSI* (Process for *A*gent *S*ocieties *S*pecification and *I*mplementation) (Burrafato and Cossentino, 2002; Cossentino, 2005) offers a step-by-step requirement-to-code process for the development of a MAS (Figure 8.1), integrating models and concepts from both the object-oriented software engineering and the agent-oriented paradigms. The methodology adopts (and largely extends/adapts) the UML notation for its work products and targets the FIPA implementation environment. *Prometheus* (Padgham and Winikoff, 2002a, 2002b, 2004), on the other hand, is an agent-oriented methodology that reuses elements from object technology only as appropriate, including several UML diagram types. There are three phases of systems specification. In the first phase, the basic functionality of the system is identified, using percepts (inputs), actions (outputs), and any necessary shared data storage. This is followed by the architectural design stage; here, the agents and their interactions are identified. Finally, there is the detailed design phase in which the internal details of each agent are addressed.

From the published literature, it is not possible to identify any direct influences from OO methods (although, of course, some may exist implicitly) for Cassiopeia, CAMLE, and Agent Factory (Figure 8.1). *Cassiopeia* (Collinot, Drogoul, and Benhamou, 1996) provides an (arguably incomplete) methodological framework for the development of collective problem-solving MASs. This method assumes that, although the agents can have different aims, the goal of the designer is to make them behave cooperatively. It adopts an *organization-oriented approach* to MAS design, as do some other AO approaches, viewing a MAS as an organization of agents that implement/encapsulate *roles*. These roles reflect not only the agents' individual functionality but also the structure and dynamics of the organization of the MAS. *CAMLE* (Shan and Zhu, 2004) is described as a caste-centric agent-oriented modeling language and environment. It is caste-centric because *castes*, analogous to classes in object-orientation, are argued to provide the major modeling artifact over the life cycle by providing a type system for agents. A significant difference is claimed between castes and classes: while objects are commonly thought of as statically classified (i.e., an object is created as a member of a class, and that is a property for its whole lifetime), agents in CAMLE can join and leave castes as desired, thus allowing dynamic reclassification. CAMLE provides a graphical notation for caste models (similar to class models in OO modeling languages), collaboration models, and behavior models. Caste diagrams also include support for the non-OO relationships of congregation, migration, and participation. CAMLE relies heavily on the fact that an information system already exists when a new project is started, so that the new system is designed as a modification to the current one. Although this situation is indeed common, the construction of systems from scratch also happens. CAMLE, however, seems to ignore this possibility. Finally, in this group, *Agent Factory* (Collier et al., 2003, 2004) offers a four-layer framework for designing, implementing, and deploying multi-agent systems. It contains (1) an agent-oriented software engineering methodology, (2) a development environment, (3) a FIPA-compliant run-time environment, and (4) an agent programming language (AF-APL); with a stated preference for the belief-desire-intention (BDI) agent architecture according to the analysis of Luck, Ashri, and D'Inverno (2004). By employing UML and Agent UML, the Agent Factory methodology provides a visual, industry-recognized notation for its models—regarded by its authors as a major advantage over other approaches, such as Gaia (Wooldridge et al., 2000) and Tropos (Bresciani et al., 2004), which have nonstandard (i.e., non–UML-compliant) notations. These models are capable of promoting design reuse (via the central notion of *role*) and being directly implemented by automated code generation (Collier et al., 2004).

In a slightly different class, *Tropos* (Bresciani et al., 2004; Castro, Kolp, and Mylopoulos, 2002; Perini et al., 2001) uses agent, rather than object, concepts and was designed to support agent-oriented systems development with a particular emphasis on the early requirements engineering phase. The stated aim was to use agent concepts in the description and definition of the methodology rather than using OO concepts in a minor extension to existing OO approaches. Tropos takes the BDI model (Kinny, Georgeff, and Rao, 1996; Rao and Georgeff, 1995), formulated to describe the *internal* view of a single agent, and applies those concepts to the *external* view in terms of problem modeling as part of requirements engineering. It also relies heavily on the *i** framework of Yu (1995) for concepts and notation.

In summary, there is a tendency to reuse significant portions of object-oriented methodological approaches, supplementing them with a new focus on organizations, social interactions, proactivity, and roles. There is still discussion about the extent to which UML can be useful. Several AO methodologies use existing UML as a pragmatic option or, often, AUML diagrams but, at the same time, find deficiencies for which they supply new diagrammatic representations.

COMPARING AGENT-ORIENTED METHODOLOGIES

Several authors have made direct comparisons of these (and other) AO methodologies. Cernuzzi and Rossi (2002) proposed a framework containing a set of internal attributes (autonomy, reactivity, proactiveness, and mental notions), a set of interaction attributes (social ability, interaction with the environment, multiple control, multiple interests, and subsystems interaction), and four other requirements (modularity, abstraction, a system view, and communication support). They used this framework in a case study to evaluate a BDI-focused methodology (Kinny, Georgeff, and Rao, 1996; variously referred to as AAII or BDIM) and MAS-CommonKADS (Iglesias et al., 1998) both qualitatively and, with an appropriate set of metrics, quantitatively. This study and other comparative evaluations of both AO and OO methodologies were used as input to the framework proposals of Dam and Winikoff (2004), who proposed four categories: concepts, modeling language, process, and pragmatics. Their contribution is that the evaluation was done not only by the authors but by surveying a set of students who had used the case study methodologies (MaSE, Prometheus, and Tropos) on a design problem of a mobile travel planner. The same four categories were used by Sturm and Shehory (2004) and used to evaluate Gaia (as a single example) using a seven-point quantitative metric scale. The framework of Tran, Low, and Williams (2003) also has four categories, but these are said to be process-related (fifteen criteria), technique-related (five criteria), model-related (twenty-three criteria), and other supportive features (eight criteria). The framework was applied by Tran, Low, and Williams (2004) to five well-referenced AO methodologies—namely, MaSE, Gaia, BDIM, Prometheus, and MAS-CommonKADS. Different ordinal scales are used for the several-criterion sets. A more extensive set of results (the evaluation of ten AOSE methodologies) is shown in Table 8.1 (page 125), and a statistical evaluation of nine (seven overlapping and two new) is presented by Elamy and Far (2006).

AN ALTERNATIVE TO A SINGLE AGENT-ORIENTED
METHODOLOGY: SITUATIONAL METHOD ENGINEERING

Using a single fixed AO methodology (e.g., any of those outlined in the second section of the chapter) works well if that methodology and the project demands are in good alignment. This is rarely the case. More likely is the situation when the user of the XYZ methodology finds he/she needs something different or something additional. Improvisation can follow, but this runs the risk of introducing incompatibilities and inconsistencies—as well as incurring high effort-overhead costs.

An alternative is to use the well-founded tenets of "situational method engineering" or SME (e.g., Brinkkemper, 1996; Kumar and Welke, 1992; Ter Hofstede and Verhoef, 1997). SME provides a flexible way of constructing a methodology from a set of method fragments in such a way that the process requirements of the individual project are fully satisfied and the methodology is aligned to the personal and organizational cultures of the organization. In addition, SME provides sufficient flexibility to support the valuable process of Software Process Improvement or SPI, as advocated by, for example, CMMI or ISO/IEC 15504 (SPICE).

SME suggests that the elements of one (or more) methodology can be modularized and encapsulated as "method fragments" (van Slooten and Hodes, 1996) and stored in a repository or methodbase (e.g., Brinkkemper, 1996; Ralyté and Rolland, 2001). From the methodbase are then extracted only those fragments relevant to the current situation. These fragments are then connected together using "construction guidelines" to form the situational method(ology).

Ideally, the method fragments in the methodbase should all be instances of one of the concepts captured in a metamodel underpinning the methodbase (Ralyté and Rolland, 2001; Henderson-Sellers, 2003). The metamodel provides essentially a set of rules and prescriptive descriptions of all of the kinds of method elements permissible within the methodbase.

The challenge for the method engineer, as noted above, is to select appropriate and compatible fragments and to construct the final methodology (e.g., Wistrand and Karlsson, 2004). This may be from scratch or as an extension to an existing methodology (Ralyté, Deneckère, and Rolland, 2003). Thus, construction guidelines (e.g., Brinkkemper, Saeki, and Harmsen, 1998; Klooster et al., 1997; Ralyté and Rolland, 2001; Ralyté, Rolland, and Deneckère, 2004; Rolland, Prakash, and Benjamen, 1999) are critical in the SME approach. Creating a project-specific methodology is currently one of the more difficult and time-consuming jobs of the method engineering approach, since the method engineer has to understand the methodology, the organization, the environment, and the software project in order to select the appropriate fragments from the repository to use on the project as well as to understand the rules of construction. Traditionally, this process is carried out using predefined organizational requirements and the experience and knowledge of the method engineer or process engineer (e.g., Fitzgerald, Russo, and O'Kane, 2003), although significant tool support is likely in the near future (Saeki, 2003; Wistrand and Karlsson, 2004).

THE OPEN PROCESS FRAMEWORK: ITS USE IN AGENT-ORIENTED METHOD ENGINEERING

One example of a method engineering approach that provides fragment support for both object-oriented and agent-oriented methodological thinking is the OPEN Process Framework or OPF (Firesmith and Henderson-Sellers, 2002; Henderson-Sellers, 2005). The OPF adopts a framework approach based on an underpinning metamodel (Figure 8.2, page 132).[3] Originally created to support object-oriented software development, the OPF methodbase (repository) has recently been extended to include methodological support for agents (see, e.g., Debenham and Henderson-Sellers, 2003; Henderson-Sellers, 2005). As with any method engineering approach, OPF provides a repository of method fragments offering direct as well as extensible support for the construction of individually tailored (i.e., situational) methodologies for use in both industry and research environments. The current OPF repository contains many tens of method fragments for each metamodel element—in total over 1,000 standardized fragments are available for the user.

To create a situational methodology, various method fragments are then chosen from the OO/AO repository of the OPF and combined to describe the process, associated people and social issues, deliverables, and so on. Using the tenets of SME outlined above, such a methodology can be specifically constructed and tailored toward a specific project or a specific organizational "standard" using the supplied construction guidelines together with a set of deontic matrices (Figure 8.3, page 133). These matrices support the identification of fuzzy relationships between pairs of method fragment types—for example, linkages between tasks and techniques. This gives

Table 8.1

Comparison of Ten Agent-Oriented Methodologies

A. Comparison Regarding Steps and Usability of Techniques

Steps	Gaia	Tropos	MAS-CommonKADS	Prometheus	PASSI	Adelfe	MaSE	RAP	MESSAGE	INGENIAS
1. Identify system goals		H	H	H			H	H	H	H
2. Identify system tasks/behavior	M	H	H	H	H	H	H	H	H	H
3. Specify use case scenarios		H	H	H	H	H	H	H		H
4. Identify roles	H				H		H	M	M	M
5. Identify agent classes	H	H	M	H	M	H	H	L	M	H
6. Model domain conceptualization			M		M				M	
7. Specify acquaintances between agent classes	M	M	H	H	H	M	H	M	M	H
8. Define interaction protocols	H	H	H	H	H	M	H		H	H
9. Define content of exchanged messages		M	H	L	H	M	H	M	L	M
10. Specify agent architecture		L		H	H	H	M		H	
11. Define agent mental attitudes (e.g., goals, beliefs, plans, commitments . . .)		M	M	H	M	H	M	H	H	H
12. Define agent behavioral interface (e.g., capabilities, services, contracts . . .)	H		L	H	H	M				
13. Specify system architecture (i.e., overview of all components and their connections)			M	H	H	H			H	H
14. Specify organizational structure/ control regime/interagent social relationships	H	H	L						H	H
15. Model MAS environment (e.g., resources, facilities, characteristics)	M	H	M	M		H			L	H
16. Specify agent-environment interaction mechanism				H		L				H
17. Specify agent inheritance and aggregation	H		M			M				
18. Instantiate agent classes	M		L	L			H	L	L	
19. Specify agent instances deployment					L			H		

Key: H = high; M = medium; L = low; Y = yes; N = no; P = possibly.

Table 8.1

Comparison of Ten Agent-Oriented Methodologies *(continued)*

B. Comparison Regarding Concepts

Concepts	Gaia	Tropos	MAS-CommonKADS	Prometheus	PASSI
System goal		Actor diagram, rationale diagram	Goal cases	Goal diagram	
System task/behavior	Role model	Actor diagram, rationale diagram	Task model	Functionality descriptor	System requirement model
Use case scenario			Use cases	Use case descriptor	System requirement model
Role	Role model				System requirement model, Agent society model
Domain conceptualization			Expertise model		Agent society model
Agent goal/task		Actor diagram	Agent model	Agent class descriptor	System requirement model
Agent-role assignment	Agent model		Agent model		Agent society model
Agent belief/knowledge		As resources in each agent in agent class diagram	Expertise model	Data descriptor	Agent implementation model
Agent capability/service	Service model		Agent model, organizational model	Capability diagram	Agent society model
Agent plan/reasoning rule/problem-solving method		Plan diagram	Expertise model	Plan descriptor	Agent implementation model
Agent percept/method			As events in state transition diagrams of coordination model	Percepts descriptor	
Agent architecture		BDI architecture	Design model	Agent overview diagram	Agent implementation model

Adelfe	MaSE	RAP	MESSAGE	INGENIAS
	Goal hierarchy diagram	Goal-based use case model	Goal/task model	Goals and tasks model
Use case model	Extended role diagram	Goal-based use case model	Goal/task model	Goals and tasks model
Use case model	Use case diagram	Goal-based use case model		Use case diagram
	Role diagram	Agent model	Agent/role model	Agent model, organization model, interaction model
		Information model	Domain model	
Detailed architecture document		Goal-based use case model		Agent model
	Agent class diagram	Agent model	Agent/role model	Agent model
Detailed architecture document		Information model		N.b. Can be recorded in mental states, but not mentioned in methodology
Detailed architecture document				
	Task state diagram	Behavior model		Agent model
		Interaction model		
Detailed architecture document	Agent class architecture diagram			

Table 8.1 *(continued)*

Comparison of Ten Agent-Oriented Methodologies *(continued)*

B. Comparison Regarding Concepts

Concepts	Gaia	Tropos	MAS-CommonKADS	Prometheus	PASSI
Agent acquaintance	Acquaintance model	Sequence diagram/ collaborative diagram	Coordination model	Interaction diagrams	System requirement model
Interaction protocol	Interaction model	Sequence diagram	Coordination model	Interaction protocols	Agent society model
Content of exchanged messages		Sequence diagram/ collaborative diagram	Coordination model	Interaction diagrams and protocols	Agent implementation model
Interagent contract/ commitment					
System architecture			Organization model	System overview diagram	Agent implementation model
Organizational structure/ interagent social relationship	Organizational structure model	Nonfunctional requirements framework	Organization model		
Environment resource/facility	Environmental model		Organization model, design model	System overview diagram	
Environment characterization					
Agent aggregation relationship	Agent model		Organization model		
Agent inheritance relationship			Organization model		
Agent instantiation	Agent model		Organization model	Agent class descriptor	
Agent instances deployment					Deployment model

Adelfe	MaSE	RAP	MESSAGE	INGENIAS
Software architecture document	Agent class diagram	Interaction model	Organization model	Interaction model
Interaction languages document	Communication class diagram		Interaction model	Interaction model
Interaction languages document	Communication class diagram	Interaction model	Interaction model	Interaction model
		Interaction model		
Detailed architecture document			System architecture diagram	Organization model
			Organization model	Organization model
Environment definition document			Organization model	Environment model
Environment definition document				
Detailed architecture document				
	Deployment diagram			
	Deployment diagram	UML deployment diagram		

Table 8.1

Comparison of Ten Agent-Oriented Methodologies *(continued)*

C. Comparison Regarding Model-Related Criteria

	Gaia	Tropos	MAS-CommonKADS	Prometheus	PASSI	Adelfe	MaSE	RAP	MESSAGE	INGENIAS
Completeness/expressiveness	M	H	H	H	H	H	H	M	M	H
Formalization/preciseness (a)	H	H	M	H	H	H	H	H	H	H
Formalization/preciseness (b)	Y	Y	Y	Y	Y	Y	Y	Y	Y	Y
Model derivation	Y	Y	Y	Y	Y	Y	Y	Y	Y	Y
Consistency (a)	Y	Y	N	Y	Y	Y	Y	N	N	Y
Consistency (b)	Y	Y	Y	Y	Y	Y	Y	Y	Y	Y
Complexity (a)	Y	Y	Y	Y	Y	Y	Y	Y	Y	N
Complexity (b)	Y	Y	Y	Y	Y	Y	Y	Y	Y	N
Ease of understanding	H	H	H	H	H	H	H	H	H	M
Modularity	Y	Y	Y	Y	Y	Y	Y	Y	Y	Y
Abstraction	Y	Y	Y	Y	N	Y	Y	Y	Y	Y
Autonomy	Y	Y	Y	Y	Y	Y	Y	Y	Y	Y
Adaptability	P	N	N	N	N	Y	N	N	P	P
Cooperative behavior	Y	Y	Y	Y	Y	Y	Y	Y	Y	Y
Communication ability	N	Y	Y	Y	Y	Y	Y	Y	Y	Y
Inferential capability	N	Y	Y	Y	Y	Y	P	P	Y	Y
Reactivity	P	Y	Y	Y	Y	Y	Y	Y	Y	Y
Deliberative behavior	Y	Y	Y	Y	Y	Y	Y	N	Y	Y
Personality	N	N	N	N	N	N	N	N	N	N
Temporal continuity	N	N	N	N	N	N	N	N	N	Y
Concurrency	N	N	N	N	Y	N	Y	N	N	N
Human computer interaction	N	Y	Y	Y	Y	Y	N	Y	Y	Y
Models reuse	Y	P	Y	P	Y	P	Y	P	P	P

Source: After Tran and Low (2005).

Key: H = high; M = medium; L = low; Y = yes; N = no; P = possibly.

Table 8.1

Comparison of Ten Agent-Oriented Methodologies *(continued)*

D. Comparison Regarding Supportive-Related Criteria

	Gaia	Tropos	MAS-CommonKADS	Prometheus	PASSI	Adelfe	MaSE	RAP	MESSAGE	INGENIAS
Software and methodological support	N	N	N	Y	Y	Y	Y	Y	Y	Y
Open systems	Y	N	N	N	N	Y	N	N	N	N
Dynamic structure	N	N	N	N	Y	N	P	N	N	N
Agility and robustness	N	N	Y	Y	N	Y	Y	Y	N	N
Support for conventional objects	N	N	N	Y	N	Y	N	Y	Y	Y
Support for mobile agents	N	N	N	N	Y	N	N	N	N	N
Support for ontology	N	N	Y	N	Y	N	N	N	Y	N

Source: After Tran and Low (2005).
Key: H = high; M = medium; L = low; Y = yes; N = no; P = possibly.

a high degree of flexibility to the process engineer, perhaps assisted by an automated tool (Nguyen and Henderson-Sellers, 2003), who can allocate appropriate deontic values to any specific pair of process components depending upon the context, that is, the specific project, skills set of the development team, and so on. Linkage decisions are made either subjectively/experientially or by means of an overall assessment of a number of factors relating to the project. These factors include maturity/capability level (such as CMM or SPICE), specific skills in the workforce, domain of the project, and so forth.

As noted earlier, one of the hardest tasks currently in SME construction is the selection of the optimal set of method fragments to suit any specific situation. Syntactic coupling can be verified in terms of the matching of the output from one fragment to the input for a second. This is facilitated by generating fragments from a metamodel and also by using a standard way of documenting the fragments. Nevertheless, the current reality is that the semantic aspect of the fragments must be analyzed "by hand," usually by a skilled method engineer (either in-house or as a visiting consultant or mentor). Work toward a more objective approach is under way (e.g., McBride, 2004; Nguyen and Henderson-Sellers, 2003; Ralyté, 2004), and prototype tools (MethodComposer, MET) have been developed.

Creation of a project-specific or organization-specific agent-oriented methodology then proceeds using the agent-oriented method fragments contained in the OPF repository together with many non-agent-oriented method fragments (typically the earlier object-oriented method fragments) that are needed for those elements of software development that are not technology/paradigm-dependent. These include method fragments to describe project management, some metrics, reusability, and so on. A fully comprehensive methodology, suitable for direct industry usage, can be constructed

Figure 8.2   **The Five Top-Level Metaclasses of the OPEN Process Framework's Metamodel**

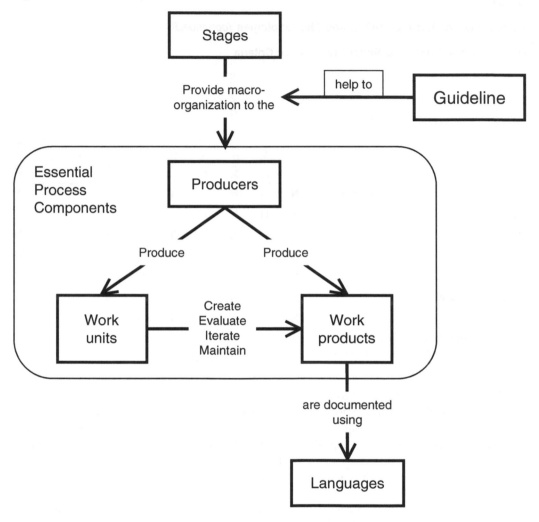

Source: After Firesmith and Henderson-Sellers (2002). Copyright © 2002 Addison-Wesley.

in this way; alternatively, one of the existing AO methodologies (e.g., Prometheus or Tropos) can be reconstructed by using only those specific AO fragments. For instance, Henderson-Sellers (2005) shows in more detail how a version of the Prometheus methodology enhanced with some Tropos concepts can be put together from the method fragments in this newly enhanced OPF repository (Figure 8.4).

Overall, the strength of this SME approach is that the finally constructed methodology is highly attuned to local conditions and the people in the organization. The challenge is to construct the several deontic matrices, ensuring that (a) linkages accord to the local situation and (b) the interfaces of any pair of method fragments to be "plugged together" are compatible.

Figure 8.3 **One of the Deontic Matrices Is Used to Link Tasks to Techniques**

Tasks

M	D	F	F	F	
D	D	F	F	D	**5 Levels of Possibility**
D	D	O	O	D	
F	O	O	O	F	M = Mandatory
F	M	O	D	F	R = Recommended
R	R	M	R	O	O = Optional
D	R	F	M	O	D = Discouraged
D	F	M	D	D	F = Forbidden
R	R	D	R	R	
O	D	O	O	R	
F	M	O	F	D	

(Techniques on the vertical axis)

Source: Redrawn from Henderson-Sellers, Simons, and Younessi (1998). Copyright © 1998 Addison-Wesley.

Note: The values in the matrix represent the likelihood of the occurrence of that pair using five levels of possibility.

Figure 8.4 **A Reconstruction of Prometheus from OPF AO Fragments Supplemented by Two Fragments** (AND/OR Decomposition and Means–End Analysis) **Derived from the Tropos Methodology**

Technique	Tasks					
	1	2	3	4	5	6
Abstract class identification						
Agent internal design			Y			
AND/OR decomposition	Y					
Class naming	Y	Y				
Control architecture		Y				
Context modeling	Y			Y		
Delegation analysis	Y	Y				
Event modeling				Y		
Intelligent agent identification		Y				
Means–end analysis	Y					
Role modeling	Y	Y			Y	Y
State modeling		Y				
Textual analysis	Y	Y				
3-layer BDI model		Y	Y			

Source: Modified from Henderson-Sellers, 2005.
Key:
1. Model dependencies for actors and goals
2. Construct the agent model
3. Design agent internal structure
4. Model the agent's environment
5. Model responsibilities
6. Model permissions

SUMMARY

To date, the evolution of AO methodologies has been disparate with many groups worldwide creating individual offerings. These vary in style and, particularly, in heritage and have a specific focus, either in terms of domain, application style, or life-cycle coverage. For industry adoption, it is essential that full life-cycle coverage is achieved in a "standardized" way. One way of achieving some degree of standardization yet maintaining full flexibility is through the use of situational method engineering, underpinned by an agreed standard metamodel. With this approach, method fragments are created and stored in a repository or methodbase. For an individual application, only a subset of these is then selected from the repository and a project-specific (or sometimes organization-specific) methodology is constructed. Here, we have demonstrated how this might work by using the OPEN approach, which already provides a significant coverage of AO method fragments as well as more traditional OO and pre-OO fragments.

The advantages of an SME approach to methodology provision lie in the flexibility and complete tailorability of the construction process. Only fragments suitable to the organization's culture and capability (e.g., in terms of ISO/IEC 15504 or CMM/CMMI), the skills of its developers, the organizational culture, and leadership style (e.g., Constantine and Lockwood, 1994) are used. Construction costs are commensurate with the costs of attempting to mold an "off-the shelf, one-size-fits-all" methodology to a specific situation. Starting with an SME approach with a large extant repository (such as that provided in the OPF) is clearly advantageous. Empirical studies, while undertaken only in OO and not AO situations (e.g., Henderson-Sellers and Serour, 2005), have shown that organizations can readily benefit from this SME approach in practice.

ACKNOWLEDGMENTS

I wish to thank Dr. Cesar Gonzalez-Perez for his useful comments on earlier drafts of this manuscript. This is Contribution number 06/03 of the Centre for Object Technology Applications and Research.

NOTES

1. For the present chapter, the words method and methodology will be used synonymously (e.g., Jayaratna, 1994).

2. A more recent manuscript in preparation does, in fact, acknowledge influences from object technology (see also later discussion).

3. In the near future, this traditional, process-focused metamodel will be supplanted by the forthcoming ISO/IEC 24744 standard: Software Engineering Metamodel for Development Methodologies. The new metamodel supports method enactment as well as method construction and brings together process-focused components of a methodology and product-focused components.

REFERENCES

Bernon, C.; Camps.,V.; Gleizes, M.P.; and Picard, G. 2005. Engineering adaptive multi-agent systems: the ADELFE methodology. In B. Henderson-Sellers and P. Giorgini (eds.), *Agent-Oriented Methodologies*. Hershey, PA: Idea Group, 172–202.

Bernon, C.; Gleizes, M.-P.; Picard, G.; and Glize, P. 2002. The ADELFE methodology for an intranet system design. In P. Giorgini, Y. Lespérance, G. Wagner, and E. Yu (eds.), *Agent-Oriented Information Systems 2002*. Proceedings of the Fourth International Bi-Conference Workshop on Agent-Oriented Information Systems, Toronto, 1–15.

Bresciani, P.; Giorgini, P.; Giunchiglia, F.; Mylopolous, J.; and Perini, A. 2004. Tropos: an agent-oriented software development methodology. *Autonomous Agents and Multi-Agent Systems,* 8, 3, 203–236.

Brinkkemper, S. 1996. Method engineering: engineering of information systems development methods and tools. *Information and Software Technology,* 38, 4, 275–280.

Brinkkemper, S.; Saeki, M.; and Harmsen, F. 1998. Assembly techniques for method engineering. In *Proceedings of CAISE 1998.* Berlin: Springer Verlag, 381–400.

Burrafato, P., and Cossentino, M. 2002. Designing a multi-agent solution for a bookstore with the PASSI methodology. In P. Giorgini, Y. Lespérance, G. Wagner, and E. Yu (eds.), *Agent-Oriented Information Systems 2002.* Proceedings of the Fourth International Bi-Conference Workshop on Agent-Oriented Information Systems, Toronto, 102–118.

Caire, G.; Coulier, W.; Garijo, F.; Gomez, J.; Pavon, J.; Leal, F.; Chainho, P.; Kearney, P.; Stark, J.; Evans, R.; and Massonet, P. 2001. Agent-oriented analysis using MESSAGE/UML. In M. Wooldridge, G. Wei, and P. Ciancarini (eds.), *Agent-Oriented Software Engineering II.* Berlin: Springer Verlag, LNCS 2222, 119–135.

Castro, J.; Kolp, M.; and Mylopoulos, J. 2002. Towards requirements-driven information systems engineering: the Tropos project. *Information Systems,* 27, 6, 365–389.

Cernuzzi, L., and Rossi, G. 2002. On the evaluation of agent-oriented methodologies. In *Proceedings of OOPSLA 2002 Workshop on Agent-Oriented Methodologies.* Sydney, Australia: Centre for Object Technology Applications and Research, 21–30.

Coleman, D.; Arnold, P.; Bodoff, S.; Dollin, C.; and Gilchrist, H. 1994. *Object-Oriented Development. The Fusion Method.* Englewood Cliffs, NJ: Prentice Hall.

Collier, R.; O'Hare, G.; and Rooney, C. 2004. A UML-based software engineering methodology for Agent Factory. In *Proceedings of SEKE 2004,* 25–30. Banff, Alberta, Canada.

Collier, R.; O'Hare, G.; Lowen, T.; and Rooney, C. 2003. Beyond prototyping in the factory of agents. In V. Marik, J. Muller, and M. Pechoucek (eds.), *Multi-Agent Systems and Applications III.* New York: Springer-Verlag, LNCS 2691, 383–393.

Collinot, A., and Drogoul, A. 1998. Using the Cassiopeia method to design a soccer robot team. *Applied Artificial Intelligence (AAI) Journal,* 12, 2–3, 127–147.

Collinot, A.; Drogoul, A.; and Benhamou, P. 1996. Agent oriented design of a soccer robot team. In *Proceedings of the Second International Conference on Multi-Agent Systems (ICMAS '96),* Kyoto, Japan.

Constantine, L.L. and Lockwood, L.A.D. 1994. Fitting practices to the people. *American Programmer,* 7, 12, 21–27.

Cossentino, M. 2005. From requirements to code with the PASSI methodology. In B. Henderson-Sellers and P. Giorgini (eds.), *Agent-Oriented Methodologies.* Hershey, PA: Idea Group, 79–106.

Cossentino, M., and Potts, C. 2002. A CASE tool supported methodology for the design of multi-agent systems. In the *2002 International Conference on Software Engineering Research and Practice (SERP '02),* Las Vegas, NV.

Dam, K.H., and Winikoff, M. 2004. Comparing agent-oriented methodologies. In P. Giorgini, B. Henderson-Sellers, and M. Winikoff (eds.), *Agent-Oriented Systems.* Berlin: Springer-Verlag, LNAI 3030, 78–93.

Debenham, J., and Henderson-Sellers, B. 2003. Designing agent-based process systems—extending the OPEN Process Framework. In V. Plekhanova (ed.), *Intelligent Agent Software Engineering.* Hershey, PA: Idea Group, 160–190.

DeLoach, S.A. 1999. Multiagent systems engineering: a methodology and language for designing agent systems. In *Proceedings of AOIS '99,* Heidelberg, Germany.

Elamy, A.-H., and Far, B. 2006. A statistical approach for evaluating and assembling agent-oriented software engineering methodologies. In A. Garcia, A. Ghose, and M. Kolp (eds.), *Proceedings of AOIS '06@ AAMAS.* Washington, DC: ACM, 17–24.

Firesmith, D.G., and Henderson-Sellers, B. 2002. *The OPEN Process Framework.* Harlow, Essex, UK: Addison-Wesley.

Fitzgerald, B.; Russo, N.L.; and O'Kane, T. 2003. Software development method tailoring at Motorola. *Communications of the ACM,* 46, 4, 65–70.

Garijo, F.J.; Gomez-Sanz, J.J.; and Fuentes, R. 2005. The MESSAGE methodology for agent-oriented analysis and design. In B. Henderson-Sellers and P. Giorgini (eds.), *Agent-Oriented Methodologies.* Hershey, PA: Idea Group, 203–235.

Henderson-Sellers, B. 1995. Who needs an OO methodology anyway? *Journal of Object-Oriented Programming,* 8, 6, 6–8.

————. 2003. Method engineering for OO system development. *Communications of the ACM,* 46, 10, 73–78.

————. 2005. Creating a comprehensive agent-oriented methodology—using method engineering and the OPEN metamodel. In B. Henderson-Sellers and P. Giorgini (eds.), *Agent-Oriented Methodologies.* Hershey, PA: Idea Group, 368–397.

Henderson-Sellers, B., and Serour, M.K. 2005. Creating a dual agility method—the value of method engineering. *Journal of Database Management,* 16, 4, 1–24.

Henderson-Sellers, B.; Simons, A.J.H.; and Younessi, H. 1998. *The OPEN Toolbox of Techniques.* London: Addison-Wesley.

Iglesias, C.A.; Garijo, M.; Gonzalez, J.C.; and Velasco, J.R. 1996. A methodological proposal for multiagent systems development extending CommonKADS. In *Proceedings of the Tenth KAW,* Banff, Canada. Available at http://ksi.cpsc.ucalgary.ca/KAW/KAW96/iglesias/Iglesias.html.

————. 1998. Analysis and design of multi-agent systems using MAS-CommonKADS. In M.P. Singh, A. Rao, and M.J. Wooldridge (eds.), *Intelligent Agents IV: Agent Theories, Architectures, and Languages.* Berlin: Springer-Verlag, LNAI 1365, 313–327.

Jacobson, I.; Booch, G.; and Rumbaugh, J. 1999. *The Unified Software Development Process.* Reading, MA: Addison-Wesley.

Jayaratna, N. 1994. *Understanding and Evaluating Methodologies: NIMSAD, a Systematic Framework.* London: McGraw-Hill.

Juan, T., and Sterling, L. 2003. The ROADMAP metamodel for intelligent adaptive multi-agent systems in open environments. In P. Giorgini, J.P. Müller, and J. Odell (eds.), *Proceedings of AOSE2003.* Berlin: Springer-Verlag, LNCS 2935, 53–68.

Juan, T.; Pearce, A.; and Sterling, L. 2002. ROADMAP: extending the Gaia methodology for complex open systems. In *Proceedings of the First International Joint Conference on Autonomous Agents and Multi-Agent Systems (AAMAS2002),* Bologna, Italy, July, 3–10.

Kendall, E.A., and Zhao, L. 1998. Capturing and structuring goals. Presented at *Workshop on Use Case Patterns, Object Oriented Programming Systems Languages and Architectures.* Vancouver, Canada.

Kendall, E.A.; Malkoun, M.T.; and Jiang, C. 1996. A methodology for developing agent based systems for enterprise integration. In P. Bernus and L. Nemes (eds.), *Modelling and Methodologies for Enterprise Integration.* London: Chapman and Hall.

Kinny, D.; Georgeff, M.; and Rao, A. 1996. A methodology and modelling technique for systems of BDI agents. Technical Note 58, Australian Artificial Intelligence Institute; also published in *Agents Breaking Away: Proceedings of the Seventh European Workshop on Modelling Autonomous Agents in a Multi-Agent World (MAAMAW '96),* Eindhoven, The Netherlands, 56–71.

Klooster, M.; Brinkkemper, S.; Harmsen, F.; and Wijers, G. 1997. Intranet facilitated knowledge management: A theory and tool for defining situational methods. In *Proceedings of CAISE 1997.* Berlin: Springer Verlag, 303–317.

Kruchten, Ph. 1999. *The Rational Unified Process. An Introduction.* Reading, MA: Addison-Wesley.

Kumar, K., and Welke, R.J. 1992. Method engineering: a proposal for situation-specific methodology construction. In W.W. Cotterman and J.A. Senn (eds.), *Systems Analysis and Design: A Research Agenda.* New York: Wiley, 257–269.

Luck, M.; Ashri, R.; and D'Inverno, M. 2004. *Agent-Based Software Development.* Boston: Artech House.

McBride, T. 2004. Standards need more rigour. *Information Age,* October/November, 65–66.

Nguyen, V.P., and Henderson-Sellers, B. 2003. OPENPC: a tool to automate aspects of method engineering. In *Proceedings of ICSSEA 2003,* vol. 5. Paris.

Odell, J.; Van Dyke Parunak, H.; and Bauer, B. 2000. Extending UML for agents. In G. Wagner, Y. Lesperance, and E. Yu (eds.), *Proceedings of Agent-Oriented Information Systems Workshop, Seventeenth National Conference on Artificial Intelligence.* Austin, TX, 3–17.

OMG. 2002. *OMG Software Process Engineering Metamodel Specification.* Available at http://www.omg. org/cgi-bin/doc?formal/02-11-14.pdf.

Omicini, A. 2000. SODA: societies and infrastructures in the analysis and design of agent-based systems. In *Proceedings of the First International Workshop on Agent-Oriented Software Engineering,* Limerick, Ireland, 185–193.

Padgham, L., and Winikoff, M. 2002a. Prometheus: a methodology for developing intelligent agents. In *Proceedings of the Third International Workshop on Agent-Oriented Software Engineering, at AAMAS '02,* Bologna, Italy, 174–185.

———. 2002b. Prometheus: a pragmatic methodology for engineering intelligent agents. In *Proceedings of the Workshop on Agent-oriented Methodologies at OOPSLA 2002*, Seattle, WA, November 4. Available at http://www.open.org.au/Conferences/oopsla2002.

———. 2004. *Developing Intelligent Agent Systems: A Practical Guide.* Chichester, UK: Wiley.

Pavón, J.; Gomez-Sanz, J.; and Fuentes, R. 2005. The INGENIAS methodology and tools. In B. Henderson-Sellers and P. Giorgini (eds.), *Agent-Oriented Methodologies.* Hershey, PA: Idea Group, 236–276.

Perini, A.; Bresciani, P.; Giorgini, P.; Giunchiglia, G.; and Mylopoulos, J. 2001. A knowledge level software engineering methodology for agent oriented programming. In J.P. Müller, E. Andre, S. Sen, and C. Frasson (eds.), *Proceedings of the Fifth International Conference on Autonomous Agents*, Montreal, Canada. May, 648–655. Available at http://sra.itc.it/tr/PGM+00.ps.gz.

Piquemal-Baluard, C.; Camps, V.; Gleizes, M.-P.; and Glize, P. 1996. Properties of individual cooperative attitude for collective learning. Presented at *Seventh European Workshop on Modelling Autonomous Agents in a Multi-Agent World (MAAMAW '96)*, Eindhoven, The Netherlands.

Ralyté, J. 2004. Towards situational methods for information systems development: engineering reusable method chunks. In O. Vasilecas, A. Caplinskas, W. Wojtkowski, W.G. Wojtkowski, J. Zupancic, and S. Wrycza (eds.), *Proceedings of the Thirteenth International Conference on Information Systems Development. Advances in Theory, Practice and Education.* Vilnius, Lithuania: Vilnius Gediminas Technical University, 271–282.

Ralyté, J., and Rolland, C. 2001. An assembly process model for method engineering. In *Advanced Information Systems Engineering.* Berlin: Springer-Verlag, LNCS2068, 267–283.

Ralyté, J.; Deneckère, R.; and Rolland, C. 2003. Towards a generic model for situational method engineering. In M.M.J. Eder (ed.), *CAiSE2003.* Berlin: Springer-Verlag, LNCS 2681, 95–110.

Ralyté, J.; Rolland, C.; and Deneckère, R. 2004. Towards a meta-tool for change-centric method engineering: a typology of generic operators. In A. Persson and J. Stirna (eds.), *CAiSE2004.* Berlin: Springer-Verlag, LNCS 3084, 202–218.

Rao, A.S., and Georgeff, M.P. 1995. BDI agents: from theory to practice. In *Proceedings of the First International Conference on Multi-Agent Systems,* San Francisco, CA, 312–319.

Rolland, C., and Prakash, N. 1996. A proposal for context-specific method engineering. In *Proceedings of IFIP WG8.1 Conference on Method Engineering.* London: Chapman and Hall, 191–208.

Rolland, C.; Prakash, N.; and Benjamen, A. 1999. A multi-model view of process modelling. *Requirements Engineering,* 4, 4, 169–187.

Rumbaugh, J.; Blaha, M.; Premerlani, W.; Eddy, F.; and Lorensen, W. 1991. *Object-Oriented Modeling and Design.* Englewood Cliffs, NJ: Prentice Hall.

Saeki, M. 2003. CAME: the first step to automated software engineering. In *Process Engineering for Object-Oriented and Component-Based Development. Proceedings of OOPSLA 2003 Workshop.* Sydney, Australia: Centre for Object Technology Applications and Research, 7–18.

Schreiber, A.T.; Wielinga, B.J.; de Hoog, R.; Akkermans, J.M.; and Van de Velde, W. 1994. CommonKADS: a comprehensive methodology for KBS development. *IEEE Expert,* 9, 6, 28–37.

Shan, L., and Zhu, H. 2004. CAMLE: A caste-centric agent-oriented modeling language and environment. In *Third International Workshop on Software Engineering for Large-Scale Multi-Agent Systems. Edinburgh, 24–25 May 2004.* Berlin: Springer-Verlag, 144–161.

Sturm, A., and Shehory, O. 2004. A framework for evaluating agent-oriented methodologies. In P. Giorgini, B. Henderson-Sellers, and M. Winikoff (eds.), *Agent-Oriented Systems.* Berlin: Springer-Verlag, LNAI 3030, 94–109.

Taveter, K., and Wagner, G. 2005. Towards radical agent-oriented software engineering processes based on AOR modeling. In B. Henderson-Sellers and P. Giorgini (eds.), *Agent-Oriented Methodologies.* Hershey, PA: Idea Group, 277–316.

Ter Hofstede, A.H.M., and Verhoef, T.F. 1997. On the feasibility of situational method engineering. *Information Systems,* 22, 401–422.

Tran, Q.-N.N., and Low, G.C. 2005. Comparison of methodologies. In B. Henderson-Sellers and P. Giorgini (eds.), *Agent-Oriented Methodologies.* Hershey, PA: Idea Group, 341 367.

Tran, Q.-N.N.; Low, G.; and Williams, M.-A. 2003. A feature analysis framework for evaluating multi-agent system development methodologies. In N. Zhong, Z.W. Ras, S. Tsumoto, and E. Suzuki (eds.), *Foundations of Intelligent Systems—Proceedings of the Fourteenth International Symposium on Methodologies for Intelligent Systems ISMIS '03*, Maebashi, Japan, 613–617.

————. 2004. A preliminary comparative feature analysis of multi-agent systems development methodologies. In *Proceedings of AOIS@CAiSE*04*. Riga, Latvia: Faculty of Computer Science and Information, Riga Technical University, 386–398.

van Slooten, K., and Hodes, B. 1996. Characterizing IS development projects. In S. Brinkkemper, K. Lyytinen, and R. Welke (eds.), *Proceedings of the IFIP TC8 Working Conference on Method Engineering: Principles of Method Construction and Tool Support*. London: Chapman and Hall, 29–44.

Wagner, G. 2003. The Agent-Object Relationship metamodel: towards a unified view of state and behavior. *Information Systems,* 28, 5, 475–504.

————. 2004. AOR modelling and simulation: towards a general architecture for agent-based discrete event simulation. In P. Giorgini, B. Henderson-Sellers, and M. Winikoff (eds.), *Agent-Oriented Information Systems*. Berlin: Springer-Verlag, LNAI 3030, 174–188.

Wagner, G., and Taveter, K. 2005. Towards radical agent-oriented software engineering processes based on AOR modeling. In B. Henderson-Sellers and P. Giorgini (eds.), *Agent-Oriented Methodologies*. Hershey, PA: Idea Group.

Wistrand, K., and Karlsson, F. 2004. Method components—rationale revealed. In A. Persson and J. Stirna (eds.), *CAiSE2004*. Berlin: Springer-Verlag, LNCS 3084, 189–201.

Wood, M., and DeLoach, S.A. 2000. An overview of the multiagent systems engineering methodology. In *Proceedings of the First International Workshop on Agent-Oriented Software Engineering (AOSE-2000)*, Limerick, Ireland, 207–222.

Wooldridge, M.; Jennings, N.R.; and Kinny, D. 2000. The Gaia methodology for agent-oriented analysis and design. *Autonomous Agents and Multi-Agent Systems,* 3, 285–312.

Yu, E. 1995. Modelling strategic relationships for process reengineering. Ph.D. diss., University of Toronto, Department of Computer Science.

Zambonelli, F.; Jennings, N.; and Wooldridge, M. 2003. Developing multiagent systems: the Gaia methodology. *ACM Transactions on Software Engineering and Methodology,* 12, 3, 317–370.

Zhang, T.I.; Kendall, E.; and Jiang, H. 2002. An agent-oriented software engineering methodology with applications of information gathering systems for LLC. In P. Giorgini, Y. Lespérance, G. Wagner, and E. Yu (eds.), *Agent-Oriented Information Systems 2002*. Proceedings of the Fourth International Bi-Conference Workshop on Agent-Oriented Information Systems, Toronto, 32–46.

PART IV

NEW APPROACHES AND ARCHITECTURES FOR INFORMATION SYSTEMS DEVELOPMENT

APPLICATION OF THE FACT-BASED APPROACH TO DOMAIN MODELING OF OBJECT-ORIENTED INFORMATION SYSTEMS

KINH NGUYEN AND THARAM DILLON

Abstract: *In order for an information system to satisfy the information needs for which it is built, the design must be based on a correct domain model, which must capture precisely all the classes and relationships that are relevant to the information needs being addressed. To perform this task, the text analysis approach—whereby one tries to discover classes and relationships by examining the nouns and verbs in the language of the domain stakeholders—is commonly adopted. However, there are situations where the construction of the domain model can be too complex a task for the text analysis approach to handle effectively. In this chapter, we identify a number of problems associated with the text analysis approach, and propose the use of the fact-based approach (also known as Object-Role Modeling) as an alternative technique. In particular, we show how the fact-based approach can be used effectively, in conjunction with the use case approach, in the construction of domain models for object-oriented information systems.*

Keywords: *Information System, Domain Modeling, Text Analysis, Fact-Based Modeling, Object-Role Modeling, Use Case*

INTRODUCTION

In the development of information systems, it is increasingly common for the modeling task to be approached from the object-oriented perspective, regardless of the eventual implementation platform. One obvious advantage of this approach is that it allows the analyst to capture both the structural and behavioral features of the problem as well as the solution space. In addition, the widespread use of UML greatly facilitates both the modeling activities and the communications among the people involved. Moreover, with recent advances in practical object persistence solutions such as object-relational mapping, the implementation of information systems can be truly object-oriented—that is, the domain objects are directly represented and manipulated as software objects. Consequently, the use of object-oriented modeling has become even more compelling.

Among the tasks of object-oriented modeling, the construction of a correct domain model—one that captures all the relevant domain classes and their relationships—is critical. A successful information system must, by necessity, provide the correct functionality in order to satisfy the business's information needs for which the system is built. The domain model is in fact a model of those information needs, and as such, it plays a crucial role in the development process.

The construction of the domain models for industry-strength information systems can be a difficult task. Most business information systems typically present the analyst with a large number of business-related concepts, complex relationships among business entities, intricate business rules, and operational procedures, most of which are often not obvious and have to be carefully unearthed and documented. In such cases, the popular text analysis method, as will be illustrated in this chapter, may not be able to handle the task effectively. The aim of the chapter is to identify a number of problems associated with the text analysis approach, and to propose the use of a fact-based approach, also known as Object-Role Modeling or ORM, as a supporting technique for the construction of domain models for object-oriented information systems.

The following three sections present a brief review of current approaches to domain modeling; briefly introduce the basic concepts of ORM; and describe the Gymnastics System case study, which will be used throughout the chapter. The next section examines in detail a particular domain modeling process that applies the text analysis approach to the Gymnastics System case study, and identifies various shortcomings of the text analysis approach in general. We then show how ORM can be combined with the use case approach to provide a very effective method for the construction of the domain model. Finally, to provide further insights, we examine the difference between the text analysis and ORM on a more theoretical basis.

A REVIEW OF APPROACHES TO DOMAIN MODELING

The domain model is made up of the following main elements: classes, relationships (inheritance, association, and aggregation), attributes (for classes and associations), and methods. Of all of the elements, classes and relationships are of primary importance. The two most basic issues are: (1) how are we to discover the relevant classes? and (2) how are we to discover the relevant relationships? Once these two questions have been resolved, other issues can be more readily addressed.

As expected, a number of approaches have been suggested to identify classes and relationships. To help make sense of what seems to be a diversity of approaches, it is useful to observe that they can be broadly described in terms of two dimensions: perspective and discovery techniques. The perspective can be *top-down*, or *bottom-up*, and the discovery techniques can be *text analysis*, *collaboration analysis*, or *fact analysis*.

Perspective relates to whether or not we divide the subject matter into various parts and work on those parts in the process of developing the complete model. Considering that the majority of methods propose the use of nouns and noun phrases for identifying classes, we may ask: Where are we to look for these nouns and noun phrases? As stated in Delisle, Barker, and Biski (1999), the answer varies: in a concise summary of the subject matter (Coad and Yourdon, 1990), in a description of the problem space (Pressman, 1997), in a description of the user requirements (Rumbaugh et al., 1990), or in descriptions of use cases, scenarios (Whitten, 1998). To make some sense of all of these answers, let us note that the *ultimate* source for relevant concepts must be the subject matter itself—that is, anything that can be uttered about the system at hand. But the *practical* source has to be a manageable *subset* of the ultimate source. Any of the following may be part of that practical source: a summary description of the subject matter, the transcripts of interviews, a set of use case descriptions, and so forth. The kind of practical source we use depends on our perspective. We may adopt a *top-down* perspective and simultaneously concern ourselves with the whole system, or we may construct the domain model incrementally from considerations of parts of the system (e.g., use cases), that is, by pursuing a *bottom-up* approach.

Let us now consider a sample of methods. George and colleagues (2004, pp. 208–209) suggest that domain modeling can be done from a top-down or a bottom-up perspective or by using a combination of both. The top-down approach derives the model from an "intimate understanding of the nature of the business, rather than from any specific information requirements in computer displays, reports, or business forms." To help develop a model from this perspective, a number of key questions are suggested. To identify classes, it is suggested that we ask: "What are the subjects/ objects of business?" "What types of people, places, things, and materials are used or interact in this business?" "How many instances of each object may exist?" Similar sorts of questions are suggested for identifying attributes, associations, aggregations, compositions, generalization, and so on, including integrity rules and security controls. These authors also embrace the bottom-up approach by "reviewing specific business documents—computer displays, reports, business forms—handled within the system. These displays, reports, forms can be attached to the relevant use case." Thus, this approach can be broadly characterized as being both top-down and bottom-up in perspective, and using text-analysis as the discovery technique.

Bennett, McRobb, and Farmer (2002) strongly advocate the identification of classes and relationships through analysis of use cases by (1) first trying to identify the actors and the classes (or objects) that are involved, then (2) trying to sketch an initial collaboration diagram, and (3) from there, trying to determine the relevance of the classes (identified earlier in the analysis of the use case) and their relationships (Bennett et al., 2002, 176–195). Thus, the main approach these authors recommend is bottom-up in perspective and uses collaboration analysis as the discovery technique. However, they also take the view that it is feasible to develop a domain model that is "independent of any particular use cases." In addition, they advise that it helps to know what you are looking for by keeping in mind (1) a set of categories of things and concepts that can be potential candidates for representation (people, organizations, structures, physical things, etc.), and (2) some guidelines to eliminate unsuitable candidates. Thus, the method is mainly, but not exclusively, bottom-up in perspective and uses collaboration and text analysis as discovery techniques.

Object modeling technique (OMT; Rumbaugh et al., 1990) is largely top-down and text analysis in character. As is common with text analysis approaches, two kinds of heuristics are provided to help the analyst identify the appropriate concepts: (1) a set of categories of things to watch out for as potential candidates, and (2) a set of guidelines to evaluate the suitability of a candidate concept. The evaluation guidelines of OMT will be discussed in detail in a later part of the chapter.

The Responsibility-Driven approach (Wirfs-Brock, Wilkerson, and Wiener, 1990) places an emphasis on behavior. The approach's starting point is the perceived responsibilities of the system. The tasks to be done by the system are considered in turn. And, for each task, the first question is: Which class is responsible for carrying it out? The next question is: With which other classes does this class have to collaborate in order to perform its duty? And so on. The classes and their collaborations are usually recorded using the Class-Responsibility and Collaborator (CRC) cards (Beck and Cummingham, 1989). This approach is thus bottom-up in perspective and uses collaboration analysis as the main discovery technique. Note that this approach still needs to initially identify the relevant classes, and this is usually done by simple brainstorming or by some text analysis technique.

The Unified Process or UP (Jacobson, Booch, and Rumbaugh, 1999) provides a general development process framework that can be customized for specific projects. Judging by the published literature on UP in relation to domain modeling, UP domain modeling can be broadly described as embracing both the top-down and bottom-up approaches with text analysis and collaboration analysis as its discovery techniques.

Extreme Programming or XP (Beck, 2000) advocates the writing of stories (scenarios, use cases) and test cases, and possibly with a minimum amount of analysis, proceeding to programming— relying on refactoring techniques to incorporate additional functionality and to cope with changes.

Any domain modeling engaged in by XP could be said to be bottom-up and text analysis (at least in identifying classes).

Recognizing the challenge of domain modeling for data-intensive systems, the use of analysis patterns, such as those proposed in Fowler (1977), has been seen as a way to improve productivity. Works on analysis patterns seek to describe commonly recurring analysis situations and their associated solutions, forming an explicit, shareable knowledge-base. Analysis patterns are a form of knowledge reuse, which derives its inspiration from the influential works on design patterns (Gamma et al., 1995). Despite being analogous to design patterns, the impact of analysis patterns has been quite moderate. Most likely, this lack of impact is due to the fact that in practice we encounter a great variety of situations, which, after all, reflects the great variety of human activities.

Quite distinct from the approaches mentioned so far is the fact-based modeling approach, formally known as Object-Role Modeling (Halpin, 2001). The fact-based approach captures information structure in terms of *elementary fact types* and the *constraints* on these fact types. In simple terms, elementary fact types are types of sentences that allow us to describe the state of the application domain (often referred to as the universe of discourse). The elementary fact types effectively form a well-defined ontology. This ontology, in turn, allows the analyst to precisely express, as logical statements, the constraints (invariants) on the possible states of the universe of discourse. A distinguishing feature of ORM is that its key abstraction mechanism is *attribute-free*. Though in ORM parlance elementary fact types are about "objects" playing roles, objects in ORM can correspond to both objects and attributes in object-oriented models. This attribute-free property is the key factor that allows ORM to be used effectively to construct the domain models in an *incremental* and *stable* manner. ORM strongly advocates the bottom-up approach, working with user views of the data (reports, forms, etc.) rather than with the general description of the application domain. The practice of working with user views of data can naturally be adopted to work with use cases, as will be shown. Thus, ORM can be characterized as being bottom-up in its perspective and fact-based in its discovery technique.

Another well-known attribute-free approach is that proposed by Embley (1998). While ORM is concerned more or less exclusively with the information structure, Embley's method includes the dynamic aspect of the system.

Though it is not normally regarded as being in the field of domain modeling, Resource Description Framework or RDF (Beckett, 2004), is closely related to ORM. RDF expresses information in terms of RDF triples, which consist of a subject, a predicate, and an object. The "subjects" and "objects" of RDF closely correspond to "objects" of ORM, and RDF triples are a form of ORM binary fact type.

Given the important role played by natural language in the modeling process, techniques developed for natural language processing, such as part-of-speech tagging, pronoun resolution, sentence normalization, and so on, have been applied to facilitate object-oriented modeling (e.g., see Delisle, Barker, and Biski, 1999; Overmyer, Lavoie, and Rambow, 2001; Rayson et al., 2000). These tools use as their major input various sorts of textual descriptions about the domain and the system, such as requirements statement, use case descriptions (or task scripts), transcripts of interviews, and so on. The tools can annotate the textual descriptions with part-of-speech tags, and extract and present the analyst with sets of content words in context, which helps the analyst determine candidate elements for the domain model. The combination of the techniques of tagging, pronoun resolution, and sentence transformation can produce descriptions made up of sentences that clearly indicate the information structure (e.g., customer/NN has/VBZ ID/NN) or various kinds of relevant behavior (e.g., customer/NN can/MD reserve/VBZ ticket/NN). The treatment of attributes may be more complicated. The consideration of adjectives for attributes

Figure 9.1   **A View of an Order**

Order Number: ORD-10
Order Date: 15 March 2006
Customer ID: CUST-10, Sam Smith, Ph: 9800-1234

Product Code	Name	Qty	Unit Price	Amount
PROD-10	Table	2	180.00	360.00
PROD-20	Chair	10	50.00	500.00
				$860.00

is problematic because, as observed in Delisle, Barker, and Biski (1999), the English language can and does convey information in complex noun phrases, whose treatment requires the use of a noun modifier relationship analyzer.

The brief survey above shows that text analysis is the prevalent technique for domain modeling. Even when collaboration analysis is used, a certain amount of text analysis is employed to identify the classes. From the survey and the techniques it covers, we can see that for data-intensive systems, the identification of domain classes and relationships can be a challenging task.

BASIC CONCEPTS OF THE FACT-BASED APPROACH

As a source of both introduction and reference to ORM, we recommend Halpin (2001), which provides a comprehensive treatment of ORM. A comparison of ORM and UML is given in Halpin and Bloesch (1999). Further information can be found on the ORM Web site (2007), which includes information about ORM tools. In this section, we provide a brief introduction to the two most fundamental concepts of ORM, namely, "elementary fact type" and "uniqueness constraint," and how they work. To do this, we apply the ORM approach to the design of a relational database that is based on—that is, able to support—an external view of an order shown in Figure 9.1.

With the fact-based approach, we can start by noting that all the information contained in the above view can be expressed by the following statements or facts: (1) Order ORD-10 is made on 15 March 2006; (2) Order ORD-10 is for customer CUST-10; (3) Customer CUST-10 has the name Sam Smith; (4) Customer CUST-10 is on the phone 9800–1234; (5) Product PROD-10 has the name "Table"; (6) Product PROD-10 has a unit price of $180.00; (7) Product PROD-20 has the name "Chair"; (8) Product PROD-20 has a unit price of $50.00; (9) Order ORD-10 requests 2 units of product PROD-10; and (10) Order ORD-10 requests 10 units of product PROD-20. (We omit the facts about subtotals and the total amount, which can be derived from other facts.)

The above statements are known as *elementary facts* because they cannot be broken down any further without losing their ability to assert facts about the view. Some of the facts, such as facts 5 and 6, have the same structures. They are instances of the same *elementary fact type*. Below are all the elementary fact types that can be used to state all the facts (except for the derived ones) in the given external view:

Order (number) . . . is made Date (dd/mm/yyyy) . . .
Order (number) . . . is for Customer (ID) . . .
Customer (ID) . . . has Name . . .
Customer (ID) . . . is on Phone (code) . . .
Product (code) . . . has Name . . .
Product (code) . . . has UnitPrice ($) . . .
Order (number) . . . for Product (code) . . . has Quantity (nr+) . . .

(A more stringent standard would require the second-to-last fact type to be written as "Product (code) . . . has unit price MoneyAmount ($) . . .")

The third elementary fact type represents a fact or relationship between type Customer and type Name. Type Customer is an entity type. Its instances are nonlexical objects, and they are identified by lexical objects IDs. Type Name is a value type. Its instances are lexical objects and are therefore self-identifying. Every entity type is required to have a reference scheme (e.g., ID is the reference scheme for Student). The elementary fact types can be graphically represented in a conceptual schema diagram as shown in Figure 9.2.

A number of constraints can be applied to the elementary fact types, the most important among them being the uniqueness constraints. These constraints are represented by arrows such as those shown in Figure 9.2. The arrow over the elementary fact type F1, for example, indicates that a Customer can have at most one Name. As a more complicated example, the arrow over fact type F7 (which is broken into two parts) indicates that each combination of Order and Product can have at most one Quantity.

With the elementary fact types and uniqueness constraints defined, the following simplified procedure can be applied to map the conceptual schema to a relational schema: (1) First, put in the same table all the fact types that are attached to the same object with a key of length 1; and (2) then, put each of the remaining fact types in a separate table.

Applying that procedure, we get the tables:

Customer (ID, Name, Phone)
Product (Code, Name, UnitPrice)
Order (OrderNr, Date, CustomerID)
OrderedQuantity (OrderNr, ProductCode, Quantity)

In addition to the basic concepts above, ORM provides a rich collection of graphical constraints. Apart from the internal uniqueness constraints that we have seen, there are other constraints such as: external uniqueness constraints (that apply to more than one fact type), mandatory constraints, value constraints, frequency constraints, subset constraints, equality constraints, exclusion constraints, and so on. Furthermore, due to the availability of the elementary fact types, which allows us to make well-defined statements, we can express any other static constraints, if we need to, as predicates in predicate calculus. These are known as textual constraints.

Earlier it was remarked that ORM provides models that are capable of evolving in a stable manner. As a simple illustration, suppose that in the example above, the price of a product is determined by contracts the supplier makes with the customers; that is, the price of a product may vary from customer to customer. Then, all we have to do with the ORM model is to replace the fact type "Product . . . has UnitPrice . . ." with a ternary fact type "Product . . . for Customer . . . has UnitPrice . . . ." With an entity-relationship or object-oriented model, we would need to remove an attribute from the class Product, and add a new class and some relationships to represent

Figure 9.2   **Conceptual Schema Diagram for the Order**

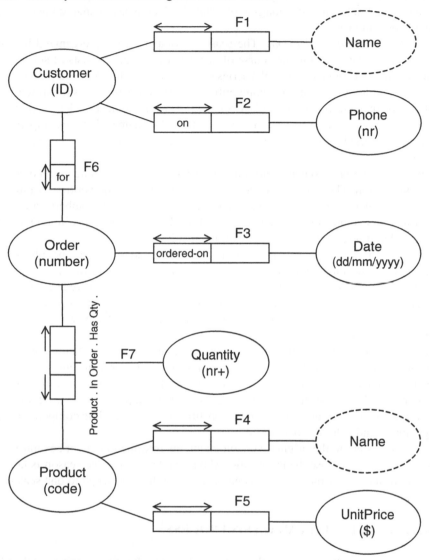

the new information. It is useful to note that with ORM, (1) not only is the stability of the model preserved but also (actually the other side of the same coin) (2) the changes to the model reflect precisely the changes in our cognition of the domain.

THE GYMNASTIC CASE STUDY

This case study was originally published in White (1994). The problem statement below is a paraphrase of the original version, with some minor modifications that will be pointed out.

The purpose of the Gymnastics System is to keep information on the gymnasts, their clubs, and the competitions among the clubs during one season.

- *Gymnasts and Clubs.* For each gymnast, we record an ID (unique), a name, a date of birth, and a gender. Each gymnast belongs to one club. Each club has a name (unique), an address, and a phone number.
- *Meets, Competitions, and Events.* The season's competitions are organized in a series of meets. Each meet is held in the course of one day. Each meet consists of several competitions. Each competition consists of a series of events run on different equipment. Figure 9.3 shows a sample of the result of a competition in a meet. Each meet is identified by a name and has the date on which it is held. A competition within a meet is identified by its name. The competition names come from a small set of standard names. Thus, a competition within a meet is identified across the system by the combination of the meet name and the competition name.
- *Teams in Competitions.* When a club enters a meet, the club enters some subset of its members in a competition. This subset is a team. When a team is in a competition, it must enter all the events of that competition. A team must have the same set of members entered for each event within a competition (White, 1994, p. 34). Thus, a team is identified by the name of the club that it represents and the competition that it enters.
- *Scoring.* Each event in a meet has a judging panel assigned to it. These people are qualified to give scores for this event. Each judge rates each gymnast on his/her performance in the event. The highest and lowest scores will be thrown out, and the rest are averaged to produce the gymnast's score for the event. The event score of a team for an event is the sum of all its members' scores for the event. The competition score of a team (which is also its meet score) is the sum of its event scores.
- *System Operations.* The Gymnastics System is used to prepare the schedule of meets for the season, to ensure that qualified judges are assigned, to register teams and gymnasts, to run the meets, and to publish the results in various forms. Its main system operations include: (1) registering a club in a meet; (2) registering a team in a competition; (3) assigning a judge to an event; (4) scoring trials, events, and competitions; and (5) mailing competition schedules to gymnasts and judges, and so forth.
- *Note:* The system in the original version maintains information about several leagues for several seasons. Because the information about one league for one season is largely independent of the rest, without loss of generality, we confine the scope to one season and one league.

THE ORTHODOX DOMAIN ANALYSIS PROCESS

In the treatment given in White (1994), the first model to be built is the domain model and the first task for its construction is to find the candidate classes. Below is part of the analysis presented by the author in Chapter 4 of the book, which is displayed in extracts, followed by our comments, some of which contain comparisons with ORM.

> We are about to model a *gymnastics* scoring *system.* Our mission is to automate the *definition, registration, scoring,* and *record keeping* of a gymnastics *season.* (p. 33)

Comment 1. This is the opening paragraph of the problem statement. The nouns are italicized as candidates for further analysis. Note that the approach is highly sensitive to the way the problem statement, the interview scripts, and other documents are written.

Figure 9.3 **The Scoring of a Competition**

Meet: Town Invitational
Date: 12/02/2006
Competition: Women's Senior Team

Event Scores

Club	Beam	Vault	Bar	Floor
Flippers	41.5	40.3	44.6	43.7
Acrobats	42.2	38.5	41.0	40.7
Tumblers	38.4	39.8	42.6	41.3
Jugglers	36.2	41.0	37.4	39.6

Source: Based on Figure 3–4 in White (1994).

> *Gymnastics System* is the entire system, not one object. The project is best named "Gymnastics System." (p. 33)

Comment 2. Few of us, if any, would include the Gymnastics System as a class in the domain model (though we could argue that it is an object in the application domain). In ORM modeling, there will be no fact type involving "gymnastic system" as a participating entity. Consequently, "gymnastic system" will not be part of the domain model. The issue would not arise in the first place.

> *Definition, registration, scoring,* and *record keeping* are operations that the system will have to carry out. These are general functions, not classes. (p. 33)

Comment 3. In ORM modeling, we would not have any fact types that involve terms describing the system's functions. Therefore, these terms will automatically be excluded from consideration for the domain model.

> Here is a brief description of a gymnastic *league* and one of their *contests*: a league is a group of *clubs* that compete against each other. Each *team* recruits *members* to participate in the contests. . . . [Keywords are italicized for subsequent analysis]

> "*Contests*" is a vague word. Certainly contest will be a key abstraction, but a bit farther down in the statement are several other terms that could be considered as contests. (p. 34)

Comment 4. We may wonder: by what criteria is "contests" a vague word? In fact, this issue is never revisited. And when the key classes are later listed (p. 38), it is simply not there.

Club is an entity in the Gymnastics System. A club and its members will need to be tracked. At this stage, *team* appears to be a synonym for *club*. To clarify the role of club and team in the system, return to the system function statement and identify the use cases involved in this portion of the system. List each of the actions that must be taken to complete the use case.

Comment 5. Beyond the simplest concepts, the going can quickly get tough. Considerable effort is needed in order to recognize potential hidden dangers and deal with them.

Use case: Register a club in a meet

1. Register the club in a meet.
2. For every competition in the meet, register the club members that are participating in that competition.

Comment 6. The idea of using the relevant use case for clarification is sensible, but thinking in terms of general collaboration does not seem to bring much benefit. It would be better to consider some sample data showing a meet, a competition or two, a club, and some members of the clubs. Using such examples, one can articulate the information content more easily.

Club, competition, and meet are collaborators in this scenario. When a club is registered for a meet, must it enter all competitions? The answer is "no." Must a club have the same set of gymnasts entered in all competitions within a meet? Categorically "no," or you could not have men's and women's competitions. In fact, the club enters some of its members in a competition. This subset is a team.
. . . Clearly, club and team are both abstractions in the Gymnastics Systems. (p. 34)

Comment 7. The concept of "team" is correctly identified in this context, but later it is confused with other concepts of "team."

The analysis continued in this fashion, and other candidate classes such as event, judge, and the like were identified. One piece of reasoning, regarding the "judging panel," appears to be questionable:

Each event has a *judging panel* assigned to it. These people are *qualified scorers* for this event. Each judge rates each gymnast on the event and reports the *score* to a *score keeper*. The score keeper throws out the high and low scores and averages the rest. . . .
A *judging panel* is a collection of judges assigned to judge an event. *Judge* is the class being collected and is a key abstraction. *Judging panel* is a relationship between event and *judge* that identifies the judges assigned to score the event. (p. 36)

Comment 8. But it can be argued convincingly that "judging panel" is a key abstraction. It makes perfect sense, for example, to ask: Who is on the judging panel for such and such event? We may represent it as a relationship for some reason, but in the language of the problem domain, it is an abstraction (a concept).

After about five pages of analysis, seven candidate classes (not counting "Season" and "League") are listed as resulting candidate classes: Competition, Event, Judge, Team, Gymnast, Club, and Meet.

From the extracts and comments above, we can make a number of observations. First, the process is quite *labor-intensive*. Effectively, we have to consider each of the nouns we encounter, even the ones that we may immediately discard. For other nouns, we may have to engage in some heavy reasoning as recorded above.

Second, the process can be *unsystematic* and, on occasions, chaotic. While engaging in this process, it is hard to determine whether we are really making progress toward our final goal. Results are not building up in a steady manner. At any moment, there may occur a new understanding that can profoundly disrupt the whole picture. Some of our reasonings may be tentative or based on shaky grounds (e.g., the reasoning about "contest"), and they need to be followed up. The necessary follow-ups and subsequent resolutions are not something that can be easily planned for in a systematic manner.

Third, the method is *error-prone*. Because the method relies mainly on the analyst's intuitive understanding of the application domain, and because of the unsystematic nature of the analysis process, it is easy to make mistakes.

Note: Regarding the above shortcomings—and others as well—natural language processing tools can be very helpful. Tools such as LIDA (Overmyer, Lavoie, and Rambow, 2001) and REVERE (Rayson et al., 2000), for example, can handle large amounts of textual information, extract and present keywords in context, analyze sentences and transform and present them in standard forms, and exhibit links between the elements of the domain model to textual information to facilitate insights and validations, and so on.

Going back to the case study, it can be seen that the domain class model given in White (1994) contains some serious inconsistencies. These inconsistencies are caused by what we call the problem of *mutating concepts*. This problem arises in situations where several concepts in the same application domain are referred to (by the domain experts) by the same term. Thus, in one part of the problem description (or an interview), the term is used with one particular meaning, and then often without warning, in another part of the description it is used with another meaning. This type of problem is very common. It is likely to occur in most nontrivial applications. We coin the term "mutating concept" to draw attention to the potential dangers.[1]

How does the problem of mutating concepts arise in the Gymnastics case study? Some of the terms, such as "club" and "gymnast," have a single meaning and do not pose any problem. In contrast, other terms such as "competition," "event," and "team"—as it turns out—have multiple meanings and must be handled very carefully. For example, a careful reading of the problem statement reveals two concepts of "competition":

- One refers to the "competition type" (such as "Women's Senior Team");
- The other refers to the "competition in a meet" (such as "Women's Senior Team" in the "Town Invitational Meet").

The two meanings of the term refer to two different—though closely related—concepts. The fact that the concepts are closely related actually increases the danger of confusion.

The concept of "team" requires even greater care. As explained in White (1994):

> When a club enters a meet, must it enter all the competitions in the meet? The answer is "no." Must a club have the same set of gymnasts entered in all competitions of a meet? Categorically "no," or you could not have men's and women's competitions. In fact, the club enters some subset of its members for a competition. This subset is a team. (White, 1994, p. 34)

The quotation alludes to one meaning of "team." But it is not the only one. In fact, the term can be used in three different senses:

- In the first sense, a team is a kind of team, for example, Women's Senior Team. This concept of "team" turns out to be equivalent to the concept of "competition type."
- In the second sense, a team is a team of gymnasts in a club, for example, Women's Senior Team of the Flippers Club.
- In the third sense, a team is a team from a club that actually participates in a competition, for example, Women's Senior Team of the Flippers Club for Town Invitational Meet. This is the concept of the term "team" explained in the above quotation.

The models in the book seem to confuse these different concepts of "team."

- In Figures 4–9 (White, 1994, p. 50) and 5–4 (ibid., p. 60), the relationship cardinalities show that each gymnast can belong to only *one* team and each team can participate in *many* competitions. These cardinalities are correct if the term "team" is used in the first or second sense.
- Then, in Figure 6–6 (ibid., p. 71), the relationship cardinalities show that a gymnast can belong to many teams (correct for "team" in the third sense), and a team can participate in many competitions (correct for "team" in the first or second sense).

To support the operations of the Gymnastics System, at least two concepts of "team" (the first and the last) have to be distinctly represented. As the given model stands, it does not capture and represent the first concept of "team" or "competition type."

In addition to the problem of identifying classes and relationships, numerous constraints need to be identified and enforced. For example:

- A judge for an event in a meet must be qualified for that *type* of event.
- A gymnast participating in a competition as a member of team T must be of a certain age and gender, and must belong to team T's club.
- Or, when a gymnast G participates in a competition C, and the competition has event E, then gymnast G must receive a score for event E of the competition.

Of these three constraints, only the first one is explicitly identified in White (1994). There is no evidence that any of them is actually enforced (e.g., by reading the collaboration diagrams and the class specifications).

USING ORM AS A SUPPLEMENTARY TECHNIQUE

Dealing with the Problem of Mutating Concepts

With ORM, when writing down the fact types, we have to specify the "reference schemes" (how "objects" are identified). In this way, related concepts can be easily distinguished and the problem of mutating concepts is overcome.

Consider, for example, the "Scoring of a Competition" report in Figure 9.3. In the ORM approach, we can start by reading a few facts from the report. For example, the fact related to the score of 41.5 for club Flippers may be expressed as follows:

The *Women's Senior* team from club *Flippers* for event *Beam* in meet *Town Invitational* receives the score of *41.5*. (Sentence A)

This sentence forms a meaningful unit of information. Note that in order to talk about the score of 41.5, we need to include the other four data items (italicized in sentence A). For example, it is obvious that we cannot omit the club's name from this sentence; if we do that, we get a meaningless sentence. To derive a fact type from sentence A, we note that 41.5 is the score that a team receives for an event. That is, the fact type is of the form:

Team ( ) . . . receives Score ( ) . . . for Event ( ) . . . (Sentence B)

In the context provided by sentence A, we can see clearly what we mean by a "team": a "team" is "a team from a club for a competition type in a meet." Therefore, it is identified by the combination of the club's name, competition type's name, and the meet's name. And similarly, an event is identified by a combination of the meet's name, the competition type's name, and event type's name. Adding the reference scheme to sentence B, we have the fact type (with informal notation being used for reference schemes):

Team (club name + competition type name + meet name) . . . receives Score (number) . . .

for Event (meet name + competition type name + event type name) . . . (Sentence C)

It is conceptually clearer to write the above fact type (sentence C) using the following "nonstandard" format in which square brackets are used to denote the reference schemes of the entity types they enclose:

Team ([Club] + [Competition Type] + [Meet]) . . . receives Score (number) . . . for Event ([Meet] + [Competition Type] + [Event Type]) . . . (Sentence D)

As a validity check, we note that sentence A can be rewritten in the format of sentence D as the sentence E below, which contains precisely the same information:

Team identified by Club Name *"Flippers"* and Competition Type Name *"Women's Senior Team"* and Meet Name *"Town Invitational"* receives Score of *41.5* for Event identified by Meet Name *"Town Invitational"* and Competition Type Name *"Women's Senior Team"* and Event Type Name *"Beam."* (Sentence E)

(*Note:* In the above sentence, there is an important constraint regarding the Competition Type Name and Meet Name. The same values for them should appear as part of the identification of both the Team and the Event. This situation is sometimes known as "derived redundancy." The constraint can be formally expressed if desired. Perhaps more important, in implementing any use case that involves the creation of facts of these fact types, we need to ensure that the constraints are satisfied. As far as the single fact type D is concerned, we can eliminate the redundancy using an objectified relationship. In doing so, however, concepts such as "team" may not be represented explicitly, which generally is not a desirable outcome.)

The key to the above analysis is actually sentence A. It provides a "context" in which we can easily see that a team (which is an entity that participates in a meet) should be identified by a meet name, a competition type name, and the club name. With this reference scheme, the current concept of "team" can be clearly distinguished from other possible concepts of "team" that may also be relevant to this application domain: other concepts of "team," if applicable, must have different reference schemes. Thus, in the practice of fact-based analysis, the problem of mutating concepts is resolved as a matter of routine: *In forming the fact types, because we are required to specify the reference schemes explicitly, all the issues related to mutating concepts are naturally resolved. The reference schemes clearly identify the concept that a particular term stands for and clearly distinguish it from other concepts that may be expressed by the same term.*

Identifying Fact Types on the Basis of Use Cases

We now consider the practical problem of how to efficiently identify fact types for large-scale information systems. In theory, we can identify fact types in any order. But in practice, especially for large-scale information systems, in order for the process to be carried out effectively, we need some strategy to divide and conquer. Our suggested divide-and-conquer strategy is based on a kind of *ordering* of use cases.

Theoretical considerations and experience have convinced us that the fact-identifying process can be carried out most effectively in the order of "data entry dependency." Informally speaking, this is the order in which the data are stored in the system. This order entails a certain amount of "existence dependency." For example, we must first create a particular *meet* before we can enter information about a *competition* that belongs to the *meet* (and this is what we mean by "data entry dependency"). So quite naturally, in identifying fact types, it makes sense—and it is much more efficient—to proceed in that same order; that is, we should identify the fact types related to meets before those related to competitions. This leads to the technique of considering use cases based on their order of dependency.

For the Gymnastics System, the fact types can be effectively identified by considering use cases in the following order: (1) Add a club, (2) Enter a gymnast, (3) Enter a competition type, (4) Enter an event type, (5) Enter a judge, (6) Create a meet, (7) Enter a competition (for a meet), (8) Enter an event (for a competition), (9) Enter judges for events, (10) Register a team (for a competition), and (11) Enter a score.

Note that for the purpose at hand, which is to identify fact types, it is sufficient in most cases to consider only those use cases that cause data to be *added* to the information base. The idea is to perceive a sequence of use cases or events, such as the one listed above, that can generate all the relevant fact types (except possibly for the derived fact types). Moreover, while identifying fact types generated by an event, we can also identify the constraints applied to these fact types. In the context of use cases, fact types and constraints are easier to identify (because of the temporary focus on specific use cases). The use cases can also be used to organize the recording of the fact types for documentation purposes.

The application of the suggested process for the Gymnastics case study is outlined below.

Fact Types About Clubs and Gymnasts

Add a club. When a club is formed and registered, the following fact types are generated:

> Club (name) . . . has Phone (code) . . .
> Club (name) . . . is at Address (text) . . .

Enter a gymnast. This event generates the following fact types:

> Gymnast (id) . . . has Name . . .
> Gymnast (id) . . . was born on Date (dd/mm/yyyy) . . .
> Gymnast (id) . . . is a member of Club (name) . . .

Fact Types About Competition Types, Event Types, and Judges

Enter competition types. By considering facts such as CompetitionType (name) "Women's Senior Team" is for gender (code) "female," and so on, we can identify the following fact types:

> CompetitionType (name) . . . is for Gender (code) . . .
> CompetitionType (name) . . . has lower limit of Age (years) . . .
> CompetitionType (name) . . . has upper limit of Age (years) . . .

Enter event types. Note that this use case must be preceded by the "Enter competition type" use case. It generates the following fact type:

> EventType (name) . . . is for Gender (code) . . .

Enter data about judges. Note that this use case must be preceded by the "Enter event types" use case.

> Judge (name) . . . is on Phone (code) . . .
> Judge (name) . . . is qualified for EventType (name) . . .

Fact Types About the Meets

Create a meet.

> Meet (name) . . . is held on Date (dd/mm/yyyy) . . .
> Meet (name) . . . is held at Location (name) . . .

Fact Type About Competitions, Events, and Judges for Events

Enter a competition for a meet

> Competition ([Meet] + [CompetitionType]) . . . belong to Meet (name) . . .
> Competition ( ) . . . is of CompetitionType (name) . . .

Enter an event for a competition

> Event ([CompetitionType] + [EventType]) . . . belongs to Competition ( ) . . .
> Event ( ) . . . is of EventType (name) . . .

Enter judges for events

> Judge (name) . . . is assigned to Event ( ) . . .
> Constraint: If Judge *j* is assigned to Event *e*, and Event *e* is of EventType *t*, then Judge *j* is (must be) qualified for EventType *t*.

Note: As mentioned earlier, while identifying fact types, we are in a good position to identify the constraints applied to the fact types under consideration, and we can then express the constraints in terms of these fact types. In this section, to save space, we will record only the "less common" constraints. In particular, we omit "common" constraints such as uniqueness constraints (e.g., each club must be at one address) or mandatory constraints (e.g., each club must have a phone number). In practice, these common constraints, due to their importance, are routinely specified on the conceptual schema diagram, especially when tools such as VisioModeler (see ORM, 2007) are used.

Fact Types About the Team Registrations

Register a team and its members in a meet (for a competition). Similar to the notion that a team is a club in a competition, we have the concept of a "member" (for want of a better term) as a gymnast participating in a team. The inclusion of "member" makes it a little clearer to express, for example, in the case of the awarding of a score, which the gymnast receives as a member of a team rather than just as a gymnast of a club.

> Team ([club] + [Competition]) . . . enter Competition ( ) . . .
> Member ([Gymnast] + [Team]) . . . is Gymnast ( ) . . .
> Member ( ) . . . belongs to Team ( ) . . .
> Constraint (informally expressed): A gymnast (member) can belong to a team, which is registered for a particular type of competition, only if the gymnast is eligible (having suitable gender and age) for that type of competition.

Fact Types About Scoring

The fact types related to scoring are listed below. Note that the last two fact types can be derived from the first fact type and other relevant fact types that have been identified earlier. For example, the score received by a gymnast for an event is calculated by discarding the highest and the lowest scores of the judges.

Enter a score

> Judge ( ) . . . gives Score (number) . . . to Member ( ) . . . in Event ( ) . . .
> Member ( ) . . . receives Score ( ) . . . for Event ( ) . . . [derived]
> Team ( ) . . . receives Score ( ) . . . for Event ( ) . . . [derived]
> Constraint (informally expressed): A gymnast participating in a competition must have a score for each event of that competition from each of the judges of the event.

Conceptual Schema Diagram

From the fact types that have been identified above, we construct the ORM conceptual schema shown in Figure 9.4.

Figure 9.4   **The ORM Conceptual Schema Diagram for Gymnastics System**

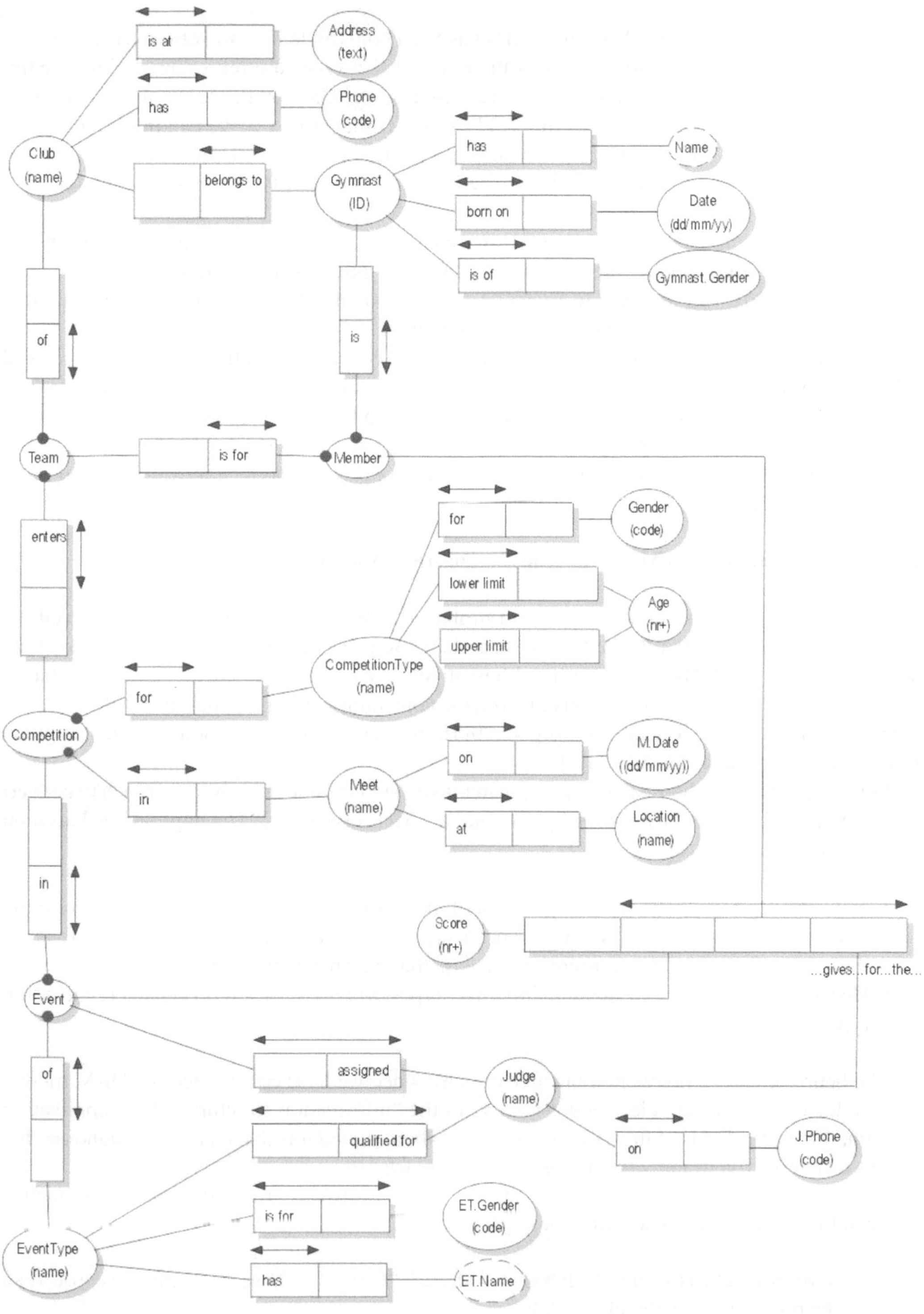

Validating by Traversing the Conceptual Schema Diagram

Once the conceptual schema diagram (CSD) has been constructed, it is useful to *traverse* it as a validation check, in order to verify that the relevant fact types are represented. Once again, the order of data entry comes in handy: we can traverse the CSD on the basis of this ordering. Thus, given the ordering: (1) Add a club, (2) Enter a gymnast (3) . . . , we can inspect the CSD and say to ourselves: "Obviously, I can enter facts about a club. Now I can enter facts about a gymnast including the club to which he or she belongs. That fact type is here on the diagram. And so on."

As we go over the fact types in the CSD in this manner, we can also identify the constraints among the facts. For example, when it comes to register a judge for an event, not only do we need fact type Judge ( ) . . . is assigned to Event ( ) . . . , but we also have the constraint that a judge can judge only those events for which he/she is qualified.

Note: Another validation technique, which is not time-consuming at all, is to derive a relational schema from the ORM conceptual schema, and then subject it to an inspection. Again, this can be done systematically by walking through the use cases in the order suggested above and seeing how the relational schema can support the use cases. Experience has shown that by inspecting the relational schema, a lot of sense can be made of the data model, and mistakes, if any, can often be easily picked up.

Deriving a Domain Class Model for the Gymnastics System

Mapping attribute-free models to models with attributes has been an active area of research in ORM. On a formal basis, Bollen (2002) describes an elaborate procedure to map an ORM conceptual schema diagram to a UML class diagram. Alternatively, we can apply a schema abstraction based on major object types, which are derived from the constraint patterns in the given ORM model. A brief introduction to this technique is given in Halpin (2001), and a detailed treatment is given in Campbell, Halpin, and Proper (1996).

For this chapter, we choose to use a simple intuitive, and yet quite effective, approach to convert the ORM model for the Gymnastics System into a UML class model. The approach is based on two simple heuristic rules:

- Heuristic Rule 1. There are groups of fact types with a simple key attached to a common object type, which can be an entity type, a subtype, or an objectified relationship. Each of these groups, *in most cases,* represents a class that we are trying to identify.
- Heuristic Rule 2. Each of the remaining fact types, *in most cases*, represents a relationship type.

The heuristic rules work well in practice because, once we have constructed the ORM model, we will have gained a very clear understanding of the "information structure" of the application domain, that is, the kinds of things that we can say about it, and it is this clear understanding that allows us to effectively apply the heuristic rules to reach our goal.

For the Gymnastics case study, most of the fact types fall into groups with simple keys attached to a common object. Let us consider these groups.

1. Group attached to *Club:* "Club is at Address," "Club has Phone." Clearly, this group can be represented by the class Club.

2. Group attached to *Gymnast:* "Gymnast has Name," "Gymnast is born on Date," "Gymnast is of Gender," "Gymnast belongs to Club." Clearly, we should have the class Gymnast, which would capture the first three fact types, and let the last one be represented by an association between Gymnast and Club.

3. Group attached to *CompetitionType:* Clearly, we should have the class CompetitionType to capture these fact types (related to gender, lower and upper age limits).

4. Group attached to *EventType:* "EventType has Name." We should have the class EventType to capture this fact type.

5. Group attached to *Judge:* "Judge has Phone." We should have the class Judge.

6. Group attached to *Meet:* "Meet is on Date," "Meet is at Location." We should have the class Meet.

7. Group attached to *EventType:* "EventType has Name." We should have the class EventType to capture this fact type.

Note: So far, the choices have been very straightforward. In fact, we do not have any other choices. However, this is not the case for the next group of fact types.

8. Group attached to *Competition:* "Competition is for CompetitionType," "Competition is in Meet." Obviously, we can represent these two fact types by class Competition (let us call it choice A).

On the other hand, because a Competition is identified by the combination of Meet and CompetitionType, we can, if we so wish, represent the two fact types by an association between class Meet and class CompetitionType (let us call this choice B).

Though both choices are equivalent in the sense that both resulting models allow us to store the required information, we will prefer choice A because it represents the concept of "competition" explicitly. It is also important to note that this "competition" concept plays an important role in expressing other facts about the application domain (as will be seen next).

9. Group attached to *Event:* "Event is of Event Type," "Event is for Competition."

Suppose we have made choice A for the "Competition group" and have the class Competition at our disposal. What choices can we have in this case? An obvious choice is to introduce a class Event and represent the two fact types as associations between this class and classes EventType and Competition (let us call this choice A for this fact type group). But we could also represent the two fact types by an association between Competition and EventType (choice B).

Now, if we had made choice B for "Competition group" (group 8 above) and thus do not have class Competition to work with, a possible choice would be to represent the fact types by a ternary association between Meet, CompetitionType, and EventType (choice C). Here, the implicit representation of the concept of "Competition" makes it harder (and messier) to capture the concept of "event."

Similar to the previous case, we prefer choice A, which explicitly represents the concept of "event."

10. Group attached to *Team:* A similar sort of observation applies. Our preference is to introduce the class Team.

11. Group attached to *Member:* Similarly, we would introduce the class Member.

Figure 9.5   **A Domain Model for the Gymnastics System: The Preferred Model**

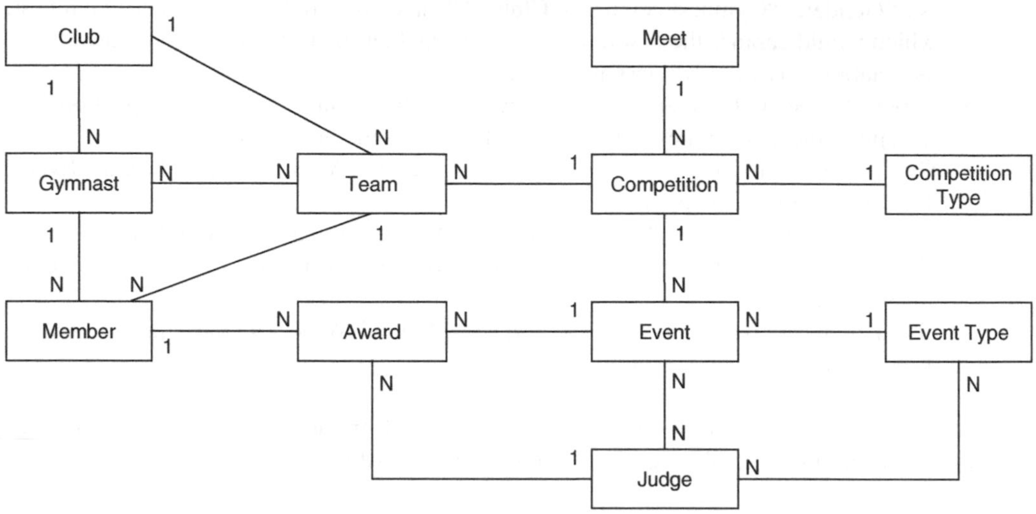

Now, there remain three binary fact types without a simple key and a quaternary fact type. The three fact types (EventType is for Gender, Judge is qualified for EventType, Judge is assigned to Event) are to be represented by three associations. The quaternary fact type can be represented by class Award (or Score)—though an association class is also a possible choice.

With the choices that we have made, where most concepts are explicitly represented, we arrive at the class diagram shown in Figure 9.5.

Additional Insight into Possible Class Diagrams

The above simple approach clearly shows the considerable extent to which the fact-based model can facilitate the construction of the class model. Furthermore, the analysis also leads to an interesting consequence, that is, we can have an understanding of a *range* of possible domain models.

Here is how we arrive at this understanding. First, we note that for the model in Figure 9.5, every important concept is represented explicitly. Now, if we go to the other extreme and represent the fact type groups for Competition, Event, Team, Member (groups 8–11) implicitly as associations, we would get the model shown in Figure 9.6. Though strange-looking and not intuitively appealing, it is still a legitimate domain model in which information about the application domain is represented as objects (instances of classes) and links (instances of associations). The two models presented are essentially the two extremes. Other possible models are those between these two extremes, depending on how we choose to represent certain groups of fact types.

A COMPARISON ON THEORETICAL GROUNDS

Having covered the practical use of the text analysis and the fact-based approach, we now examine and contrast their basic premises. The comparison should provide a deeper insight into the differences between the two approaches.

Figure 9.6 **Another Domain Model for the Gymnastics System: With Minimum Number of Classes**

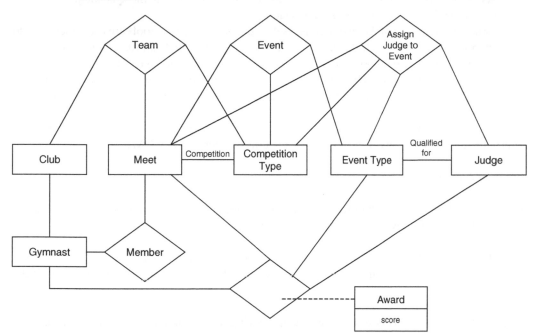

A Typical Procedure of Text Analysis Method

The following is a summary of the description of the text analysis method given in Rumbaugh and colleagues (1990, p. 153). It is a typical procedure and has been adopted by various other authors. It consists of the following steps:

- Extract the nouns and noun phrases from the problem statement.
- Make a list of candidate classes.
- Separate the good classes from the bad ones. Eliminate the following: (1) Redundant classes, (2) Irrelevant classes, (3) Vague classes, (4) Attributes, (5) Operations, (6) Roles, and (7) Implementation constructs.

How the Procedure Would Perform in Practice

Upon reflection, it can be seen that the procedure is based on the following premises:

- Premise 1: The classes for the analysis model can be found among the nouns and noun phrases contained in the problem statement.
- Premise 2: The nouns and noun phrases contained in the problem statement can be a valid or an invalid candidate class. The way to distinguish between them is to apply a number of criteria (such as the ones in the procedure above).

The first premise places a lot of responsibility on the problem statement. How should the problem statement be written so that it can fulfill these responsibilities—that is, to ensure that it can supply an exhaustive, or at least nearly so, list of potentially valid candidate classes for the analysis model? How do we tell whether or not a given problem statement is adequate for this purpose? And what can we do if it is inadequate?

Another consequence of the first premise is that, unless appropriate tools are used, there would be problems with scaling up. If the problem statement is written in detail for a large system, there will be a large number of "good" nouns and a huge number of "bad" ones. The list of candidate classes could be quite long. The elimination process, being unsystematic, would be quite unmanageable. As mentioned earlier, linguistic analysis tools could be very useful for dealing with these problems.

As to the second premise, how effectively can the suggested criteria be applied to eliminate improper candidate classes? Let us consider the criteria suggested by OMT.

Relevant Classes

What is meant by "relevant"? In Rumbaugh and colleagues (1990) (from which the above procedure is taken), the following explanation is given:

> If a class has little or nothing to do with the problem, it should be eliminated. This involves judgment, because in another context the class could be important. (Rumbaugh et al., 1990, p. 155)

Thus, the explanation defines "irrelevant" as "having little or nothing to do with the problem." But this kind of elaboration offers very little help. Indeed, we can ask, if a concept has little or nothing to do with the problem, why is it included in the problem statement at all? More important—*How can we tell if a concept that occurs in the problem statement has little or nothing to do with a problem?*

Let us try to look at this issue from the fact-based point of view. A very important property of those classes to be included in the domain class model is that they *carry information* required for the operation of the enterprise. This is obviously true, for example, for the domain model of the Gymnastics System. The analysis model has classes such as Club, Gymnast, CompetitionType, EventType, Judge, Meet, Team, Score, and so on. Each of these classes carries certain information required for the running of the competitions.

To be clearer on this point, let us consider an application that manages bank accounts. When we observe what is happening in the real world, we see, for example, that people use automatic teller machines (ATMs) to carry out banking transactions. Then, should we include ATM in the domain class model? The answer is: it depends! If we need to keep records of the ATM involved in the transactions, then the answer is definitely "yes." But suppose we do not need to do that; then the answer is "no." In the latter case, the ATM will play exactly the same role as a desk in a library, or a screen on a computer terminal. It may or may not be modeled as a control class, but certainly not as a domain class.

From the fact-based perspective, clearly if a class carries certain information required for the enterprise's operation, then it must appear in some fact type. Thus, we have the following characterization for "relevant": *A concept is relevant for the domain model if, and only if, it appears in at least one elementary fact type.*

Thus, "relevant" is linked ultimately to "information." If a concept represents some sort of information to be maintained by the system, then it is relevant and it should be included in the domain model as a class, an attribute, or a relationship.

Redundant Classes

What is a redundant class? The following explanation is given:

> If two classes express the same information, the most descriptive name should be kept. For example, although customer might describe a person taking an airline flight, passenger is more descriptive. (Rumbaugh et al., 1990, p. 153)

But in general, how do we know that two terms express the same concept? For example, in the Gymnastics System, how do we know whether or not "competitor" and "member" of a team refer to the same kind of objects? To find out, we need to carefully examine how these terms are actually used by the stakeholders in the context of the application domain. But as to how we are to carry out this examination, the text analysis approach seems to leave it entirely to the initiative of the analyst.

The fact-based approach offers more definite criteria for discrimination. A concept (or an ORM entity type) must have a reference scheme (how we identify an instance of this entity type), and it must participate in a number of fact types. With that in mind, we can arrive at the following clearer, and more workable, characterization: *Two terms represent the same concept/class if their instances have the same reference scheme and participate in the same set of fact types.*

Vague Classes

This point is explained as follows:

> A class should be specific. Some tentative classes may have ill-defined boundaries or be too broad in scope. For example, *Recordkeeping provision* is vague. In the ATM problem, this is part of *Transaction*. In other applications, this might be included in other classes, such as *Stock sales, Telephone calls*, or *Machine failures*. (Rumbaugh et al., 1990, p. 155)

But as before, how do we recognize that a concept is ill-defined or too broad in scope? A few examples of such classes, as given in the explanation above, will not be of much help when an analyst faces a "vague" concept (which he or she may not recognize as such) in the analysis of some particular application domain (with which he or she may not be quite familiar).

From the fact-based perspective, a "vague" concept, such as *recordkeeping* or *recordkeeping provision*, if it is indeed vague, will not appear in a fact type. Why? Because at the very least we have to ask: how are we going to identify an instance of this concept (its reference scheme)? If we cannot find a reference scheme, then indeed it is vague or, in the language of the fact-based approach, it is not a proper entity, and it will not appear in any fact type. On the other hand, if there is some reference scheme for such a concept, then it may well represent a legitimate class no matter how strange the term may sound to us. Thus, we have: *If a concept is vague (ill-defined, not representing a valid entity), then it will not appear in any fact type, and therefore will not be in the domain model.*

Attributes

How do we know, or decide, whether or not a concept is an attribute? The following advice is given:

Names that primarily describe individual objects should be restated as attributes. For example, name, age, weight, and address are usually attributes. If the independent existence of a property is important, then make it a class, not an attribute. For example, an employee's room would be a class in an application to reassign rooms after a reorganization. (Rumbaugh et al., 1990, p. 155)

Should "independent existence" be used as a basic criterion to distinguish between attributes and classes? If something, let us call it A, cannot exist without something else, let us call it B, then should we make A an attribute of B?—Not necessarily! We frequently have objects whose existence requires the existence of another kind of object (e.g., copies of books in a library cannot exist without the abstract books, often identified by their ISBN).

So really, how can we decide whether a concept should be an attribute or a class? Let us look at this issue from the fact-based approach. Consider, for example, the case where we have fact of type:

A Person (name) . . . was born in a City (name) . . .

Should City be an attribute? The answer is: it depends! If City is involved in no other fact type, then it is reasonable to answer "yes." However, if it is also involved in other fact types such as

City (name) . . . has Postcode (code) . . .
City (name) . . . has Population (nr+) . . .

then it is no longer feasible to represent City as an attribute. Therefore, whether or not a concept should be regarded as an object depends largely on the *relationships* it has with other concepts. More precisely, *the issue of whether a concept should be represented as an object or an attribute can be resolved only by considering (explicitly or implicitly) (1) all the fact types in which the concept is involved, and (2) whether or not some of these fact types contain other information about the concept.*

Operations

The following advice is given:

If a name describes an operation that is applied to objects and not manipulated in its own right, then it is not a class. For example, a telephone call is a sequence of actions involving a caller and a telephone network. If we are simply building telephones, then *Call* is part of the dynamic model and not a class. [. . .] An operation that has features of its own should be modeled as a class, however. For example, in a billing system for telephone calls a *Call* would be an important class with attributes such as date, time, and destination. (Rumbaugh et al., 1990, p. 155)

Clearly, from the fact-based point of view, the above advice is an obvious consequence of the following simpler and more general guideline: *We do not need to consider whether or not a name is an operation. If a concept, irrespective of whether or not it normally indicates some sort of operation, carries information to be maintained, that is, it appears in some fact type, then include it in the domain model. Otherwise, do not.*

Roles

The following advice is given:

> The name of a class should reflect its intrinsic nature and not a role that it plays in an association. For example, *Owner* would be a poor name for a class in a car manufacturer's database. What if a list of drivers is added later? What about persons who lease cars? The proper class is *Person* (or possibly *Customer*), which assumes various different roles, such as owner, driver, and lessee. (Rumbaugh et al., 1990, p. 155)

But in practice, we do model *Owner, Driver*, or *Lessee* as classes, most likely as subclasses of *Person*, or *BusinessEntity* (because an owner can be a company). So what can really help us to decide whether a particular name represents a role rather than a class?

From the fact-based perspective: *We do not need to consider whether or not a name represents a role. We need to be concerned only with whether the name would appear in some fact type and how it is identified. Moreover, the technique of subtype analysis (which is done in terms of fact types [see Halpin, 2001] would take care of the case where a certain object appears to play different roles.*

Implementation Constructs

Further explanation is given as follows:

> Constructs extraneous to the real world should be eliminated from the analysis model. They may be needed later during design, but not now. For example, CPU, subroutine, process, algorithm, and interrupt are implementation constructs for most applications [and should be excluded from the analysis model]. . . . (Rumbaugh et al., 1990, p. 155)

From the fact-based point of view: *Nouns that represent implementation constructs (CPU, subroutine, etc.), though they may appear in the problem statement, will not appear in any fact type and therefore will be automatically excluded from the domain model.*

Note: Another commonly given piece of advice concerns the kinds of things we may be looking for as potential candidates for domain classes. In Bennett, McRobb, and Farmer (2002, p. 184), for example, we are advised to look for the following kinds of things: (a) People (e.g., Mr. Smith); (b) Organization (e.g., Jones & Co.); (c) Structures (e.g., teams, projects); (d) Physical things (e.g., car, truck); (e) Abstractions of people (e.g., employee, supervisor); (f) Abstractions of physical things (e.g., vehicle, goods); (g) Conceptual things (e.g., project, qualification); (h) Enduring relationships (e.g., sale, contract). But it can easily be seen that this kind of advice has quite limited use. After all, a concept such as "judging panel," which fits really well into the category of "structure," is rejected in the analysis of the Gymnastics case study. Similarly, it is also the case for the rejected concept of "contest," which fits well into the category of "enduring relationship." Clearly, the categories enumerated above can be used to classify the kinds of things that a concept (or a noun) may fall into, but that "classifying" ability cannot be a means of telling us which concept (or noun) should or should not be kept as candidate domain classes. As a matter of fact, note that most nouns, regardless of whether or not they can be candidates for classes, would belong to one or more of the suggested categories.

Comparing the Underlying Perspectives

We have seen that, by being aware of the information about the application domain that the system must maintain, we can eliminate many of the issues arising from the text analysis approach. Let us pursue this point a little further.

It is clear that whether or not a concept expressed by a noun can be a class depends on the kind of information it carries and the kinds of relationships it has with other concepts. In other words, a noun derives its meaning from the context in which it is found. Its significance depends on the relationships it has with other concepts in a network of concepts. It is very similar to the way a concept derives its meaning from the semantics network in which the concept occurs.

It can be observed that the text analysis approach generally does not effectively exploit the interrelation upon which the significance of the concept is based. In contrast, the fact-based approach seeks to exploit that valuable source of interrelations, and does so effectively, with a clear focus. All we ask consistently is: "What are the facts about the application domain that the system is expected to maintain?" (And we would answer that question by examining the problem statement, or more effectively, by examining the user views such as input/output screens, reports, etc.)

Questions regarding facts and fact types are much more fundamental and much easier to answer. Consider, for the sake of argument, a concept or a noun "X"; instead of asking "Is X a class?" or "Is X an attribute?" we simply ask, "Do we need to maintain some information about X?" or "Are there any fact types involving X?" To take an example, if "X" is "Customer," then we do not have to ask "Is 'customer' a class?" or "Is it an attribute?" or "Is it a role?" We ask, "What is the information we maintain for a customer?" or "Does 'customer' appear in any fact type?" These questions, being directly related to matters of information, are more to the point. They are also easier to answer. Clearly, if we cannot answer the latter questions ("Can we have a fact type with 'customer' in it?"), we would have no hope of answering the former ones ("Is 'customer' a class?" or "Is 'customer' an attribute?" etc.). In fact, with ORM, in most cases, we do not have to consciously ask such questions; by working with the user's data views (reports, forms, screens), we can read the facts or fact types off the user views. The fact-oriented viewpoint of ORM allows us to work directly with the information content aspect of the application domain.

SUMMARY

In this chapter, we have examined in detail the text analysis approach to class and relationship discovery, and pointed out several problems with it. We have also shown how, with the use of the fact-based approach, we can eliminate or effectively handle these problems. We have illustrated how the fact-based analysis can be incorporated into the overall object-oriented domain modeling process. In particular, we have demonstrated (a) how the order of data entry dependency can be used in identifying and organizing the fact types; (b) how the conceptual schema (that is, the fact-type model) can be validated in several simple but effective ways; and (c) how to convert the conceptual schema into a domain class model.

In addition, we have delved deeper into the issue and examined the basic premises of the text analysis and the fact-based approach. We have pointed out that the significance of a concept depends on its relationships with other concepts in a semantic network (expressed in terms of fact types) and that the fact-based approach is one that effectively exploits these all-important relationships with a clear and consistent focus.

NOTE

1. The problem of mutating concepts is closely related to what is known in the literature as the problem of "homonym." However, most treatments of the "homonym" problem are mainly concerned with discovering and reconciling the locally valid uses of the *same name* in *different models* to represent *different concepts*. In such cases, the concepts in question are modeled correctly in each of the models. The mutating concept problem is about a different kind of situation where the *same term* is used for *different concepts* in the *same discourse*.

REFERENCES

Beck, K. 2000. *Extreme Programming Explained: Embrace Change.* Reading, MA: Addison-Wesley.

Beck, K., and Cunningham, W. 1989. A Laboratory for teaching object-oriented thinking. *Proceedings of OOPSLA '89,* New York, NY: ACM Press, 1–6.

Beckett, D. 2004. *RDF/XML Syntax Specification, W3C Recommendation 10 February 2004.* Available at www.w3.org/TR/rdf-syntax-grammar (accessed September 2007).

Bennett, S.; McRobb, S.; and Farmer, R. 2002. *Object-Oriented Systems Analysis and Design Using UML.* London: McGraw-Hill International.

Bollen, P. 2002. *A Formal ORM-to -UML Mapping Algorithm.* Research Memoranda 015, Maastricht, The Netherlands: METEOR, Maastricht Research School of Economics of Technology and Organization.

Coad, P., and Yourdon, E. 1990. *Object-Oriented Analysis.* Englewood Cliffs, NJ: Yourdon Press, Prentice Hall.

Campbell, L.; Halpin, T.; and Proper, H. 1996. Conceptual schemas with abstractions: making flat schemas more comprehensible. *Data and Knowledge Engineering,* 20, 39–85.

Delisle, S.; Barker, B.; and Biski, I. 1999. Object-oriented analysis: getting help from robust computational linguistic tools. *Fourth International Conference on Applications of Natural Language to Information Systems (OCG Schriftenreihe 129).* Klagenfurt, Austria, 167–171.

Embley, D. 1998. *Object-Database Development.* Reading, MA: Addison-Wesley.

Fowler, M. 1997. *Analysis Patterns: Reusable Object Models.* Reading, MA: Addison-Wesley.

Gamma, E.; Helm, R.; Johnson, R.; and Vlissides, J. 1995. *Design Patterns: Elements of Reusable Object-Oriented Software.* Reading, MA: Addison-Wesley.

George, J.; Batra, D.; Valacich, J.; and Hoffer, J. 2004. *Object-Oriented Systems Analysis and Design.* Upper Saddle River, NJ: Pearson Prentice Hall.

Halpin, T. 2001. *Conceptual Schema and Relational Databases.* San Francisco, CA: Morgan Kaufmann.

Halpin, T., and Bloesch, A. 1999. Data modeling in UML and ORM: a comparison. *Journal of Database Management,* 10, 4, 4–13.

Jacobson, J.; Booch, G.; and Rumbaugh J. 1999. *The Unified Software Development Process.* Reading, MA: Addison-Wesley.

ORM. 2007. ORM—The Official Web Site for Conceptual Data Modeling. Available at www.orm.net (accessed September 2007).

Overmyer, S.; Lavoie, B.; and Rambow, O. 2001. Conceptual modeling through linguistic analysis using LIDA. *Proceedings of the Twenty-third International Conference on Software Engineering,* ICSE, Toronto, 401–410.

Pressman, R. 1997. *Software Engineering: A Practitioner's Approach.* New York, NY: McGraw-Hill.

Rayson, P.; Emmet, L.; Garside, R.; and Sawyer, P. 2000. The REVERE project: experiments with the application of probabilistic NLP to system engineering. *Proceedings of the Fifth International Conference on Applications of Natural Language to Information Systems,* Versailles, France, 288–300.

Rumbaugh, J.; Blaha, M.; Lorensen, W.; Eddy, F.; and Premerlani, W. 1990. *Object-Oriented Modeling and Design.* Englewood Cliffs, NJ: Prentice Hall.

White, I. 1994. *Using the Booch Method: A Rational Approach.* Redwood City, CA: Benjamin-Cummings.

Whitten, J. 1998. *Systems Analysis and Design Methods.* Boston, MA: Irwin/McGraw Hill.

Wirfs-Brock, R.; Wilkerson, B.; and Wiener, L. 1990. *Design Object-Oriented Software.* Englewood Cliffs, NJ: Prentice Hall International.

CHAPTER 10

SYSTEMATIC DERIVATION AND EVALUATION OF DOMAIN-SPECIFIC AND IMPLEMENTATION-INDEPENDENT SOFTWARE ARCHITECTURES

K. Suzanne Barber and Thomas Graser

Abstract: *Software architectures have been demonstrated to be effective representations for expressing system stakeholder concerns and prescribing software systems to satisfy those concerns. However, research is only beginning to emphasize systematic processes for deriving and evaluating those architectures from stakeholder requirements. The research described in this chapter offers a systematic process and a supporting tool, Reference Architecture Representation Environment (RARE), for deriving and evaluating a high-level software architecture, the Domain Reference Architecture (DRA), such that the resulting architecture reflects quality goals prioritized by the architect, including reusability, maintainability, performance, integrability, reliability, and comprehensibility. The DRA is an implementation-independent architecture composed of Domain Reference Architecture Classes (DRACs), each of which specifies some portion of domain data and functionality. Thus, the essential DRA derivation process consists of identifying DRACs and allocating domain data and functionality to those DRACs. While disciplines such as object-oriented analysis and design offer selective guidance for deriving class-based architectures, the current state of the art is largely ad hoc. The approach used in this research focuses on defining a deterministic transformation, such that for a given model of functional and data requirements and a prioritized set of architect quality goals, the derivation process yields a particular DRA structure, and the evaluation of that DRA with respect to quality goals is consistent.*

Keywords: *Software Architecture, Software Engineering*

INTRODUCTION

Software architectures have been used to represent a variety of concerns in the software development process, including requirements, domain-specific knowledge, implementation structure, and component connectivity (Bass, Clements, and Kazman, 1998; Tracz, 1995). To accommodate these concerns, a variety of architecture representations have been proposed (Clements, 1996). In an effort to promote large-scale reuse over time, one form of architecture, the "reference architecture," has proved to be particularly effective for prescribing a series of systems within a domain without constraining developers by current technology. The reference architecture is designed to describe anticipated system component functionality and relationships between those components without specifying implementation details (Gacek, 1995). Avoiding such details allows the architecture specification to be reused for multiple application instantiations over time as new and innovative technologies become available.

While there has been a definite trend toward utilizing all forms of software architecture (including reference architectures) as analysis frameworks during the development cycle, research has only recently emphasized formalizing the derivation and concurrent evaluation of these architectures (Bosch and Molin, 1999; Egyed, Gruenbacker, and Medvidovic, 2000). The objective of a formal derivation and evaluation process is to generate an architecture capable of fulfilling a variety of concerns expressed by stakeholders. These concerns may include exhibiting a particular behavior at runtime, performing acceptably on a particular piece of hardware, and being easy to customize. The architect translates these concerns into a series of system qualities, such as reusability, flexibility, performance, comprehensibility, maintainability, and reliability (Bass, Clements, and Kazman, 1998), and uses the software architecture as a framework for analyzing a potential system in the context of these qualities. Since an architecture is intended to prescribe a software system, the resulting system's ability to respond to these qualities is strongly impacted by decisions made during the architecture derivation process. However, given that inherent conflicts exist between system qualities (e.g., performance often opposes reliability), it is rare for a single architecture to be capable of satisfying all qualities effectively without some tradeoff (Bosch and Molin, 1999). Combining this observation with the realization that each architect tends to approach the derivation problem differently further underscores the need for capturing architect rationale as an essential part of the derivation process. Moreover, rationale must be supported by formal evaluation approaches to provide evidence that a given architecture adheres to qualities of interest (Perry and Wolf, 1992). The combined rationale and evaluation results become valuable artifacts complementary to the architecture itself, facilitating knowledge transfer and helping to ensure that the architecture evolves in the spirit intended by the original architect.

In response to the motivations above, the research described in this chapter focuses on devising a formal process and developing a supporting tool, Reference Architecture Representation Environment (RARE), to guide the system architect in deriving a high-level software architecture, the Domain Reference Architecture (DRA), designed to capture domain functional and data requirements intended to be domain-specific/technology-independent, and thus reusable across implementations within a domain.[1]

Software Architectures and Their Derivation and Evaluation

Every software system has an architecture, since every system can be shown to be composed of components and relations among those components (Bass, Clements, and Kazman, 1998; Jacobsen, Kristensen, and Nowack, 1999). In fact, a system may be described by *multiple* architectures, each providing a different perspective at a different level of abstraction. Depending on the content being conveyed by the architecture description, the semantics of a component and corresponding relations will be different. Figure 10.1 depicts two similarly appearing architectures using the "box and line" notation often seen in architecture diagrams (Barber, Graser, and Holt, 2001; Bass, Clements, and Kazman, 1998; Gujral, Ahn, and Barber, 2005; Shaw and Garlan, 1996). The "Domain Architecture" on the left captures domain modeling knowledge, where a component represents a class of task performers in the health care domain, each of which is responsible for selected domain tasks (Barber, Graser, and Holt, 2001). Component relations in this example describe data dependencies between performer classes. In the "Implementation Architecture," a component symbolizes a single machine with relations representing network connections among machines

Figure 10.1   **Sample Software Architectures: "Domain Architecture" vs. "Implementation Architecture"**

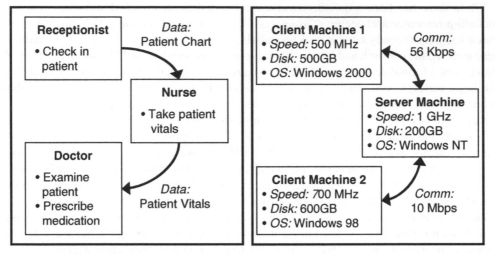

"Domain Architecture"
Describing roles, tasks
(functionality), and data exchange
in the health care domain

"Implementation Architecture"
Describing computing resource
specifications and their connectivity

(Barber, Graser, and Holt, 2001). Each architecture emphasizes particular types of information, while certain details are distilled away for clarity (Barber, Graser, and Holt, 2001).

Architectures at different levels may also be related. For each Domain Architecture conveying functionality from an implementation-independent point of view, there may be many associated Implementation Architectures that not only represent domain data and functionality but also consider specific implementation requirements and site installation constraints.

Taking into account all forms of software architectures, the software architecture derivation process can be generalized as (1) identifying *components* appropriate for a given level of abstraction, (2) describing their *properties*, and (3) determining their *relationships*, such that the resulting architecture prescribes a system that satisfies selected quality attributes.

Architectural qualities are typically grouped into major categories based on how they are ultimately measured. Bass and colleagues (1998) suggest four categories: (1) discernible at runtime, (2) not discernible at runtime, (3) business qualities, and (4) relevant to the architecture itself. Table 10.1 lists typical quality attributes along with their associated categories.

Regardless of when a quality attribute is measured (e.g., reliability and performance are observable only at runtime), the software architecture of a system can be structured in such a way as to promote or inhibit certain qualities (Bass, Clements, and Kazman, 1998; Kavi and Browne, 1999). Thus, the architect has the ability to tailor an architecture to act as a "blueprint" for building one or more systems that exhibit selected qualities.

Certainly, it would be optimal to achieve *all* of the attributes listed in Table 10.1. However, inherent tradeoffs exist between quality attributes, such that no quality can be maximized without sacrificing some other quality. Changes in architecture content or structure to improve a given quality often affect other qualities of interest (Bass, Clements, and Kazman, 1998; Kazman et al.,

Table 10.1

Typical Software Architecture Quality Attributes

Quality attribute	Description	Category
Reusability	Degree to which system's structure or some of its components can be reused	Not discernible at runtime
Integrability	Ability to make the separately developed components of the system work together	Not discernible at runtime
Maintainability	Ability to make changes quickly and cost effectively	Not discernible at runtime
Reliability	Ability of the system to keep operating over time	Discernible at runtime
Performance	Responsiveness of the system	Discernible at runtime
Cost	System development cost	Business quality
Comprehensibility	Ease by which architecture can be understood by stakeholders	Relevant to the architecture
Completeness	Scope of architecture content as a percentage of source documents	Relevant to the architecture
Correctness	Accuracy and consistency of content validated against source documents	Relevant to the architecture

Source: Bass, Clements, and Kazman (1998).

1998; Shaw and Garlan, 1996). For example, an architecture intended to emphasize reusability may be organized as small, cohesive modules. On the other hand, focusing on performance may suggest optimizing data flow between critical functions that might be separated in a more reusable architecture. Thus, the decision to colocate critical functions during architecture derivation may increase performance in systems built from the architecture blueprint at the expense of greater reusability of system modules.

To manage such tradeoffs while yielding an acceptable architecture, the derivation process must be capable of maximizing satisfaction of the architecture based on the priorities of competing quality attributes. As the architect makes decisions at each stage during the derivation process, choices must be made when conflicts arise. Because there are likely many possible architectures for a given set of constraints, the capture of rationale for such choices becomes an integral part of the architecture and the derivation process (Perry and Wolf, 1992).

Given the categories of quality attributes shown in Table 10.1, a variety of architecture evaluation methods have proved useful during the derivation process. Methods range from "static" approaches—such as (1) measuring properties of architecture and component structure (Li-Thiao-Te, Kennedy, and Owens, 1997), (2) rating an architecture based on its ability to support various scenarios (Kazman et al., 1994, 1998), and (3) subjectively judging an architecture with respect to specific attributes (Kalyanasundaram et al., 1998)—to "dynamic" approaches such as simulation of an architecture specification (Bose, 1999).

The objective of this research is to define a formal process to derive a high-level Domain Reference Architecture analogous to the "Domain Architecture" shown in Figure 10.1 from a computational Domain Model (DM) such that the resulting architecture prescribes systems exhibiting a prioritized set of quality attributes (Barber, Graser, and Holt, 2001; Graser, 2001). In the

Figure 10.2   **Domain Reference Architecture Class (DRAC) Representation**

DECLARATIVE MODEL (D-M)	BEHAVIORAL MODEL (B-M)
Attributes	State Chart
Name: Name of attribute Type: Data type of attribute Cardinality: Attribute data cardinality Value constraints: Expression	States: High-level states Transitions: High-level transitions Events: Transition-enabling events Guards: Transition-enabling guards
Services	**INTEGRATION MODEL (I-M)**

Name: Name of service
Preconditions: Expression
Postconditions: Expression
<u>Input Events</u>
    Received from DRAC service
<u>Input Data</u>
    Received from DRAC service
<u>Output Events</u>
    Sent to DRAC service(s)
<u>Output Data</u>
    Sent to DRAC service(s)
	Subsystem Dependencies

	DRACs: Elements of subsystem
	Service Dependencies
	DRAC Services: Required events and data generated by other DRACs
	Attribute Dependencies
	DRAC Attributes: Required attributes from other DRACs

context of this research, a "formal" process can be considered to be one that is "explicitly defined and repeatable" (Merriam-Webster, 2005). This is in contrast to existing approaches for software architecture derivation from requirements, which are essentially ad hoc.

The Domain Reference Architecture

The DRA is composed of Domain Reference Architecture Classes (DRACs), each of which specifies some portion of domain data and functionality (Barber et al., 2000; Graser, 2001). These classes and their relationships become a reusable blueprint that guides subsequent development efforts in terms of:

1. *Functional, data, and timing requirements*—the domain functions, data, and ordering of functions to be satisfied, and
2. *Prescribed architectural structure*—the relationships between DRACs that dictate the relationships between participating applications implementing those DRACs.

Since it is likely that DRACs will be instantiated by different implementation solutions each time the blueprint is reused for a new system development effort (e.g., computer programs, hardware devices, personnel), the DRA representation is designed to be highly implementation independent.

The functionality and data allocated to a DRAC and the relationships between a DRAC and other DRACs are represented in the three submodels shown in Figure 10.2: the *Declarative Model (DRAC D-M)* defines the attributes (i.e., data and events) and services (i.e., functionality) that

Figure 10.3   **Domain Reference Architecture Derivation Positioned Among System Development Activities**

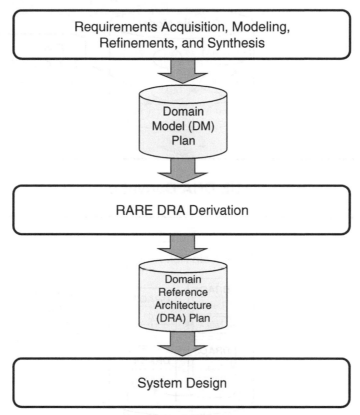

should be offered by an instance of the DRAC specification; the *Behavioral Model (DRAC B-M)* describes the behavior expected from an instance of the DRAC through a high-level state chart; and the *Integration Model (DRAC I-M)* defines the constraints and dependencies between DRAC instances resulting from the distribution of dependent domain functions across DRACs. These dependencies are based on the input and output of data and events as well as the clustering of classes into subsystems to represent domain functionality typically colocated.

The next section provides a detailed explanation of the DRA derivation process, followed by a discussion of related work and the benefits and limitations of RARE and the DRA in the context of a standard software engineering process. The chapter then concludes with summary remarks and future work.

DERIVING THE DOMAIN REFERENCE ARCHITECTURE USING THE REFERENCE ARCHITECTURE REPRESENTATION ENVIRONMENT

The RARE DRA derivation process is positioned among phases associated with typical software engineering methodologies as shown in Figure 10.3 (Barber, 2004; Barber and Graser, 2000a, 2000b; Barber, Graser, and Jernigan, 1999; Barber et al., 1999; Graser, 2001). DRA derivation follows requirements acquisition, modeling, refinement, and synthesis activities that yield a DM,

Figure 10.4   **DRA Derivation as a Transformation from a Functional Representation to a Class-Based Representation**

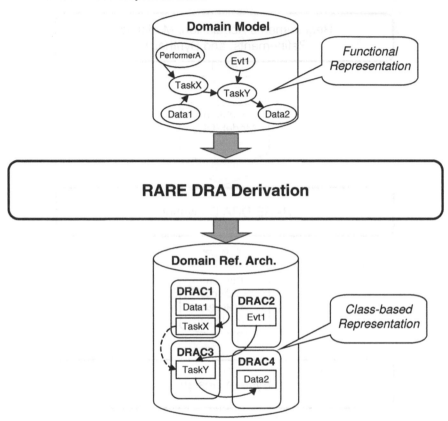

a computational representation of Domain Requirements. The resulting DRA becomes input to system design activities when technology-related decisions are made with respect to implementation of selected functionality in the DRA.

As a product of requirements acquisition, modeling, and refinement activities, the DM provides RARE with a single, computational requirements specification. RARE then guides the architect in restructuring DM information by defining a collection of DRACs to which domain functionality and data are assigned.

Figure 10.4 summarizes the transformation from the DM to the DRA. The DM representation is designed to accommodate requirements capture, synthesis, and verification. Specifically, the DM is a "functional" model centered around domain tasks and their relationships, often the focal point of requirements acquisition sessions with domain experts. However, the DRA is designed to act as a developer and integrator specification, where DRACs encapsulate domain requirements to be satisfied by applications. Since the DM is the primary source for DRA content, the transformation should be lossless, resulting in direct traceability from DRA model elements (e.g., classes, data, events, tasks) back to DM model elements.

While the DRA does not incorporate any additional domain requirements, the DRA derivation process is nonetheless considerably complex due to the many possible configurations when defining

DRACs and allocating data and functionality to those DRACs. Since these allocation decisions are driven by quality goals prioritized by the architect (reusability, integrability, maintainability, reliability, performance, and comprehensibility), the resulting DRA *also* suggests a structure (topology) that reflects given qualities. An important premise of this work is that designs satisfying DRA content requirements (i.e., domain functionality and data) and adhering to the DRA topology will likewise exhibit the qualities possessed by the DRA. In summary, the DRA specifies two forms of requirements to be satisfied by new or existing applications:

1. *Content Requirements:* the collections of data and functionality in DRACs to be provided by an application, and
2. *Topology Requirements:* the integration requirements specified in the DRAC I-M that describe dependencies between DRACs, and therefore dependencies between respective applications implementing those DRACs.

The complexity of the allocation process is rooted in a number of issues. These issues are described below.

How should derivation proceed to create an architecture exhibiting selected qualities?

Given that different architectures are appropriate for different systems and domains, not all architects emphasize the same quality attributes, and the architecture may take on different forms depending upon which quality attributes are emphasized. One architect may hold the opinion that reusability should be the primary driver for class definition, while another may place greater emphasis on the comprehensibility of the overall class model.

How should conflicts between qualities be managed?

While it would be ideal to create an architecture capable of maximizing all qualities of interest, inherent conflicts exist between qualities, making this infeasible. For example, while both reusability and performance may be important to the architect, the optimal set of reusable classes may look completely different from the optimal set of classes resulting from an emphasis on performance, and resolutions/tradeoffs made by respective architects can/will differ (Bosch and Molin, 1999). The architect must manage these conflicts, making tradeoffs as necessary. Certainly, emphasizing one quality over another is one consideration when resolving such conflicts. In attempting to resolve these conflicts, the architect may benefit from exploring multiple possible architectural structures.

How can the architecture be evaluated with respect to the qualities selected, and how does the architect know when quality goals have been achieved?

Certainly, if the architect intends to emphasize particular qualities, there must be some means for evaluating the architecture with respect to these qualities. While intuition may often drive architecture derivation, an intuitive approach is unable to provide evidence that qualities are being met and that systems generated from the architecture will exhibit those qualities. To improve upon an intuitive approach, quantitative evaluation is necessary to justify the architect's decisions. As with any software engineering process, architecture derivation cannot be improved without a measurement mechanism to provide feedback to the architect (Basili, Briand, and Melo, 1996).

While there are various metrics related to architectural structure that are easily computed (e.g., number of classes, number of services per class, degree of coupling), evaluating with respect to high-level qualities such as reusability and maintainability is not so straightforward. The challenge is to establish explicit correlation between specified qualities and measurable characteristics of derived architectures. Such a correlation will also help determine the contribution of individual DRA elements to the satisfaction of specific quality attributes.

By combining features such as derivation heuristics, conflict management, formal evaluation, and rationale and process capture, the RARE process has evolved architecture derivation from an ad hoc activity to a deterministic process. Nonetheless, it is unrealistic to expect that such a process can fully automate architecture derivation. Even with such support, derivation remains an iterative, exploratory process, where architect involvement is essential. The RARE process is designed to reduce the burden of managing information during iterative derivation, yet allow the architect to contribute where automation is not suitable.

The following subsections elaborate on the RARE derivation approach, addressing the steps in the formal derivation process, the supporting representations that drive derivation based on the qualities selected by the architect, conflict detection and resolution, and methods for evaluating the architecture with respect to selected qualities using relevant metrics.

RARE Formal DRA Derivation Process

Architecture derivation is an iterative process analogous to a guided search of the space of possible architectures for a given DM. The search begins with a complete Domain Model and an empty DRA. The search space represents (1) the degree to which the DRA covers the information represented in the DM and (2) the many possible structuring options available to the architect given a particular set of desired quality goals. A search path represents a sequence of derivation iterations, where each DRA version builds upon the one produced in the previous iteration.

The detailed steps involved in DRA derivation are shown in Figure 10.5. The process is divided into two phases: (1) *Plan-Generation*—when goal priorities are assigned and a "Derivation Plan" is generated and (2) *Plan-Execution*—when strategies in the plan are applied and the resulting DRA is evaluated with architect oversight. Figure 10.5 outlines the steps associated with each phase in a process flow diagram. Boxes in Figure 10.5 symbolize processes, black arrows represent process flow, and gray arrows indicate data flow. The diagram distinguishes between processes associated with Plan-Generation and those related to Plan-Execution. Font styles in the process boxes indicate performer: italics—the architect; underlined—RARE; both italics and underlined— a joint process between the architect and RARE. The following section describes the two phases and their constituent processes.

DRA Plan-Generation

During DRA Plan-Generation, the architect selects and prioritizes goals from the RARE knowledge base (KB) (described in a subsequent section). From the prioritized goals, RARE builds the Derivation-Plan and subsequently prunes conflicting strategies. The processes in this phase (see Figure 10.5) are described below:

1. *Select and Prioritize Goals Based on Qualities Identified (performed by the architect):* From the goals available in the RARE KB, the architect selects and prioritizes a set of

Figure 10.5   **RARE Derivation and Evaluation Process Flow**

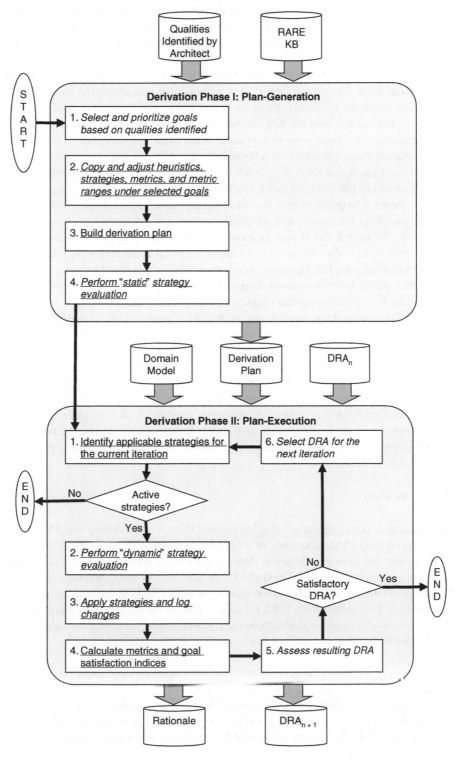

goals to derive a particular DRA. The goals selected will be accompanied by corresponding heuristics (guidance on satisfying goals), metrics (means for measuring characteristics related to heuristics), and strategies (approaches for achieving heuristics).

2. *Copy and Adjust Heuristics, Strategies, Metrics, and Metric Ranges under Selected Goals (performed jointly by RARE and the architect):* Following selection and prioritization of goals, RARE copies the goals and corresponding heuristics, strategies, and metrics to a working set of "Derivation Goals" that will become part of the Derivation Plan. While it is not necessary to modify the heuristics, metrics, and strategies under a selected goal after being copied from the KB, the architect has the option to prune heuristics, adjust heuristic weights, prune strategies, prune metrics, adjust metric weights, and change metric acceptance range values. Such adjustments allow the architect to tailor the plan when deriving a particular DRA. For example, the architect may want to define subsystems (collections of DRACs) manually, and thus would want to remove strategies for creating subsystems. The architect may also modify acceptable metric ranges, since the tolerance for a metric in the context of a particular project (e.g., "Number of services in DRAC" must be between 2 and 8) may be more or less than the range defined in the KB.

    In most cases, the architect (particularly a novice architect) would accept the guidance offered by the KB. However, given the ability to massage heuristics, strategies, and metrics, a company may choose to install its own guidelines or an architect may decide to customize to accommodate project-specific exceptions.

3. *Build Derivation Plan (performed by RARE):* From the set of goals and associated heuristics, metrics, and strategies selected by the architect, RARE builds a Derivation Plan, a sequence of steps that determines when selected strategies can be applied during derivation.

4. *Perform "Static" Strategy Evaluation (performed jointly by RARE and the architect):* Strategies assigned to the Derivation Plan may conflict based on conflict declarations in each strategy definition. When two strategies conflict, RARE suggests that the strategy associated with the lower priority goal and/or lower weight heuristic be pruned from the Derivation Plan. The resulting set of pruned and nonpruned strategies is presented to the architect for review.

DRA Plan-Execution

The Plan-Execution phase processes the Derivation Plan created during the Plan-Generation phase by stepping through the sequence of strategies in the plan in an iterative fashion. During each iteration, relevant strategies from the Derivation Plan are applied and associated metrics are calculated. Following strategy application and metric calculation, the architect reviews the resulting DRA and evaluation results against metrics to determine if the DRA is satisfactory or requires further refinement. Evaluation of the DRA is based in part on the value of goal satisfaction indices calculated from low-level metrics. Refinement can continue as long as unexecuted strategies remain in the Derivation Plan. The processes in this phase (see Figure 10.5) are:

1. *Identify Applicable Strategies for the Current Iteration (performed by RARE):* For the current step in the Derivation Plan, determine whether any strategy preconditions are satisfied based on the input architecture, DRA_n. Active strategies are added to a pending execution list. If no strategies in the current plan step are active, the subsequent step is examined. If no more steps are available, the derivation process ends.

2. *Perform "Dynamic" Strategy Evaluation (performed jointly by RARE and the architect):* Some problems cannot be detected during "static" detection and resolution during Plan-Generation. In particular, if the same sequence of strategies continues to be executed over a series of iterations, the derivation process may cease to make progress. RARE compares the set of pending strategies with a "strategy log" to determine whether such "looping" is taking place and suggests strategy pruning when appropriate. As with static conflict detection and resolution, the architect is given the opportunity to review the set of suggested strategies and finalize the strategies to be executed.

3. *Apply Strategies and Log Changes (performed jointly by RARE and the architect):* RARE executes the set of strategies approved by the architect. Each strategy generates a series of low-level architecture transformation actions (e.g., "Add Class X"). The architect reviews the actions to be applied and changes parameters as desired (e.g., "Add Class Y" instead of "Add Class X"). All strategies and actions are logged as part of rationale capture.

4. *Calculate Metrics and Goal Satisfaction Indices (performed by RARE):* RARE calculates the metrics associated with all selected goals and computes corresponding goal satisfaction indices.

5. *Assess Resulting DRA (performed by the architect):* The architect reviews the new DRA version (DRA_{n+1}) along with associated metric values and goal satisfaction indices. The architect has the option of ending derivation with the current DRA version or continuing the derivation process.

6. *Select DRA for the Next Iteration (performed by the architect):* If the architect opts to continue the derivation process, a prior DRA version must be selected for further refinement in the next iteration (i.e., the next DRA_n). The DRA selected may be the version produced from the current iteration or one generated in a prior iteration. The process then continues with step 1 above, *Identify Applicable Strategies for the Current Iteration.*

The phases of the derivation process are guided by content in the RARE KB and the generated Derivation Plan. The following section defines the KB and describes how the architect expresses desired qualities using the Derivation Plan.

Guiding Derivation through the Knowledge Base and the Derivation Plan

Since different qualities can result in different architectures, the structure of the DRA derived reflects the qualities emphasized. The KB captures the expertise for deriving an architecture in light of a particular quality, while the Derivation Plan allows the architect to express the qualities desired for a given architecture. The discussion begins by describing the fundamental elements of the KB and the Derivation Plan: goals, heuristics, strategies, and metrics.

Since attributes such as maintainability, reusability, integrability, performance, comprehensibility, and reliability describe overall architectural qualities, their presence is not easily verified by direct observation. On the other hand, low-level architecture characteristics (e.g., class size, depth of inheritance tree, class coupling) that are easily measured do not always have a direct relationship to the high-level architectural qualities. In fact, there is often a many-to-many relationship between the high-level qualities and the low-level characteristics, such that no single metric provides conclusive evidence that a quality attribute has been satisfied.

RARE attempts to bridge this gap by correlating high-level architectural quality attributes, or *goals*, with low-level characteristics, or *metrics*, through *heuristics* and *strategies* (Figure 10.6). Each of these elements can be described as follows:

Figure 10.6   **Relationships Between RARE Goals, Heuristics, Strategies, and Meta-strategies**

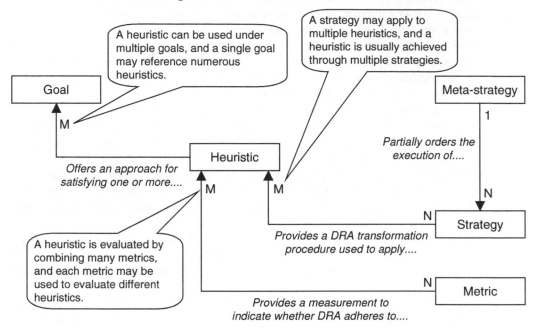

Heuristic

A "rule of thumb" compiled from expert experience on past projects that assists the architect in making rational decisions when defining DRACs. For example, a well-known object-oriented heuristic recommends reducing coupling among classes to encourage reuse (Riel, 1996). An architectural goal associated with a given quality (e.g., reusability) is typically associated with multiple heuristics.

Strategy

An architecture transformation procedure (sequence of actions) used to apply a given heuristic. Following the "reduce coupling" example, a strategy might explicitly state, "move service S1 from DRAC D1 to DRAC D2" to eliminate the need to exchange data between DRACs D1 and D2. More than one strategy may contribute to a heuristic, and a strategy may apply to more than one heuristic. A strategy becomes "active" (i.e., may be applied by the architect) when specific preconditions encoded in the strategy evaluate to true. These preconditions are based on particular metric values or conditions in the architecture. For example, the "reduce coupling" strategy may be triggered by an unsatisfactory value for "Degree of Coupling," a metric used as a measure of DRAC-to-DRAC coupling.

Metric

A measurement of a particular architecture characteristic that provides an indication as to whether the architect adhered to a given heuristic. Continuing with the previous example, the DRAC in-

Figure 10.7   **Using Meta-strategies to Enforce a High-level Order for Derivation**

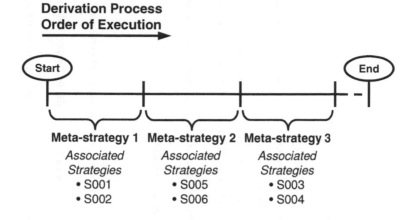

heritance hierarchy and/or number of data/event dependencies passed between DRACs (e.g., one service in one DRAC required as input data held by another DRAC) provide some evidence as to the degree of coupling in the DRA (Rosenberg and Hyatt, 1997). Typically, multiple metrics are used in combination to evaluate an architecture in the context of a heuristic and its parent goal.

Meta-strategy

Meta-strategies establish a high-level order for the derivation process and determine when a strategy is applicable during derivation. The derivation process executes only one meta-strategy at a time, and only strategies associated with the active meta-strategy may be executed. Figure 10.7 illustrates this relationship. Each Derivation Plan Entry in a Derivation Plan is associated with a meta-strategy (Meta-strategy 1–3 in Figure 10.7). The derivation process begins by executing Meta-strategy 1, during which only strategies S001 and S002 can be applied. Meta-strategy 1 completes when neither S001 nor S002 becomes active (i.e., each strategy has respective preconditions that must evaluate to true for the strategy to be selectable), and derivation proceeds with Meta-strategy 2, during which strategies S005 and S006 may be applied. The process continues until no more meta-strategies are available for execution. One portion of the derivation process that relies on the order enforced by meta-strategies is subsystem definition. Based on experiences deriving DRAs manually, it is recommended that functional and data allocation be completed before defining subsystems (Barber, 2004). RARE enforces this order through meta-strategies that ensure allocation strategies are executed prior to subsystem definition strategies.

Table 10.2 illustrates a sample set of goals, heuristics, and strategies represented in the RARE KB. The quality goals depicted have been prioritized based on an architect's understanding of the needs of a particular architecture: *Priority 1:* "Reusability," *Priority 2:* "Performance," *Priority 3:* "Comprehensibility," and *Priority 4:* "Maintainability." Examining the "Reusability" goal more closely, four contributing heuristics have been defined, each associated with corresponding strategies. Metrics applicable to the "Reduce class coupling . . ." heuristic may include familiar object-oriented metrics such as "Coupling Between Objects" and "Degree of Cohesion" (Chidamber and Kemerer, 1991; Rosenburg and Hyatt, 1997). Since strategies and metrics may apply to more than one heuristic under more than one goal, the "Redistribute services . . ." strategy is an

Table 10.2

Sample Set of RARE KB Goals, Heuristics, Strategies, and Metrics

Priority	Goal	Heuristics	Strategy
1	Reusability	Increase possibilities for reuse by encouraging inheritance and factoring services.	Create parent classes based on domain model performer hierarchies.
			Define new parent classes to reduce coupling.
		Create more finely granular classes so that applications will be better candidates for reuse.	Split classes dependent on a significant number of other classes.
			Split classes to increase cohesion.
			Split classes to reduce total number of inputs and outputs.
		Reduce class coupling and increase cohesion to increase application independence.	Redistribute services to reduce input/output dependencies between classes.
			Redistribute attributes to reduce input/output dependencies between classes.
			Consolidate classes to reduce coupling.
		Create self-sufficient subsystems comprised of strongly coupled classes.	Collect classes into subsystems.
2	Performance	Create classes based on suggested architecture style to increase performance.	Apply client/server style to accommodate highly used services/attributes.
		Reduce I/O performance bottlenecks by reducing message passing between applications.	Redistribute services to reduce input/output dependencies between classes.
			Redistribute attributes to reduce input/output dependencies between classes.
			Consolidate classes to reduce coupling.

Priority	Goal	Heuristics	Strategy
3	Comprehensibility	Improve architecture readability by reducing architecture, class, and service complexity.	Split classes dependent on a significant number of other classes.
			Split classes to increase cohesion.
			Split classes to reduce total number of inputs and outputs.
		Enhance architecture understandability by aligning classes with task performer roles.	Ensure classes are created corresponding to all domain task performers.
4	Maintainability	Reduce class size to facility application extensibility.	Split classes dependent on a significant number of other classes.
			Split classes to increase cohesion.
			Split classes to reduce total number of inputs and outputs.
		Reduce class coupling since highly interconnected applications may complicate maintenance.	Redistribute services to reduce input/output dependencies between classes.
			Redistribute attributes to reduce input/output dependencies between classes.
			Consolidate classes to reduce coupling.
		Reduce architecture size to facility maintenance.	Collect classes into subsystems.

appropriate technique for both reducing coupling under the "Reduce class coupling . . ." heuristic and reducing message passing under the "Reduce I/O performance bottlenecks . . ." heuristic. Strategies may be triggered based on the stage of the DRA during the derivation process. For example, "Collect classes into subsystems" may be executed after DRACs have been defined and functionality allocated. Strategies are also triggered by certain structural arrangements detected in the DRA, based on the value of related metrics. For example, "Redistribute services . . ." under the "Reduce class coupling . . ." heuristic could be triggered, in part, by an unsatisfactory value for metric "Coupling Between Objects."

To express the intentions for a particular architecture being derived, the architect selects and prioritizes goals from the RARE KB prior to initiation of the derivation process (step 1 in the Plan-Generation phase Figure 10.5). To enable customization, the architect is provided with a working copy of the goals selected and may modify any portion of the associated heuristics, metrics, or strategies. Modifications may include (step 2 in the Plan-Generation phase Figure 10.5):

- pruning heuristics,
- adjusting heuristic weights,
- pruning metrics,
- adjusting metric weights,
- adjusting acceptable ranges for metric values, and
- pruning strategies.

Managing Strategy Conflicts and Identifying Potential Strategy Problems During Derivation

Given that there are often inherent conflicts leading to tradeoffs between high-level architectural quality attributes, conflicts will naturally arise between suggested architectural transformations during the derivation process. While it is not uncommon for multiple strategies to be suggested during a particular stage of derivation (i.e., during a Derivation Plan Entry), a conflict arises when the projected effects of different strategies will likely drive the derivation process into opposing directions or stagnate the derivation progress altogether. For example, a strategy associated with one goal may suggest combining services into a single class, while another strategy may become active that suggests further dividing the existing classes into smaller classes.

During Plan-Generation, RARE detects conflicts based on explicit strategy-to-strategy conflict declarations in strategy definitions. Regardless of the rationale for selecting a particular strategy for a given heuristic, the strategy itself describes a deterministic transformation of the DRA's structure and content (e.g., combining classes, splitting classes, allocating functionality, allocating data); therefore, conflicts can be explicitly encoded at the strategy level because it is readily apparent that two strategy transformations will likely interfere with each other (e.g., combining DRACs vs. splitting DRACs). Nonetheless, due to the relationship between strategies and their associated heuristics and goals, such strategy conflicts also suggest conflicts between respective goals and heuristics. Correspondingly, RARE attempts to resolve these conflicts during "static strategy evaluation" by suggesting to the architect that selected strategies be pruned based on their associated goal priorities and heuristic weights.

After RARE generates a Derivation Plan based on the goal priorities and heuristic weights set by the architect, it is highly likely that conflicts will exist between strategies based on the conflict declarations in each strategy. RARE resolves strategy conflicts by suggesting that certain strategies be pruned, retaining only strategies with higher priorities (i.e., where strategy priority is a function

Figure 10.8   **"Static" Conflict Resolution During Plan Generation**

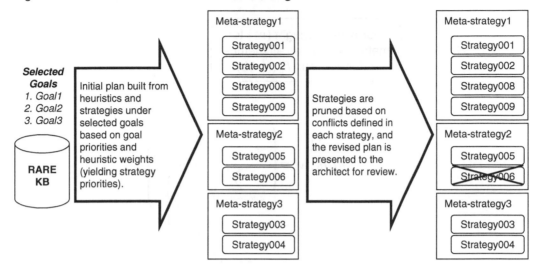

of goal priority and heuristic weight). At the termination of Plan-Generation, the Derivation Plan is presented to the architect for review prior to Plan-Execution.

Figure 10.8 shows an example of this process. The architect selects three goals from the KB, prioritized as *Goal1*, *Goal2*, and *Goal3*. RARE builds an initial derivation plan from the heuristics and strategies under the selected goals, taking into account the goal priorities and associated heuristic weights to calculate strategy priorities. The resulting plan in Figure 10.8 is composed of three meta-strategies with respective prioritized strategies. If the strategy definitions in the KB indicate that *Strategy005* conflicts with *Strategy006*, RARE suggests that *Strategy006* be pruned, since *Strategy005* has a higher priority in the derivation plan. The revised plan is presented to the architect for final review.

The following section discusses the RARE approach for DRA evaluation with respect to selected quality goals.

Formally Evaluating the DRA with Respect to Quality Goals

In RARE, metrics defined under heuristics have two functions: (1) to evaluate the current state of the architecture with respect to achieving respective goals and heuristics (i.e., "how good is the DRA?" and "is DRA derivation complete?") and (2) to provide direction as to how derivation should proceed to more fully satisfy quality goals (i.e., "what transformations are suggested to improve the DRA?"). To support these decisions, the RARE tool must be able to determine whether a metric value is acceptable, and if not acceptable, in which direction it deviates and how severe the deviation is. Since it is highly unlikely that a single, desired value can be achieved for every metric under consideration, defining an "acceptable range" and a set of "deviation ranges" is more practical (e.g., "highly deviated," "slightly deviated," and "acceptable" ranges). Furthermore, while a metric can apply to more than one heuristic, what may be considered an acceptable value under one heuristic may not be acceptable under another. Thus, when evaluating the current state of the architecture with respect to quality goals, it is the degree of deviation, rather than the metric value itself, that contributes to overall goal evaluation. In addition, some metrics are better

Figure 10.9   **Calculating Normalized Metric Weight Under a Heuristic**

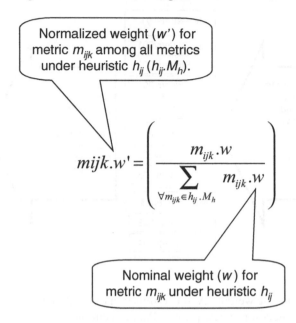

Normalized weight (w') for metric m_{ijk} among all metrics under heuristic h_{ij} ($h_{ij}.M_h$).

$$mijk.w' = \left(\frac{m_{ijk}.w}{\displaystyle\sum_{\forall m_{ijk} \in h_{ij}.M_h} m_{ijk}.w} \right)$$

Nominal weight (w) for metric m_{ijk} under heuristic h_{ij}

indicators than others regarding how well a quality goal has been achieved. To reflect this, a metric weighting can be assigned that indicates how well the metric is able to predict a given goal. For example, metrics such as "coupling between objects" and "degree of cohesion" are often suggested as independence indicators linked to reusability (Lorenz and Kidd, 1994; Morris, 1989). Assuming that reducing coupling is considered to be a strongly recommended heuristic to improve chances for reusability, these metrics would be assigned a higher weight. Weights are relative among all metrics under a heuristic, such that a metric value's contribution is determined by the proportion of its weight to the sum of all weights under the heuristic (Figure 10.9).

In addition to providing a foundation for quantitative evaluation of the reference architecture with respect to quality goals, metrics also help guide the derivation process. Through assigned deviation ranges, RARE becomes aware not only that a metric value is not within an acceptable range but also how severely it is askew from that range. To refine the architecture accordingly, specific strategies become activated from the Derivation Plan based on the metric and the metric deviation value, leading to corresponding changes to the DRA content and structure (only strategies belonging to the Derivation Plan are considered for execution since only those strategies are associated with selected quality goals). For example, to significantly reduce the average class coupling in the architecture, one strategy may suggest combining classes, thereby affecting not only architecture coupling, but other factors as well, such as the total number of classes in the architecture. A more subtle approach may suggest rearranging services among the existing classes. The former strategy may be selected when a particular coupling-related metric is two deviations from being acceptable, while the latter strategy may be suggested with only one deviation. In summary, one strategy is selected over another based on the impact it has on metric values and thereby associated heuristics and goals.

The evaluation process (step 4 of the Plan-Execution phase) is represented by the formula depicted in Figure 10.10, where σ_g represents the resulting goal satisfaction index for goal g_i

Figure 10.10 **Goal Satisfaction Calculation**

$$\sigma_{g_i \in G_{Deriv}} = \frac{1}{W_i} \sum_{\forall h_{ij} \in g_i.H_{g_i}} h_{ij}.w \left[\frac{1}{W_{ij}} \sum_{\forall m_{ijk} \in h_{ij}.M_{h_{ij}}} (m_{ijk}.w)(performance(m_{ijk})) \right]$$

G_{Deriv}	Sequence of "Derivation Goals" selected and prioritized by the architect and represented in the Derivation Plan
$g_i \in G_{Deriv}$	Goal with priority i among goals selected by the architect, where g_1 is the highest priority goal
$h_{ij} \in H_{g_{ij}}$	Heuristic j belonging to the set of heuristics associated with goal g_i
$m_{ijk} \in M_{h_{ij}}$	Metric k belonging to the set of metrics related to heuristic h_{ij} under goal g_i
σ_{g_i} :float | $0.0 \le \sigma_{g_i} \le 10.0$	satisfaction of quality goal g_i
$h_{ij}. w$: float	weight of heuristic h_{ij} under goal g_i, where $W_i = \sum_{\forall h_{ij} \in g_i.H_{g_i}} h_{ij}.w$ is the sum of all heuristic weights under g_i
$m_{ijk}. w$: float	weight of metric m_{ijk} under heuristic h_{ij}, where $W_{ij} = \sum_{\forall m_{ijk} \in h_{ij}.M_{h_{ij}}} m_{ijk}.w$ is the sum of all metric weights under h_{ij}
$performance(m_{ijk}) \rightarrow$ $\{0.0, 2.5, 5.0, 10.0\}$	normalized performance value for metric m_{ijk} under heuristic h_{ij}*

*See Figure 10.11.

selected by the architect.[2] The goal satisfaction index is a value between 0 and 10 that is computed via a weighted average of heuristic "performance" values, calculated using each heuristic weight $h_{ij}.w$ and the corresponding weighted average of metric performance values under the heuristic. The weighted average metric performance values are computed using metric weights $m_{ijk}.w$ and a performance value for the respective metric, $performance(m_{ijk})$. A goal satisfaction index value of 0 symbolizes that no metrics associated with the goal are within an acceptable range. A satisfaction value of 10 indicates that the values for all related metrics fell within an acceptable range. The metric performance value calculation is presented in Figure 10.11 and discussed below.

Each metric m_{ijk} under a heuristic h_{ij} yields a normalized performance value, $performance(m_{ijk})$, of 0.0, 2.5, 5.0, or 10.0 (Figure 10.11). These values correspond to the qualitative notions of "acceptable," "near acceptable," "somewhat acceptable," and "unacceptable." The "acceptable," "near acceptable," and "unacceptable" assessments were chosen based on the "safe," "flag," and "alarm" ranges suggested in Henderson-Sellers (1996). Dividing the range 0 to 10 among these assessments resulted in assignments of 10.0, 5.0, and 0.0, respectively. However, during experimentation it was determined that the cut-off between "near acceptable" (5.0) and "unacceptable" (0.0) was too sharp, justifying an interim value of 2.5. The effectiveness of these ranges will be explored by future work.

A metric performance value is based on where the metric value falls with respect to the acceptable value ranges defined for the metric under the heuristic (ranges defined by $m_{ijk}.ld2$, $m_{ijk}.ld1$, $m_{ijk}.ld0$, $m_{ijk}.rd0$, $m_{ijk}.rd1$, and $m_{ijk}.rd2$). Since this comparison requires a single scalar value, metrics computed against DRA elements other than the DRA itself must be aggregated into a single value, a_{ijk}, and the aggregation method is defined by $m_{ijk}.sumRule$ as "minimum," "maximum," or "average." For example, if "DRAC Coupling" is calculated for every DRAC in the DRA, a set of values (V_{ijk}) is produced. After applying the $sumRule$ associated with "DRAC Coupling" to the

Figure 10.11 **Metric Performance Calculation**

$performance : HeurMetric \rightarrow \{0.0,2.5,5.0,10.0\}$

$performance : HeurMetric \rightarrow \{0.0,2.5,5.0,10.0\}$

normalized performance value based on acceptable ranges and a summarized value for a metric under a heuristic.

$$performance(m_h) = \begin{cases} 10.0, & \text{if } m_{ijk}.ld0 \leq a_{ijk} \leq m_{ijk}.rd0 \\ 5.0, & \text{if } m_{ijk}.ld1 \leq a_{ijk} \leq m_{ijk}.rd1 \\ 2.5, & \text{if } m_{ijk}.ld2 \leq a_{ijk} \leq m_{ijk}.rd2 \\ 0,0, & \text{if } a_{ijk} < m_{ijk}.ld2 \text{ or } a_{ijk} > m_{ijk}.rd2 \end{cases}$$

$a_{ijk} : float$ aggregate value of metric value set V_{ijk} for metric m_{ijk} based on summarization rule $m_{ijk}.sumRule$
if $m_{ijk}.sumRule$ = MIN then a_{ijk} = min(V_{ijk})
if $m_{ijk}.sumRule$ = MAX then a_{ijk} = max(V_{ijk})
if $m_{ijk}.sumRule$ = AVG then a_{ijk} = avg(V_{ijk})

$V_{ijk} : \{v_{ijk} : float\}$ set of values produced by calculating metric m_{ijk} for every relevant element in the DRA, whether that be (1) the DRA, (2) every DRAC, (3) every attribute, (4) every service, or (5) every subsystem.
If $m_{ijk}.m.scope$ = DRA then
$$V_{ijk} = \{v_{ijk} : float \bullet v_{ijk} = m_{ijk}.m.calc(DRA)\}$$
If $m_{ijk}.m.scope$ = DRAC then
$$V_{ijk} = \{v_{ijk} : float \bullet \forall d : DRAC \mid d \in DRA \bullet v_{ijk} = m_{ijk}.m.calc(d)\}$$
If $m_{ijk}.m.scope$ = SVC then
$$V_{ijk} = \{v_{ijk} : float \bullet \forall s : Svc \mid s \in DRA \bullet v_{ijk} = m_{ijk}.m.calc(s)\}$$
If $m_{ijk}.m.scope$ = ATTR then
$$V_{ijk} = \{v_{ijk} : float \bullet \forall a : Attr \mid a \in DRA \bullet v_{ijk} = m_{ijk}.m.calc(a)\}$$
If $m_{ijk}.m.scope$ = SUBSYS then
$$V_{ijk} = \{v_{ijk} : float \bullet \forall b : Ssubsys \mid b \in DRA \bullet v_{ijk} = m_{ijk}.m.calc(b)\}$$

set V_{ijk}, the resulting value is compared to the respective acceptable ranges to yield a performance value of 0, 2.5, 5.0, or 10.0. In summary, a metric contributes to the evaluation of the architecture with respect to a particular goal based on (1) the metric's current value; (2) the rule for aggregating the metric to the DRA level if the metric is calculated based on characteristics of DRACs, subsystems, services, or attributes (e.g., "Coupling Between Objects" is calculated for each class in the DRA and the average, maximum, or minimum is used across all classes); (3) the acceptable ranges defined by the architect; and (4) the weight of that metric.

Ranges for well-known metrics in the RARE knowledge base were initialized based on suggestions from the literature (Lorenz and Kidd, 1994; Rosenburg and Hyatt, 1997). Other metrics are unique to the RARE process, and initial values were determined from experiences applying this process manually (Barber, 2004). These values can be adjusted by the architect in the KB and in the Derivation Plan. Modifying a Derivation Plan affects only the respective architecture being derived, while adjusting KB values will be reflected in each Derivation Plan created from the KB. As RARE has been applied to various example domains (Barber and Graser, 2001; DARPA, 2000), empirical observations have resulted in fine-tuning adjustments to the deviation ranges. In particular, initial acceptable ranges may have proved too narrow, such that achieving such a range was unrealistic. For example, assume an acceptable "Degree of Coupling" is defined to be less than 5. Thus, if the architecture exhibited a "Degree of Coupling" greater than 5, RARE strategies would be activated to refine the architecture. However, by achieving a "Degree of Coupling" less than 5, it may significantly alter the value of another metric, such as "DRAC Size," that it is no longer in an acceptable range. Thus, such tight constraints may mandate continued refinement without ever being able to achieve some equilibrium state for the architecture.

RELATED WORK

This section highlights related work in software architecture evaluation methods and object-oriented analysis and design as related to software architecture derivation and evaluation.

Software Architecture Evaluation

Approaches for software architecture evaluation cover a broad spectrum. On the one hand, evaluation approaches can be classified based on the qualities they emphasize—from methods that focus on particular qualities to broad-brush methods that provide a general evaluation framework. On the other hand, approaches can be categorized based on the evaluation technique employed, from static methods such as scenario analysis or metrics-based assessment to dynamic methods such as simulation. While dynamic methods often provide an accurate measure of system performance and other runtime qualities, such analysis is not relevant to the RARE DRA derivation and evaluation process and will not be addressed in detail. RARE evaluation focuses on the measuring characteristics of the architectural structure that results from defining DRACs and allocating DM functionality and data to those DRACs. Thus, static approaches are more applicable to the RARE process.

Much of the software architecture research has progressed as a result of individual communities focusing on specific software system quality issues such as maintainability (Bengtsson and Bosch, 1999; Briand, Morasca, and Basili, 1993), comprehensibility (Briand, Morasca, and Basili, 1993), reliability (Abd-Allah, 1997; Wang, Wu, and Chen, 1999), performance (Abd-Allah, 1997), integrability (Abowd et al., 1993), reusability (Zhao, 2000), and flexibility (Lassing, Rijsenbrij, and Van Vliet, 1999). RARE DRA derivation is concerned with structure, primarily the identification of classes and the allocation of data and functionality. Consequently, these specific evaluation methods must be applicable during the allocation activity to be relevant to RARE DRA evaluation. For example, the recommendation by Briand, Morasca, and Basili (1993) for low average coupling and high average cohesion to encourage maintainability and comprehensibility can be directly applied to DRA data and service allocation—in fact, coupling/cohesion can be considered the strongest influence in DRA derivation. However, the reliability approaches suggested by Abd-Allah (1997) and Wang, Wu, and Chen (1999) cannot be applied in whole since they rely heavily on the semantics of architectural styles, some of which imply implementation properties not addressed in the systems engineering process activities SEPA DRA.

While it is important for research efforts to focus on methods for evaluating individual qualities, real-world software systems require a balance of different software qualities (Bengtsson and Bosch, 1999; Bosch and Molin, 1999). Two approaches have been proposed for static evaluation of architectures that are not specific to a particular quality: scenario-based methods and metrics-based methods.

The most prevalent overall architecture evaluation approaches are rooted in scenario-based methods such as the Software Architecture Analysis Method (SAAM) (Kazman et al., 1994) and the Architectural Tradeoff Analysis Method (ATAM) (Kazman et al., 1998; Lougee, 2005). The success of scenario-based approaches has led to the development of a number of related evaluation methods (Asundi, Kazman, and Klein, 2001; Bengtsson, 2002; Dobrica and Niemela, 2002;

Tekinerdogan, 2004) as well as supporting tools (Benarif et al., 2004; Kazman, 1996). As evident by the name, ATAM considers multiple quality attributes and the tradeoffs between those attributes. The assumption is that attribute-specific analyses are interdependent, since attributes connect to other attributes through specific architectural elements (e.g., a property of a component), leading to tradeoffs (Kazman et al., 1998). RARE recognizes such inherent conflicts among quality goals (manifested through a given DRA structure, which promotes some attributes while inhibiting others), and the RARE approach allows the architect to establish goal priorities, so RARE can make sensible tradeoffs when conflicts arise.

Other evaluation methods that are not scenario-based have also been applied to software architectures (Dobrica and Niemela, 2002). Among those relevant to DRA evaluation in RARE are the use of static metrics to aid the evaluation of quality attributes (Kalyanasundaram et al., 1998); a method for architectural complexity evaluation described in Alhazbi (2004); and metrics for evaluating product-line architectures (the DRA was partly inspired by the notion of product-line architectures) discussed in (van der Hoek, Dincel, and Medvidovic, 2003). In Kalyanasundaram and colleagues (1998), the authors propose the Concept Selection Method to assess the effects of individual metrics on different software qualities, attempting to establish a relationship between objective metrics and subjective quality attributes. The RARE DRA derivation process improves upon the Concept Selection Method by establishing a stronger correlation between high-level goals and low-level metrics, managing the many-to-many relationships through heuristics and strategies. A number of the static metrics referenced in Kalyanasundaram and colleagues (1998) contributed to the metrics suite used in DRA derivation, although many do not apply, since they focus on implementation-level concerns.

Object-Oriented Analysis and Design and Software Architectures

The software development community has migrated away from traditional functional methodologies toward object-oriented analysis/object-oriented design (OOA/OOD) methodologies due to what many researchers and practitioners claim to be the clear advantages of OO architectures (Calio, Antiero, and Bux, 2000; Eckert, 1994; Graham, 1995; Henderson-Sellers and Edwards, 1994; Meyer, 1997; Richter, 1999; Riel, 1996). Because these benefits align so closely with the quality attributes typically targeted by software architectures (e.g., reusability, maintainability, performance, reliability), object-orientation is often selected as an appropriate architectural style for structuring an architecture to yield desired qualities.

A significant activity in all OOA/OOD methodologies involves identifying class abstractions and assigning domain data and functionality to those classes. This activity sets the foundation for the structure upon which resulting systems will be built (Meyer, 1997) and is also foundational for DRA derivation. Nonetheless, based on experiments comparing the conceptualizations offered by different people given the same problem, Stepp and Michalski (1986) conclude there is no "right" answer. The position taken by the research described in this chapter is analogous. The objective of this research is to evolve from an ad hoc DRA derivation approach toward a more formal process by leveraging advice (heuristics) from experienced architects in a rational manner that aligns with quality goals (intentions) prioritized by the architect. To provide a foundation for these heuristics, the research described in this chapter must draw upon the recommendations of popular OOA/OOD methodologies (Booch, Rumbaugh, and Jacobson, 1999; Coad and Yourdon, 1991; Graham, 1995; Kruchten, 2000; Rubin and Goldberg, 1992; Shlaer and Mellor, 1992; Wirfs-Brock et al., 1990) as well as experts in the field (Richter, 1999; Riel, 1996; Meyer, 1997).

Without the ability to objectively evaluate an object-oriented design in light of given qualities, the potential for object-oriented approaches to achieve quality goals can be easily questioned (Miller, Hsia, and Kung, 1999). Object-oriented researchers have produced a number of metrics suites designed expressly for object-oriented analysis and design (Brito e Abreu and Melo, 1996; Chidamber and Kemerer, 1991; Lorenz and Kidd, 1994; Moser et al., 1997), and complementary research efforts have attempted to associate such measures with higher level quality concerns, such as reusability, testability, and comprehensibility (Rosenburg and Hyatt, 1997). Since such metrics were designed primarily to measure characteristics of object-oriented programs and class models, their definitions were modified slightly to apply to the SEPA DRA. Nonetheless, such modification is beneficial, since DRA derivation and evaluation is concerned with many of the same structural issues as object-oriented design.

ASSESSING THE VALUE OF RARE AND THE DRA IN THE CONTEXT OF A STANDARD SOFTWARE ENGINEERING PROCESS

The research that produced RARE and the DRA was motivated by the need for an artifact that could serve as a high-level blueprint in large, complex domains where multiple deployment sites were anticipated over many years. The functionality and data required at each site was expressible by all or part of the domain requirements modeled in the DRA, while the specific technologies used to implement that functionality differed considerably across sites and over time (Barber and Graser, 2001; DARPA, 2000; Graser et al., 2002). The promise of such extensive domain requirements reuse justified the upfront effort to gather content to populate the architecture and emphasized the importance of RARE's methodical derivation and evaluation process. Similarly, the software engineering process adopted for these projects was explicitly tailored to incorporate DRA derivation activities.

In general, the ultimate usefulness of the DRA representation and the RARE process for a typical software development organization depends on the ability to integrate them into the software architecting activities associated with whatever software engineering methodology the organization has adopted. A traditional software development methodology defines phases such as problem identification, feasibility analysis, requirements gathering and representation, system design, implementation, and deployment (Schach, 2005). Software architecting in the development cycle is described by the derivation decision process followed and the chosen representation. Given that software architectures can be represented at many different levels of abstraction, software architecting decisions can occur in any development phase. In some organizations, one person is assigned the role of software architect and makes decisions with input and recommendations from others. The designated architect may also be guided by an architecture review team, where reviews focus on evaluating the architecture with respect to quality attributes expressed by stakeholders by analyzing costs, benefits, and tradeoffs among options (as per tradeoff analysis in ATAM [Kazman et al., 1998] or RARE). In terms of representation, software engineers may leverage standard notations such as the Unified Modeling Language (UML) (Richter, 1999), create semiformal box-and-line diagrams (e.g., with Visio templates), or simply describe the architecture informally in text.

In assessing the strengths and limitations of RARE in comparison with other software architecture representation and derivation approaches, the fundamental considerations are whether the RARE process and the DRA representation can fit into an organization's existing development culture and whether the output from RARE analysis will contribute to the overall decision process. Selected aspects that characterize an organization's development process and culture are discussed below. These aspects can be used as evaluation points to help a project manager determine whether

RARE and the DRA can benefit the development process. Aspects are posed as questions and grouped into process-related and representation-related concerns.

Process-Related Concerns

Does the organization plan strategically over multiple projects? Is reuse important over the long term, or are development efforts typically "one-time" investments?

The primary value of RARE and a high-level domain reference architecture is to establish a vision for the topology of multiple deployments over time, regardless of the technology that will be selected to implement those deployments. The DRA captures domain requirements, and these requirements are reused as multiple systems are produced, thereby amortizing the cost of the analysis effort over multiple projects, systems, and deployments. The DRA also provides value independent of any particular system being built, in that it captures domain knowledge; the DRA can thereby act as a knowledge transfer medium to educate new developers and other stakeholders. However, if each project is treated as a silo and analysis and design artifacts are typically not reused, it may be difficult to justify deriving a DRA, given the upfront investment required.

One software development approach that encourages leveraging modeling efforts over multiple projects is the concept of Model-Driven Architecture (MDA). MDA defines three modeling levels: platform-independent model, platform-definition model, and platform-specific model (Frankel and Guttman, 2002). A platform-independent model is a description of a software or business system that is independent of the specific technological platform used to implement it; the model may be described in a language such as UML and can be used as a basis for transformation into a family of platform-specific models. The DRA representation is analogous to the MDA platform-independent model, where domain data and functionality are allocated into prescribed components.

RARE benefits/limitations to consider. RARE provides opportunities for long-term reuse as a domain model in a component-connector "blueprint" that can establish a vision for multiple deployments. However, considerable discipline and upfront investment are necessary to derive a DRA that captures a complete set of domain requirements and considers factors that are not only applicable to current sites but also envisioned for future sites.

Would the organization reap the value of early architectural analysis?

The DRA representation is intentionally high-level to make it suitable for early, computational analysis, the objective being to make decisions as early as possible in the development process. In general, software methodologies encourage such early modeling and analysis, motivated by the observation that errors identified earlier in the software development cycle (i.e., during analysis and design phases) are less costly to fix than after implementation commitments have been made (Graser et al., 2002). The DRA takes this one step further by allowing engineers to perform analysis in terms of architecture topology, where domain functionality is allocated to components that can prescribe eventual computing platforms.

RARE benefits/limitations to consider. The DRA is a high-level architecture defined by a formal meta-model, making it suitable for early analysis, including static structural analysis (e.g., coupling) and dynamic analysis such as performance simulation. Nonetheless, as with any extensive domain modeling effort, the DRA requires the acquisition and understanding of functionality and data as well as properties on that functionality and data. These may be challenging to acquire from stakeholders within allocated project time and budget or difficult to estimate.

Is the organization concerned with how an analysis, design, development, or deployment decision was made?

Software engineering, and modeling in particular, is an evolutionary process. RARE captures a history of DRA revisions as derivation proceeds and the combination of selected goals, heuristics, metrics, and strategies collectively represent rationale for derivation decisions. As mentioned in the related work section, most software architecture research has emphasized architecture representation and evaluation techniques over a methodical derivation process.

One option for tracking the evolution of design models and other software development artifacts is through document-level versioning (e.g., a version control system); however, this approach alone does not record the decisions that resulted from each evolutionary step. In the absence of such versioning, analysts and architects may tend to incorporate new content and make structural revisions in a single "master" version, thereby losing all traceability for later consumers of the artifact.

RARE benefits/limitations to consider. By design, RARE logs chosen goals, heuristics, metrics, and strategies; derivation activity (i.c., strategies applied); and evaluation results. However, given that each revision can be quite granular, the RARE derivation log can be voluminous. Understanding the architect's overall intentions requires mining this log for general trends in the context of chosen goals.

Is it possible to map stakeholder objectives to RARE-style goals and metrics? Can heuristics be identified that help achieve those goals?

The RARE approach depends on being able to map stakeholder objectives to quality goals and to associate those goals with lower-level metrics through heuristics. The default goals, heuristics, metrics, and strategies provided in RARE represent a compilation from project experiences, commonly accepted software engineering principles, and software architecture concepts. However, this compilation is by no means exhaustive; furthermore, goals, heuristics, and metrics may be defined uniquely for a given project or influenced by organizational standards. Regardless, since all software systems are developed to address stakeholder needs, "evaluation" is conducted in some form on every project, even if the first feedback is from client acceptance testing after system delivery and the resulting "architecture refinement" comes in the form of post-deployment system rework. Thus, there is always a mapping between stakeholder objectives and the system under development, whether implicit or explicit.

RARE benefits/limitations to consider. If selected goals, heuristics, and metrics accurately reflect stakeholder objectives, RARE provides quantitative insight as to how well an architecture meets quality objectives. However, issues in the context of identifying RARE-style goals, heuristics, metrics, and strategies include the following: (1) Is it possible to identify goals and metrics that map to stakeholder objectives that can be evaluated in a high-level DRA? (2) Is ample project time allotted up front for this activity? (3) Will evaluation results be used to influence subsequent design decisions? (4) How do the structural evaluations available in RARE relate to the various analyses available in other tools (e.g., UML class model analysis) as well as comments garnered from architecture reviews?

Representation-Related Concerns

Is the organization's development centered around Unified Modeling Language, data flow diagrams (DFDs), Integrated DEFinition models (e.g., IDEF0), or other software engineering notations?

As discussed previously, software engineering practitioners and researchers have offered many different definitions for software architecture. Common among all definitions is the notion that a software architecture is a model that either describes an existing system or prescribes a system to be built. Beyond that common ground, definitions vary considerably with regard to the specific elements that constitute a software architecture. While the RARE DRA is composed of components and connectors, where components represent collections of domain functionality and data and connectors result from the input/output dependencies between those components, others have suggested that the collection of UML models (class, state chart, use case, etc.) used to describe a system under development can be construed as an architecture (Kruchten, 2000).

RARE benefits/limitations to consider. For organizations that rely solely on UML models, the RARE DRA representation is a departure from the notations/representations they use in early analysis. In particular, these organizations may not typically consider allocation to components at an early stage. However, both representations capture domain functionality and data. Therefore, the RARE DRA can coexist with UML models. Furthermore, the DRA complements those models by enabling RARE-style structural evaluation.

Is the organization's development methodology centered around data modeling (e.g., entity-relationship diagrams)?

Some organizations focus their analysis effort on developing a project-level or enterprise-level data model with minimal emphasis on functional specifications. In fact, an extensive effort to specify functionality may not be cost effective if an organization develops and maintains systems that focus on information storage, retrieval, and display with minimal data transformation or workflow management.

RARE benefits/limitations to consider. Considerations for an organization that emphasizes data modeling are similar to those for a UML-centric organization. The DRA can coexist with a data model and complements the data model by allocating data requirements to responsible components. Each representation provides a different view on the data: data concepts and their relationships are expressed in a data model, while component allocation is conveyed by the DRA.

Does the organization emphasize the use of formal requirements specifications?

Formal specification languages and their associated analyzers (e.g., Alloy and its accompanying tool ALCOA) provide a means for specifying requirements in precise terms and conducting computer-based analysis to ensure correctness based on well-defined properties (Jackson, 2006). However, using a formal specification language requires a level of discipline and rigor when gathering and representing stakeholder requirements in order to map requirements to the constructs of the chosen language and interpret evaluation results in terms of which requirements will and will not be satisfied.

RARE benefits/limitations to consider. If an organization leverages a formal requirements specification, there should be minimal resistance to the DRA. However, in practical terms, the detail and time required for formal specification and analysis may limit its use on a given project or system (e.g., performing safety and liveness analysis only for critical functionality).

The DRA, while considered formal in that it uses a designated meta-model, is specified at a high-level, offering the opportunity to evaluate systemwide concerns at a high level. For example, in addition to structural/topological evaluation of components and their relationships (e.g., coupling, cohesion, component size), service pre- and post-conditions can provide the basis for safety and liveness analysis, and service duration and frequency properties can provide input for simulation-based performance analysis. Nonetheless, as with any formal representation, such DRA evaluation is of minimal value without a well-populated representation that accurately reflects stakeholder intentions.

Every system can be described by a software architecture, so every system can benefit from an architectural prescription prior to development. However, in determining whether the benefits from adopting an explicit software architecture derivation and evaluation process such as RARE outweigh the costs, the following questions should be considered, which summarize the concerns above:

1. Does the explicit component-connector representation in the DRA offer analysis opportunities not afforded by other representations?
2. Does the project schedule allow time to represent requirements in an architecture and step through the derivation process?
3. Are organizational standards and skill sets in the area of modeling notations and development methodologies a barrier for exploring other representations and analysis methods?
4. Will results from architectural evaluations be used to influence design and development decisions in subsequent stages of the current project as well as future projects?

A fundamental objective of RARE research was to provide a means for understanding component responsibility and component dependency early in analysis through a high-level representation and a methodical derivation process. However, RARE provides minimal decision value if the architecting activity is not a sanctioned part of an organization's development methodology. As with the justification for formal methods, software engineers and project managers must be convinced there is value in populating a computational specification for the purpose of conducting evaluations and using evaluation results as rationale for development decisions.

As trends in software engineering continue toward greater reliance on off-the-shelf components and global development teams, software managers are encouraged to find new ways to save time and cost by illuminating issues early and specifying requirements using unambiguous representations ensuring that a delivered product will meet stakeholder expectations. This is especially notable in distributed development efforts, where developers must understand the scope/boundaries of the components they have been assigned, the functionality allocated to those components, and their dependency on other system components.

CONCLUSION AND FUTURE WORK

This chapter presented a formal process and an accompanying tool, Reference Architecture Representation Environment, to derive a Domain Reference Architecture from a computational

Domain Model such that the resulting DRA reflects high-level quality attributes selected by the architect to meet stakeholder needs. Prior to this research, deriving a DRA by identifying a set of DRACs and allocating data and functionality to those DRACs was more akin to an art than a science, requiring a significant amount of guesswork and intuition on the part of the architect. The primary contribution of the RARE process is to formalize the DRA derivation process and to quantify architecture evaluation in light of quality goals. Several challenges are associated with architecture derivation, which partly explains why the architecture derivation process has been largely manual to date. Selected challenges addressed by RARE include the following:

1. *Prioritizing qualities under consideration:* During RARE's "Plan-Generation" phase, the qualities selected and prioritized by the architect are represented in a "Derivation Plan" as "quality goals." For each quality goal, the "Derivation Plan" contains relevant strategies (sequences of steps that transform the DRA) from the RARE knowledge base.

2. *Selecting and applying heuristics for DRA derivation:* The RARE KB associates one or more heuristics (i.e., rules of thumb) with each quality goal, and the KB is structured such that a goal may be associated with more than one heuristic and a heuristic may be associated with more than one goal. After selecting specific quality goals for a derivation, the "Plan-Generation" phase initializes the "Derivation Plan" with the respective heuristics and corresponding strategies. Thus the KB helps determine *which* heuristics to apply given selected quality goals and *how* to apply them, based on corresponding strategies.

3. *Resolving conflicts among qualities selected:* Each strategy is defined with a list of conflicting strategies, and because strategies are associated with heuristics and heuristics are related to quality goals, conflicting strategies infer conflicts among selected quality goals. During "Plan-Generation," conflicting strategies in the "Derivation Plan" are identified and strategies associated with lower priority goals are pruned.

4. *Evaluating the architecture with respect to quality goals:* There is often a many-to-many relationship between low-level metrics (e.g., structural metrics such as class coupling, cohesion, and size) and associated high-level qualities (e.g., reusability, maintainability), making correlation difficult. To bridge this gap, metrics are associated with quality goals in the RARE KB through heuristics. Heuristics represent suggested approaches for achieving a quality goal, and low-level metrics are useful indicators in determining whether a heuristic has been achieved.

Despite the potential impact that the RARE tool promises for the architecting process, this research is not designed to replace the architect altogether. On the contrary, the capabilities of the architect remain essential to the derivation process. Unique situations arise in different domains and under different projects that require architect input and cannot be addressed in a fully automated fashion. Nonetheless, the architect is burdened with numerous concerns during derivation. Particularly difficult to manage are issues related to capturing decision rationale. Without justification, other stakeholders (e.g., other architects or project team members) may be quick to question the architect's overall "vision" as well as specific decisions. By capturing the "Derivation Plan" and logging DRA transformation actions, RARE allows the information retained during derivation to speak for the architect.

It is an even greater challenge for the architect to quantitatively demonstrate that a DRA under derivation satisfies the quality attributes expressed by stakeholders. When deriving an architecture as abstract as the SEPA DRA, there is much room for interpretation, and evaluation approaches are often subjective. The RARE approach attempts to quantify DRA evaluation through metrics measuring architectural structure that are related to quality goals through respective heuristics. While the metrics and heuristics under a quality goal may not represent perfect predictors of a system implemented from a DRA, they are nonetheless valuable to the architect by providing a "toolbox" of derivation approaches and methods for measuring their success.

The Domain Reference Architecture derivation process and tool produced by this research provide a means for quantified evaluation of architectures and an experimental apparatus by which architectures can be compared. Such an apparatus enables follow-on studies to validate goal, heuristic, strategy, and metric definitions and resulting architectures. Specific questions to be addressed in this analysis include (1) identifying the best metrics for predicting quality goals; (2) classifying preferred DRA structures, whereby the derivation process is influenced by organizational preferences; and (3) determining optimal approaches (heuristics and strategies) for achieving those DRA structures.

There exists no compendium of approaches for deriving the optimal architecture in all situations. Rather, improving the derivation process is a learning activity, taking into account feedback from archived derivation runs, downstream architecture analysis tools, actual systems designed from derived DRAs, and so on. As such, a worthwhile avenue for future work would be the application of machine learning to the derivation and evaluation process. Specifically, this would involve incorporating machine-learning approaches into RARE to automatically fine-tune the RARE KB based on feedback received.

One particularly promising area under investigation by software architecture researchers is the synthesis of architectures with given properties. The RARE process and tool move one step closer to this goal by deriving an implementation-independent architecture driven by quality goals (i.e., high-level properties). Future research will extend the DRA derivation and refinement process to incorporate additional architecture representations designed to specify site-specific implementation and installation requirements. Thus, such a process will yield an architecture customized for a given site in terms of (1) domain services needed; (2) implementation requirements specified; and (3) installation constraints imposed.

ACKNOWLEDGMENTS

This research was sponsored in part by the Defense Advanced Research Project Agency (DARPA) Taskable Agent Software Kit (TASK) program, F30602–00–2–0588. The U.S. government is authorized to reproduce and distribute reprints for governmental purposes notwithstanding any copyright annotation thereon. The views and conclusions herein are those of the authors and should not be interpreted as necessarily representing the official policies or endorsements, either expressed or implied, of the Defense Advanced Research Project Agency.

NOTES

1. For purposes of this discussion, a "domain" can be considered a bounded set of work processes related by time and functional dependency.

2. The goal satisfaction index shown in Figure 10.10 represents one possible cost function for evaluating the DRA and guiding the derivation process. Other such functions may be considered in follow-on research.

REFERENCES

Abd-Allah, A. 1997. Extending reliability block diagrams to software architectures. *USC-CSE-97–501*. Los Angeles: Center for Software Engineering, University of Southern California.

Abowd, G.; Bass, L.; Howard, L.; and Northrop, L. 1993. Structural modeling: an application framework and development process for flight simulators. *CMU/SEI-93-TR-14*. Pittsburgh, PA: Software Engineering Institute, Carnegie Mellon University.

Alhazbi, S.M. 2004. Measuring the complexity of component-based system architecture. In *2004 International Conference on Information and Communication Technologies: From Theory to Applications*. Los Alamitos, CA: IEEE Computer Society Press, 593–594.

Asundi, J.; Kazman, R.; and Klein, M. 2001. Using economic considerations to choose amongst architecture design alternatives. *CMU/SEI-2001-TR-035*. Pittsburgh, PA: Software Engineering Institute, Carnegie Mellon University.

Barber, K.S. 2004. Lecture Notes for EE382C.7, Software Architectures. University of Texas at Austin, Fall semester.

Barber, K.S., and Graser, T. 2000a. Tool support for systematic class identification in object-oriented software architectures. In *Thirty-seventh International Conference on Technology of Object-Oriented Languages and Systems*. Los Alamitos, CA: IEEE Computer Society Press, 82–93.

———. 2000b. Reference Architecture Representation Environment (RARE)—a tool to support object-oriented software architecture derivation and evaluation. In *Fourth World Multi-conference on Systematics, Cybernetics and Informatics*. Orlando, FL: International Institute of Informatics and Systemics, vol. 2, 389–394.

———. 2001. Developing a traceable domain reference architecture to support clinical trials at the national cancer institute—an experience report. In *Eighth Annual IEEE International Conference and Workshop on the Engineering of Computer-Based Systems*. Los Alamitos, CA: IEEE Computer Society Press, 144–151.

Barber, K.S.; Graser, T.; and Holt, J. 2001. A multi-level software architecture metamodel to support the capture and evaluation of stakeholder concerns. In *Fifth Multi-Conference on Systemics, Cybernetics and Informatics*. Orlando, FL: International Institute of Informatics and Systemics, 337–342.

Barber, K.S.; Graser, T.; and Jernigan, S. 1999. The systems engineering process activities: supporting early requirements integration prior to implementation design. In *Proceedings of Software Technology and Engineering Practice*. Los Alamitos, CA: IEEE Computer Society Press, 50–59.

Barber, K.S.; Graser, T.; Grisham, P.; and Jernigan, S. 1999. Requirements evolution and reuse using the systems engineering process activities (SEPA). *Australian Journal of Information Systems—Special Issue on Requirements Engineering*, 7, 1, 75–97.

Barber, K.S.; Graser, T.; Holt, J.; and Silva, J. 2000. Representing domain reference architectures by extending the UML metamodel. In *Twelfth International Conference on Software Engineering and Knowledge Engineering*. Skokie, IL: Knowledge Systems Institute, 256–265.

Basili, V.R.; Briand, L.C.; and Melo, W.L. 1996. A validation of object-oriented design metrics as quality indicators. *IEEE Transactions on Software Engineering*, 22, 10, 751–761.

Bass, L.; Clements, P.; and Kazman, R. 1998. *Software Architecture in Practice*. Reading, MA: Addison-Wesley.

Benarif, S.; Ramdane-Cherif, A.; Levy, N.; and Losavio, F. 2004. Intelligent tool based-agent for software architecture evaluation. In *Fourth International Conference on Quality Software*. Braunschweig, Germany: Institute of Information Systems, Technical University of Braunschweig, 126–133.

Bengtsson, P. 2002. Architecture level modifiability analysis. Ph.D. diss., Department of Software Engineering and Computer Science, Blekinge Institute of Technology, Sweden.

Bengtsson, P., and Bosch, J. 1999. Haemo dialysis software architecture design experiences. In *Twenty-first International Conference on Software Engineering*. Los Alamitos, CA: IEEE Computer Society Press, 516–525.

Booch, G.; Rumbaugh, J.; and Jacobson, I. 1999. *The Unified Modeling Language User Guide*. Reading, MA: Addison Wesley Longman.

Bosch, J., and Molin, P. 1999. Software architecture design: evaluation and transformation. In *IEEE Conference and Workshop on the Engineering of Computer-Based Systems*. Los Alamitos, CA: IEEE Computer Society Press, 4–10.

Bose, P. 1999. Automated translation of UML models of architectures for verification and simulation using spin. In *Fourteenth IEEE International Conference on Automated Software Engineering*. Los Alamitos, CA: IEEE Computer Society Press, 102–109.

Briand, L.C.; Morasca, S.; and Basili, V.R. 1993. Measuring and assessing maintainability at the end of high level design. In *Conference on Software Maintenance*. Los Alamitos, CA: IEEE Computer Society Press, 88–97.

Brito e Abreu, F., and Melo, W. 1996. Evaluating the impact of object-oriented design on software quality. In *Third International Software Metrics Symposium.* Los Alamitos, CA: IEEE Computer Society Press, 90–99.

Calio, A.; Antiero, M.; and Bux, G. 2000. Software process improvement by object technology (ESSI PIE 27785-SPOT). In *Twenty-second International Conference on Software Engineering.* Los Alamitos, CA: IEEE Computer Society Press, 641–647.

Chidamber, S., and Kemerer, C. 1991. Towards a metric suite for object-oriented design. *Sigplan Notices, Proceedings of Conference on Object-Oriented Programming, Systems, Languages, and Applications,* 26, 11, 197–211.

Clements, P.C. 1996. A survey of architecture description languages. In *Eighth International Workshop on Software Specification and Design.* Los Alamitos, CA: IEEE Computer Society Press, 16–25.

Coad, P., and Yourdon, E. 1991. *Object-Oriented Analysis.* Englewood Cliffs, NJ: Prentice Hall.

Defense Advanced Research Projects Agency (DARPA). 2000. JFACC Solicitation BAA99–18. Available at www.darpa.mil/iso/jfacc/ (accessed on April 20, 2000).

Dobrica, L., and Niemela, E. 2002. A survey on software architecture analysis methods. *IEEE Transactions on Software Engineering,* 28, 7, 638–653.

Eckert, G. 1994. Types, classes and collections in object-oriented analysis. In *First International Conference on Requirements Engineering.* Los Alamitos, CA: IEEE Computer Society Press, 32–39.

Egyed, A.; Gruenbacker, P.; and Medvidovic, N. 2000. Refinement and evolution issues in bridging requirements and architectures. *USC-CSE-2000-515.* Los Angeles: Center for Software Engineering, University of Southern California.

Frankel, D., and Guttman, M. 2002. *Model Driven Architecture: Applying MDA to Enterprise Computing.* Hoboken, NJ: Wiley.

Gacek, C. 1995. Exploiting domain architectures in software reuse. In *Symposium on Software Reusability.* New York: ACM Press, 229–232.

Graham, I. 1995. *Migrating to Object Technology.* Reading, MA: Addison-Wesley.

Graser, T. 2001. Reference architecture representation environment (RARE): systematic derivation and evaluation of domain-specific, implementation-independent software architectures. Ph.D. diss., Electrical and Computer Engineering Department, University of Texas at Austin.

Graser, T.; Barber, K.S.; Williams, B.; Saghir, F.; and Henry, K. 2002. Advanced consequence management program: challenges and recent real world implementations. In *AeroSense 2002, Conference on Sensors, and Command, Control, Communications and Intelligence (C3I) Technologies for Homeland Defense and Law Enforcement.* Bellingham, WA: International Society for Optical Engineering, paper no. 4708–82.

Gujral, N.; Ahn, J.; and Barber, K.S. 2005. Architectural model for designing agent-based systems. In *Seventeenth International Conference on Software Engineering and Knowledge Engineering.* Skokie, IL: Knowledge Systems Institute, 753–760.

Henderson-Sellers, B. 1996. *Object-Oriented Metrics: Measures of Complexity.* Upper Saddle River, NJ: Prentice Hall.

Henderson-Sellers, B., and Edwards, J.M. 1994. *BOOKTWO of Object-Oriented Knowledge: The Working Object.* Sydney: Prentice Hall.

Jacobsen, E.E.; Kristensen, B.B.; and Nowack, P. 1999. Architecture = abstractions over software. In *Technology of Object-Oriented Languages and Systems, 1999.* Los Alamitos, CA: IEEE Computer Society Press, 89–99.

Jackson, D. 2006. Dependable software by design. *Scientific American,* June.

Kalyanasundaram, S.; Ponnambalam, K.; Singh, A.; Stacey, B.J.; and Munikoti, R. 1998. Metrics for software architecture: a case study in the telecommunications domain. In *1998 IEEE Canadian Conference on Electrical and Computer Engineering.* Los Alamitos, CA: IEEE Computer Society Press, 715–718.

Kavi, K., and Browne, J.C. 1999. Computer systems research: the pressure is on. *IEEE Computer,* 32, 1, 30–39.

Kazman, R. 1996. Tool support for architecture analysis and design. In *Second International Software Architecture Workshop.* New York: ACM Press, 94–97.

Kazman, R.; Bass, L.; Abowd, G.; and Webb, M. 1994. SAAM: A method for analyzing the properties of software architectures. In *Sixteenth International Conference on Software Engineering (ICSE-16).* Los Alamitos, CA: IEEE Computer Society Press, 81–90.

Kazman, R.; Klein, M.; Barbacci, M.; Longstaff, T.; Lipson, H.; and Carriere, J. 1998. The architecture tradeoff analysis method. In *Fourth IEEE International Conference on Engineering of Complex Computer Systems (ICECCS).* Los Alamitos, CA: IEEE Computer Society Press, 68–78.

Kruchten, P. 2000. *The Rational Unified Process: An Introduction.* 2nd ed. Reading, MA: Addison Wesley Longman.

Lassing, N.; Rijsenbrij, D.; and Van Vliet, H. 1999. Towards a broader view on software architecture analysis of flexibility. In *Sixth Asia Pacific Software Engineering Conference.* Los Alamitos, CA: IEEE Computer Society Press, 238–245.

Li-Thiao-Te, P.; Kennedy, J.; and Owens, J. 1997. Mechanisms for interpretation of OO systems design metrics. In *Technology of Object-Oriented Languages and Systems.* Los Alamitos, CA: IEEE Computer Society Press, 221–231.

Lorenz, M., and Kidd, J. 1994. *Object-Oriented Software Metrics.* Englewood Cliffs, NJ: Prentice Hall.

Lougee, H. 2005. DO-178B certified software: a formal reuse analysis approach. *Crosstalk,* 18, 1, 20–25.

Merriam-Webster. 2005. Merriam-Webster Online Dictionary. Available at www.m-w.com/cgi-bin/dictionary (accessed on February 20, 2005).

Meyer, B. 1997. *Object-Oriented Software Construction.* Upper Saddle River, NJ: Prentice Hall.

Miller, B.K.; Hsia, P.; and Kung, C. 1999. Object-oriented architecture measures. In *Thirty-second Hawaii International Conference on System Sciences.* Los Alamitos, CA: IEEE Computer Society Press, 1–18.

Morris, K.L. 1989. Metrics for object-oriented software development environments. Masters thesis, Sloan School of Management, MIT, Cambridge, MA.

Moser, S.; Henderson-Sellers, B.; Misic, V.B.; and Migid, V.B. 1997. Measuring object-oriented business models. In *Technology of Object-Oriented Languages and Systems.* Los Alamitos, CA: IEEE Computer Society Press, 340–349.

Perry, D.E., and Wolf, A.L. 1992. Foundations for the study of software architecture. *ACM SIGSOFT Software Engineering Notes,* 17, 4, 40–52.

Richter, C. 1999. *Designing Flexible Object-Oriented Systems with UML.* Indianapolis, IN: Macmillan.

Riel, A.J. 1996. *Object-Oriented Design Heuristics.* Reading, MA: Addison-Wesley.

Rosenberg, L.H., and Hyatt, L.E. 1997. Software quality metrics for object-oriented environments. *Crosstalk,* 10, 4. Available at www.stsc.hill.af.mil/crosstalk/1997/04/quality.asp (accessed on February 1, 2006).

Rubin, K.S., and Goldberg, A. 1992. Object behavior analysis. *Communications of the ACM,* 35, 9, 48–62.

Schach, S. 2005. *Object-Oriented and Classical Software Engineering.* 6th ed. New York: McGraw-Hill.

Shaw, M., and Garlan, D. 1996. *Software Architecture: Perspectives on an Emerging Discipline.* Upper Saddle River, NJ: Prentice Hall.

Shlaer, S., and Mellor, S.J. 1992. *Object Lifecycles: Modeling the World in States.* Englewood Cliffs, NJ: Prentice Hall.

Stepp, R.E., and Michalski, R.S. 1986. Conceptual clustering: inventing goal-oriented classifications of structured objects. In R.S. Michalski, J.G. Carbonell, and T.M. Mitchell (eds.), *Machine Learning: An Artificial Intelligence Approach.* Los Altos, CA: Morgan Kaufmann, 471–498.

Tekinerdogan, B. 2004. ASAAM: aspectual software architecture analysis method. In *Fourth Working IEEE/IFIP Conference on Software Architecture.* Los Alamitos, CA: IEEE Computer Society Press, 5–14.

Tracz, W. 1995. *Confessions of a Used Program Salesman.* Reading, MA: Addison-Wesley.

van der Hoek, A.; Dincel, E.; and Medvidovic, N. 2003. Using service utilization metrics to assess the structure of product line architectures. In *Ninth International Software Metrics Symposium.* Los Alamitos, CA: IEEE Computer Society Press, 298–308.

Wang, W.L.; Wu, Y.; and Chen, M.H. 1999. An architecture-based software reliability model. In *1999 Pacific Rim International Symposium on Dependable Computing.* Los Alamitos, CA: IEEE Computer Society Press, 143–150.

Wirfs-Brock, R.; Wilkerson, B.; Wiener, L.; and Brock, R. 1990. *Designing Object-Oriented Software.* Englewood Cliffs, NJ: Prentice Hall.

Zhao, J. 2000. A slicing-based approach to extracting reusable software architectures. In *Fourth European Conference on Software Maintenance and Reengineering.* Los Alamitos, CA: IEEE Computer Society Press, 215–223.

CHAPTER 11

OO-METHOD

A Conceptual Schema-Centric Development Approach

OSCAR PASTOR, JUAN CARLOS MOLINA, AND EMILIO IBORRA

Abstract: During the past two decades, extensive research and industrial work (object-oriented methods, formal specification languages, component-based software production, etc.) have been oriented toward the goal of generating code from a high-level systems specification, which is normally represented as a conceptual schema. However, the numerous failures in the achievement of this goal have resulted in overall skepticism when any new approach offering a "press the button, get all the code" strategy is proposed. In spite of this reticence, the current hype around model-driven architecture has given new momentum to these strategies. The new methods propose appropriate model transformations that must cover all the steps of a sound software production process from an information systems engineering point of view. These must include organizational modeling, requirements engineering, conceptual modeling, and model-based code-generation techniques. The conceptual primitives must be precisely and formally defined, and the conversion between the different models involved and their corresponding software counterparts must be done in a well-defined way in order to make the full automation of the process possible through the use of "model compilers." The objectives of this chapter are: to discuss which conceptual primitives should be present in a system specification; to analyze how to use UML to represent them; and to reduce the current complexity of the proposal by identifying only those diagrams and modeling constructs that are really necessary to create a conceptual schema. This chapter also explains in detail how to accomplish the transformation process between the problem space and the solution space. Tool support is also included to make the discussion more practical.

Keywords: Model-Driven Development, Conceptual Modeling, Model-Based Code Generation

INTRODUCTION

The history of software development can be viewed as a succession of increments in the level of abstraction of a path that moves the activity of "programming" toward representations in the problem space and away from the sphere of the solution space. Computers were first "programmed" by wiring, and then programmed through the use of machine code, then through the assembly language, then by the creation of the first compilers for procedural languages, then through object-oriented programming and component-based development techniques. At each evolutionary step, the subsequent increase in the level of abstraction allowed developers to deal with problems that were larger in size and complexity as well as to increase the quality, maintainability, and lifespan of software applications.

Today developers regard this evolution as something natural, and no one marvels at programs that can automate the transformation of a program written in one programming language to an equivalent program in a different programming language that is closer to the machine. In fact, every step in this evolution of software development has been characterized by raising the level of abstraction required to define the systems to be developed in a language that abstracts away details of the language in which the system would be implemented, and automating the transformation of programs written in the higher-level language to the lower-level language.

It is therefore only natural for the next step in this evolutionary path to assist developers in overcoming today's challenges in software development. "Today's software systems are significantly large, complex and critical, that only through the use of automated approaches can such systems be developed and evolve in an economic and timely manner" (Grünbacher and Ledru, 2004, page 12),

This goal may well be reached through the adoption of Model-Driven Development (MDD) techniques in general, and specifically by leveraging the Model-Driven Architecture (MDA) approach (MDA, 2007; Miller and Mukerji, 2003). After numerous attempts in this direction (Mellor and Balcer, 2002; Mellor, Clark, and Futagami, 2003; Selic, 2003; Völter et al., 2006), the time seems to be right for going one step forward in the process of automating the software production process itself. MDA is not the only proposal that is leading researchers in that direction. Proposals such as Extreme Non-programming in response to Extreme Programming (XNP; Morgan, 2002), or Conceptual Schema-Centric Development (CSCD; Olivé, 2005) are centered on the idea that in order to develop an information system, it is both necessary and sufficient to create its conceptual schema.

Conceptual Schema-Centric Development

Olivé promoted these concepts even further when he presented his CSCD approach as a grand challenge for information systems research (Olivé, 2005). Similar to the central ideas of MDA and XNP, CSCD is based on the assumption that the definition of the conceptual schema is all that is required to develop an information system.

Since the advancement of science and engineering is the primary purpose of the formulation and promulgation of a grand challenge, the approach proposed here focuses on the advancement of IS engineering toward automation. Even if this is not at all a new, disruptive proposal (Teichroew and Sayani [1971] argued the importance of confronting the challenge of the automation of systems building to improve the software production process), the fact is that, forty years later, this goal of automated systems building has not yet been achieved. Despite the definite progress that has been made, the design, programming, and testing activities for most projects still require a substantial amount of manual effort. Not even in the two most popular development environments (Visual Studio or Eclipse) does the automation of system building play a significant role. Programming continues to be the central activity and most (if not all) of the tool improvements are directed toward helping with the complex task of writing a program, but not with the task of compiling a conceptual model to avoid the repetitive, tedious, and complex task of programming.

Many have begun to question the usefulness of pursuing this goal. Is it perhaps a waste of time to continue trying? As researchers in this area, we firmly believe that it is not. Even though numerous problems remain to be solved (technical problems, problems related to the maturity of the field, and the lack of standards), the situation has changed drastically, especially with regard to the absence of standards.

Recent progress on widely accepted and well-known standards such as UML (UML, 2007), MDA (MDA, 2007; Miller and Mukerji, 2003), XMI (XMI, 2006), MOF (MOF, 2007), J2EE (J2EE, 2007), .NET (Microsoft .NET, 2007), among others, are really providing an opportunity to reconsider the goal of automating software development processes. The MDA proposal is especially relevant in this context because it attempts to provide software processes where model transformation is a natural consequence of the view of using models at different levels of abstraction: the Computer-Independent Model (CIM) at the highest level; the Platform-Independent Model (PIM) at the subsequent level of abstraction; and moving progressively to the solution space through the Platform-Specific Model (PSM), and to the final code. The corresponding transformations between these models provide a kind of software process where all of the previous ideas fit together perfectly.

Modern, advanced industrial tools such as OptimalJ (OptimalJ, 2007) and ArcStyler (Arcstyler, 2006) allow researchers to experiment with these approaches in practice, with results that are quite promising. However, these results are only partial because a true software process that is based on a sound model transformation process has yet to be developed. Even though partial model-driven, code-generation–based approaches provide code-generation capacities from conceptual models to a major or minor degree, programming continues to be the primary task to be accomplished. As yet, no true conceptual model compiler is available on the market. By a "true" conceptual model compiler, we mean a logical programming machine that properly transforms a conceptual schema into its corresponding software product counterpart by defining the required relationships between conceptual constructs and their associated software representations.

The OO-Method presented in this work accomplishes precisely this goal. The OO-Method and its supporting set of tools (OLIVANOVA Model Execution) make the metaphor of a Conceptual Model Compiler a reality. It introduces a fixed set of conceptual constructs and a set of rules to transform these conceptual patterns into their corresponding software counterparts. The implementation of all of these mappings makes the construction of a true model compiler possible.

To develop these ideas further, in this chapter we present the foundation of MDA and discuss its weak points. Next, we introduce the OO-Method (Pastor et al., 2001). This is a Conceptual Schema-Centric Development approach, which is based on the Formal Specification Language OASIS (Pastor, Hayes, and Bear, 1992), which sets the foundation for delivering on the promises of MDA. Then, we present a strategy to define and eventually automate the transformation of conceptual models into software systems. Before the concluding, we also introduce OLIVANOVA Model Execution (Pastor, Molina, and Iborra, 2004) as an implementation of the OO-Method and, therefore, of MDA.

MDA

MDA, which is promoted by the object management group (OMG), aims at separating the logic of applications from the software platform on which this logic is to be implemented. This separation mitigates the impact of evolving technologies on the development of applications because it enables a specification to be reified in different software platforms. This has the additional benefit of shifting the intellectual property of a software system from the source code of its implementation to the conceptual model of its specification.

In the process of developing applications, MDA turns models into "first-class citizens." These models become the most valuable asset for developers because, by using them as input to a series of transformations, developers can obtain the source code of the systems defined by these models. Developing an application in an MDA fashion basically involves creating a model of the application that is agnostic about implementation details. MDA refers to these models as Platform-Independent Models. A PIM can then be transformed into another model that adds details about the platform on which the application will be developed. These are referred to as Platform-Specific Models. Transformations can be chained so that the PSM obtained by applying a certain transformation T_i becomes the PIM for the next transformation (T_{i+1}). Eventually, a PSM (or set of PSMs) will be transformed into text in order to obtain the final product of the (chain of) transformation(s): source code.

MDA proposes UML (UML, 2007) as the "standard" modeling language to define both PIMs and PSMs, although the OMG itself acknowledges that any modeling language can be used in MDA provided that it is defined in terms of the Meta-Object Facility MOF (MOF, 2007) language.

Since the inception of the MDA, many efforts have been devoted to addressing an aspect that seems to be critical for the success of the approach itself: how to define and implement transformations between models, and from models to text. These efforts have been rewarded by the definition of two specifications to establish the grounds for full-fledged MDA implementations, namely, MOF QVT (Queries/Views/Transformations) (Heaton, 2001) and MOF Model-to-Text (Eakman, 2007).

Two aspects that are even more critical than the ability to define transformations have been traditionally neglected: modeling languages and execution models. For a modeling language to be used in a model-centric development approach, it must be:

- abstract enough so that models created with it are truly implementation-agnostic, thus allowing developers to focus on the problem space and reify to multiple platforms;
- accurate enough so that models created with it provide a full description of the relevant features characterizing the system; and
- precise enough so that all elements in models created with it have a well-defined semantics with zero semantic variation points.

Any attempt to build a deterministic, repeatable process (automated or not) to transform a conceptual model of a system into a software application that is functionally equivalent to this model must be based on an execution model that states the runtime behavior of all the primitives in the specification language.

In this context, two very remarkable features in the OO-Method are introduced below:

1. A precise set of conceptual primitives is provided by the method, in accordance with its formal basis. Since a subset of UML diagrams is used as the corresponding basic representation blocks, an adequate and efficient use of this well-known standard is proposed, which avoids the problem of overspecification that occurs when having to use the hundreds of modeling elements provided by the UML notation as a whole.
2. On the other hand, every conceptual construct introduced in the model has its corresponding software counterpart when projected in the software product representation through a process of model transformation. In this way, every piece of information contained in the conceptual schema is meaningful and has a precise semantic justification: to describe a specific part of the problem domain so that it is properly converted into a software representation at the solution space (depending on the particular target software technology).

In the following, we present the specific aspects of this approach in more detail.

OO-METHOD

OO-Method is a software development methodology that is based on a clear separation between the problem space (*what* we want to build) and the solution space (*how* are we going to build it). The definition of a problem (the abstract description of a system, represented in the corresponding conceptual schema) can be enacted regardless of any particular reification (concrete implementation of a software solution). This positions OO-Method as a sound methodological foundation on which to build tools that embrace the MDA directive of separating the logic of software applications from their (multiple) possible implementations.

The formalism underlying OO-Method is OASIS, which is a formal and object-oriented specification language for the specification of information systems (Pastor, Hayes, and Bear, 1992). This formal framework provides a characterization of the conceptual elements that are needed to accurately specify an information system. It encompasses two main components: the conceptual model and the execution model.

Conceptual Model

The conceptual model comprises four complementary views: the objects model, the dynamic model, the functional model, and the presentation model. All of them together constitute the whole conceptual schema specification. These four views allow the definition of all the functional aspects of a system in an abstract (implementation-independent) yet accurate fashion by means of a set of conceptual elements (which we refer to as conceptual primitives or conceptual patterns) with a precise semantics. Most of these conceptual patterns have a UML-based graphical notation, which hides the complexity and formalism of the underlying OASIS formal specification from the developer.

Objects Model

The objects model comprises a class diagram that graphically describes the structure of the system in terms of its classes with their properties and structural relationships (generalization, association/ aggregation), thus providing a static view of the architecture of the system.

Classes have attributes of three kinds: constant attributes (those that get a value when the class is instantiated and do not change), variable attributes (those whose value can change during the lifetime of objects), and derived attributes (those whose value is calculated from the values of other attributes). In order to specify how the value of a derived attribute is calculated, a set of well-formed formulas called derivations can be defined.

Classes also have services, which define the signature of operations that can be invoked upon objects. Services, like "operations" in UML, have arguments or parameters but also fall into two categories: events, which are atomic execution units; and transactions, which are molecular execution units that encompass other services (either events or transactions).

Events, in turn, can be stereotyped as "new" (those whose semantics is that of creating a new instance of the class, assigning a value to each of its properties and relationships) and as "destroy" (those whose semantics is that of destroying an instance of the class and breaking relationships with related instances or cascade-destroy related instances, depending on the features of each relationship). Figure 11.1 shows an example of the graphical notation in the class diagram for a class with attributes and services. The semantics of events that are not stereotyped as "new" or "destroy" are defined in the functional model.

Figure 11.1 **Class Vehicle**

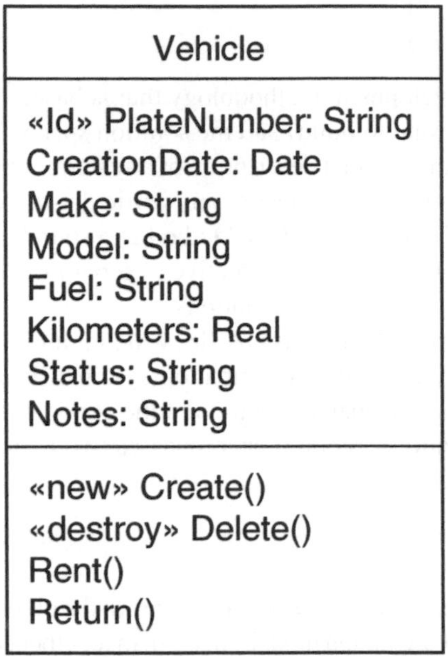

Vehicle
«Id» PlateNumber: String CreationDate: Date Make: String Model: String Fuel: String Kilometers: Real Status: String Notes: String
«new» Create() «destroy» Delete() Rent() Return()

The semantics of a transaction is defined via a formula that states:

- the set of services that comprise the transaction,
- the initialization of each argument of each of these services, and
- (optionally) Boolean conditions that must hold for each of these services to execute.

The ability to define the functionality of atomic services (events), coupled with the ability to compose an arbitrary number of services into another (molecular) service, is a clear contribution of the OO-Method and allows the functionality of services (the equivalent to UML operations) of classes to be fully specified.

The functionality of services can be further constrained by defining preconditions, well-formed Boolean formulas equivalent to precondition constraints in UML. Also, integrity constraints (class invariants) can be defined to prevent the occurrence of services from leaving objects of the system in an invalid state.

As stated above, generalization and association/aggregation relationships can be defined between classes. Generalization relationship specification deals with the inheritance specification. Both generalization and its inverse, specialization, can be specified. A child class can be seen as a role that is activated when a given event or a class condition is fulfilled and that incorporates the corresponding set of new properties characterizing the role. It can be left out when the specified event occurs or when a leaving condition is satisfied. In any case, signature compatibility is required to assure consistency between parent and child classes.

Additionally, association/aggregation relationships allow well-known binary relationships between classes to be declared, including cardinality, the static or dynamic aspect of the relationship, potential identity dependencies, and a stronger form of aggregation if composition is present. Figure 11.2 depicts sample association and generalization relationships.

Figure 11.2   **Associations Between "Vehicle" and "VehicleType," and "RetiredVehicle" and "Buyer"**

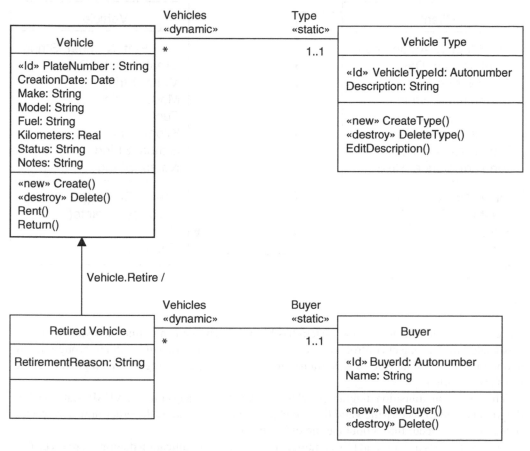

Note: Class "Vehicle" specializes into "Retired Vehicle" when event "retire" is executed.

In addition to generalization and association/aggregation relationships, OO-Method allows for the definition of agent relationships. An agent relationship is a directed relationship between two classes (one playing the role of agent class, the other acting as server class) that defines:

- which attributes in the signature of the server class the agent class is allowed to query,
- which roles (the equivalent to association ends in UML) in the signature of the server class the agent class is allowed to navigate, and
- which services in the signature of the server class the agent class is allowed to execute.

As illustrated in Figure 11.3, the graphical notation for the agent relationship is a dashed arrow from the agent class to the server class stereotyped with "agent."

This allows the modeler to specify a conceptual schema as a client-server model, where it is properly stated which services are provided to the system by classes, and what kind of permissions (agent) classes have to observe other classes' properties or activate other classes' services.

Figure 11.3 **Class "Client" Is Agent of Services "Rent" and "Return" of Class "Vehicle"**

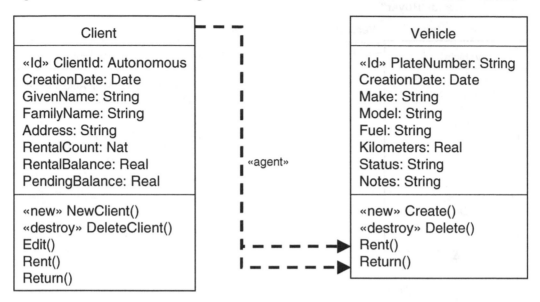

Dynamic Model

Once the static architecture of the system has been defined, we can define the dynamic aspects (associated to intraobject control and interobject communication). This is done through the dynamic model, which includes a state transition diagram per class, triggers, and a global transactions specification.

There is a state transition diagram per class present in the objects model. A UML state machine diagram is used to specify the valid lives of objects of a class, that is, the order in which services of the class can occur throughout the life of its objects.

To specify class triggers and global transactions, UML communication diagrams are used. Triggers represent those class services to be activated when a predefined condition holds in the source class. Global transactions allow global services to be defined, with *global* meaning that they group different services declared in different classes, making them constitute a single execution unit.

Functional Model

Once the system class structure has been specified and system dynamics in the form of valid lives of class objects and interobject communication mechanisms are properly defined, the only aspect to be considered is how a class service occurrence will change the local state of the involved objects. This is done through the functional model in which dynamic logic axioms of the form

$$f\,[s()]\,f'$$

are defined to specify events functionality, where f and f' are well-formed formulae built over an alphabet of class attributes and s is the corresponding service whose functionality is being specified. The informal meaning of such formulae is that "assuming that f is true, f' will express the new resulting object state after the occurrence of s." These dynamic logic axioms are the result of applying a pre/post-specification technique.

OO-Method usually refers to these dynamic logic axioms as valuations, which relate a variable attribute a of a class with a given event s so that upon the occurrence of $s,$ and if f holds, a will take the value determined by f'.

Presentation Model

Finally, user interaction has to be considered. If we want to build a complete system description, the way in which users will perceive the system when interacting with it needs to be incorporated into the constructed system specification, which is the conceptual model. Therefore, a presentation model is provided to complement the three previous system views.

To specify user interaction properties, the presentation model creates an abstract user-interface (UI) specification built from a set of UI patterns belonging to a predefined catalogue of patterns provided by OO-Method. These patterns collect the different situations that have to be considered for UI specification purposes (for instance, selection criteria for looking for specific class instances, a display set to fix which attributes should be shown to give more information about a selected object, a set of available actions to determine which actions can be executed within the scope of a given class service, etc.).

These UI patterns are structured in three different levels as shown in Figure 11.4. The first level of the hierarchy, called Hierarchical Action Tree, defines the first level of interaction. It groups the set of second-level interaction units, which are:

- The Service Interaction Unit, which is intended to represent the IU components involved in the execution of a service.
- The Class Population Interaction Unit, which is oriented to determine how to access (subsets of) the population of a class, including potential filter conditions, attributes to be viewed, potential class services available when in a particular class instance, and so on.
- The Instance Interaction Unit, which is in charge of applying a similar idea but which focuses on how to present a selected instance of a class.

Other complex interaction units can be built by composing the three previous types to deal with more sophisticated kinds of user interactions (for instance, a Master-Details Interaction Unit).

Finally, the third level of the UI pattern hierarchy is constituted by the set of UI patterns that fix the lower-level rules that guide the final specific interaction to be executed. Depending on the interaction unit type, this includes, for example: whether a service argument is to be introduced and/or to be selected using a condition built on prespecified class attributes; how to group service arguments; which attributes will be seen; what specific set of services can be activated when accessing an instance, and so on.

When all the components of the conceptual model are specified, it is time to proceed with the model transformation process that will convert every conceptual primitive into its corresponding projection in the target software development environment where the final software product is to be built. To do that, an execution model must be defined.

Execution Model

Having introduced the conceptual primitives that allow the creation of a model to describe an information system in an abstract yet accurate and precise way, the execution semantics of each

Figure 11.4 **Structure of the Presentation Model**

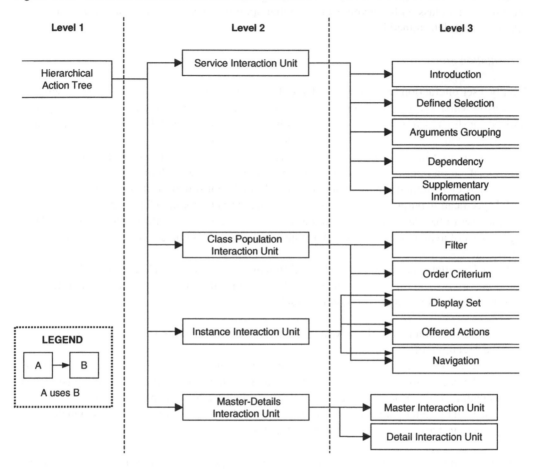

of the conceptual primitives must be defined. In other words, what will the runtime behavior of objects of the system (instances of classes of the model that represents the system) be according to the conceptual primitives that have been used to define the model that represents this system?

The execution model can be seen as an abstract machine that is capable of executing any model created with the set of conceptual primitives we have described above. It is abstract in that it does not dictate *how* to execute models in any given platform and technology. Rather, any set of rules governing the conversion of a conceptual model into a functionally equivalent software representation (implementation) in a given platform and technology must be compliant with this execution model. The execution model per se is aimed at enforcing functional equivalence between (abstract) conceptual primitives and (concrete) software representations of these primitives, and it also ensures functional equivalence between different reifications of the same conceptual model.

Therefore, in order to easily implement and animate the specified system, we define a way in which users can interact with system objects. To achieve this behavior the system has to:

1. Identify the user (access control): log the user onto the system and provide an object system view to determine the set of object attributes/services that the user can query/activate.

2. Allow service activation: once the user is connected and has a clear object system view, s/he can activate any available service in her/his worldview. Among these services, we will have system observations (object queries) or events or transactions served by other objects.

Any service activation comprises two steps: building the message and executing the service. In order to build the message, the user has to provide information to:

1. Identify the server object: the existence of this server object is an implicit (pre)condition to executing any service, unless we are dealing with a <<new>> event.
2. Provide values for service arguments.

Once the message is sent, the service execution is characterized by the occurrence of the following sequence of actions in the server object:

1. Check state transition: verify the existence of a valid transition labeled with the service being executed from the object's current state to another state in the state transition diagram.
2. Precondition satisfaction: all preconditions (if any) associated with the service must hold.
3. If 1 or 2 does not hold, an exception will arise and the message is ignored.
4. Valuations fulfillment: the induced event modifications (specified in the functional model) take place in the involved object state.
5. Checking integrity constraints in the new state: to assure that the service execution leads the object to a valid state, integrity constraints are verified in the final state. If any constraint does not hold, an exception will arise and all changes to the object are undone.
6. Testing trigger relationships: after a valid change of state, the set of condition-action rules that represent the internal system activity is verified. If any of them holds, the specified service will be triggered.

The previous steps guide the implementation of any program to assure the functional equivalence between the object system specification collected in the conceptual model and its reification in a programming environment.

COMPILING OO-METHOD CONCEPTUAL MODELS

An OO-Method conceptual model represents an application to be developed. The next natural step after building a conceptual model and validating it is to implement the application that the model represents.

We will refer to the process of transforming a conceptual model into a functionally equivalent software application as conceptual model compilation. If the creation of conceptual models results in a rise in the level of abstraction with respect to that of the source code, in much the same way that source code raises the level of abstraction from that of, say, machine code, it seems only natural to refer to this transformation process as "compilation," in the same way that the software engineering community refers to the process of transforming source code into machine code as compilation.

Traditional compilers transform a program written in a certain programming language (which abstracts away details about the hardware platform on which it will execute through the use of registers, physical organization of memory, etc.) into code that executes directly on a given machine with its requirements as a hardware platform.

Analogously, a model compilation transforms a conceptual model (which abstracts away details about the software platform on which it will execute through the use of execution control, representation of data in memory, data access, etc.) into a program written in a certain programming language that will take care of the requirements of the software platform on which it will be executed.

Since the semantics of all primitives in the conceptual model is clearly defined, the compilation of a conceptual model can be carried out in a manual way. In other words, the specification of the conceptual model contains enough details about the system to be developed that a developer with no additional information could implement it. Moreover, using the same conceptual model as input, different developers would create different implementations of it, but all of them would be functionally equivalent.

Nevertheless, to perform these transformation processes in an efficient way, there must be a set of tools that automate the compilation of models: we will refer to these tools as conceptual model compilers or, in short, as model compilers.

Regardless of whether the compilation process is performed manually or in an automated way, certain requirements must be observed in order to define a set of guidelines to perform a complete and correct compilation of a conceptual model. Compiling a conceptual model into an application must be a deterministic process that can be applied in a systematic way. To obtain this process, OO-Method establishes:

- what the representation of any conceptual model in any development environment must be (taking into account both static and dynamic aspects); and
- an execution strategy that guarantees functional equivalence between a specification and an implementation of it.

Also, the architecture of applications to be produced by the compilation process must be defined. In consequence, the way to transform elements in the conceptual model into elements in the application architecture and the way to transform the latter into code must be defined.

Application Execution Strategy

The first key aspect to be taken into account in order to implement a process to compile conceptual models is the definition of how the applications to be produced will use elements defined in the conceptual model to function. OO-Method proposes an abstract execution strategy (the execution model) that is tied to the semantics of modeling elements, but that is independent of the details of the software platforms on which applications will be implemented.

This strategy does not change with different compilation processes; it completes the semantics of modeling elements and guarantees that the applications produced as a result of applying a compilation process will be functionally equivalent to the conceptual models used as input for this compilation process.

Application Architecture

The application architecture establishes the common structure of any application compiled from an OO-Method conceptual model and must be compliant with the application execution strategy in order to preserve the functional equivalence of the application with respect to the conceptual model.

The set of mechanisms defined by the application execution strategy is abstract in the sense that it dictates only *what* mechanisms an application must have in place (e.g., verify that integrity constraints hold for an object after executing a service on it), but it does not dictate *how* these mechanisms must be implemented (e.g., a method that reads the values of the attributes of the object on which a service has been executed and verifies that every attribute has a valid value according to the integrity constraints defined in the class that this object is an instance of). Therefore, we need to define the architecture of applications.

First of all, it is obvious that the application architecture must provide mechanisms for every conceptual primitive in a conceptual model: classes, attributes, relationships, derivations, preconditions, integrity constraints, and so on. However, in addition to this, the application architecture must state how all of the mechanisms in the application execution strategy will be implemented (e.g., how the state of objects is made persistent, how derivations are calculated, how integrity constraints are enforced, etc.). Finally, the application architecture must provide mechanisms that are independent of the conceptual model but that are common in any application to be implemented on a given platform: error management, communication protocols, data access management, and so forth.

The application architecture must therefore be a reconciliation of the set of mechanisms required by the conceptual model and the execution model (application execution strategy) with the set of mechanisms imposed and/or required by the software platform, programming language, programming model, and so on, at which the application is targeted.

A clearly defined application architecture will apply the process of conceptual model compilation in a systematic way on different models, thus obtaining different applications (one per model) that have common features and quality levels. Should there be a change in the acceptance level for any feature of the application, the application architecture would be revised to achieve the new requirements, but the conceptual model would remain unchanged. After modifying the application architecture, we would apply the process of conceptual model compilation to the conceptual model again in order to obtain a new version of the application that provides the same functionality (since the conceptual model used as input would be the same) according to the new requirements.

We will refer to the set of elements and properties and elements relations that comprise the application architecture as the application model. With OO-Method defining both the set of conceptual primitives and its execution model, the intellectual effort in the creation of a model compiler is focused on defining this application execution model.

Transformation Strategy

In order to complete the definition of a conceptual model compilation process, we must define a transformation strategy to obtain the application model from the conceptual model and, in a second step, obtain the application code from the application model.

The transformation strategy comprises the definition of:

- Mappings, which establish relationships between elements in the conceptual model and elements in the application model.
- Text transformations, which state how to transform elements in the application model into text (code fragments).

Mappings define how to create instances of elements in the application model from instances of elements in the conceptual model so that the set of mappings creates an application model from a conceptual model. This set of mappings can be seen as a function whose domain is the conceptual model and whose co-domain is the application model. Mappings can include conditions that must hold for the mapping to be applied (e.g., some mappings will be applied only on elements of the conceptual model on which a certain condition is verified). Finally, mappings can be related to one another to define

- the order in which mappings are to be applied, and
- a dependency hierarchy between mappings.

Text transformations define how to obtain a code fragment from an element in the application model and the values of its properties. A text transformation can be seen as a function whose domain is an element of the application model (or a subset of its properties) and whose co-domain is a text.

OLIVANOVA MODEL EXECUTION, AN OO-METHOD IMPLEMENTATION

In Miller and Mukerji, (2003), the authors state that "To be adopted, a submitted technology must include a PIM and at least one PSM; in addition, there must be an implementation or a commitment to provide an implementation within a year."

France and Rumpe (2007, page 4) state that MDD approaches have to overcome three main challenges to succeed: to provide high-level, precise modeling abstractions; to deal properly with different viewpoints when modeling systems; and to manage models (transformations, traceability, consistency, evolution . . .). Tool support is currently a need to put these ideas successfully in practice. The OO-Method, aligned with the MDA perspective, has commercial implementations developed by CARE Technologies (Care Technologies, 2007) that work hard in this direction under the brand OLIVANOVA Model Execution. It includes, among others, the OLIVANOVA Modeler modeling tool (CARE Modeler) and a set of model compilers branded OLIVANOVA Transformation Engines (CARE Model Compiler). Therefore, OLIVANOVA Model Execution provides a Conceptual Schema-Centric Development Approach that is supported by tools aligned with the MDA initiative (Molina, 2006). Of course, this is not the "only" working implementation of MDA, but it provides an adequate workbench where the ideas previously introduced can be checked in practice.

The main components of OLIVANOVA Model Execution are illustrated in Figure 11.5:

Starting with the set of functional requirements for an application to be developed, the analyst will create an OO-Method conceptual model of the desired system in OLIVANOVA Modeler. In MDA terms, the conceptual model would be the PIM of the system since any OO-Method conceptual model is truly platform-independent because its level of abstraction lets the analyst define all the functional aspects of the system regardless of the platform (or platforms) on which this system is to be implemented. Nevertheless, it is important to note that even if the conceptual model is platform-independent, it is detailed and precise enough to enable an automated set of transformations to compile it into a full application.

Therefore, this conceptual model, or PIM, is used as input to a set of OLIVANOVA Transformation Engines or Model Compilers (the choice of which depends on the target platform) which then operate two transformations:

1. First, the conceptual model is transformed into an application model that addresses the specific details of the target platform on which the modeled system is to be implemented. In the MDA jargon, this would correspond to a PIM to PSM transformation.

Figure 11.5 **OLIVANOVA at a Glance**

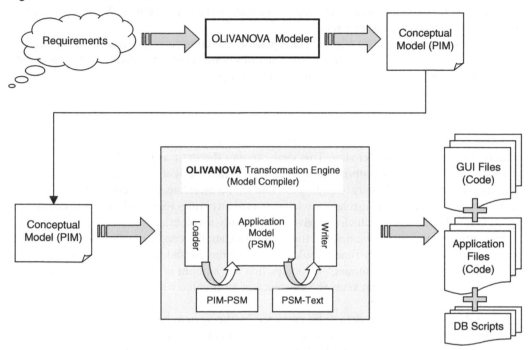

2. Second, the application model is transformed into text in the form of, for instance, source code for the GUI, source code for the application logic, or scripts for database creation (depending on the model compiler). Again, using MDA terminology, this would be a PSM to Text transformation.

OLIVANOVA MODELER

OLIVANOVA Modeler is a tool for the edition and validation of OO-Method conceptual models. Its major features include:

- Support for the four conceptual model views: objects, dynamic, functional, and presentation
- Formula editors
- Automatic validation of models
- Import of models from:
  - Total or partial models created with the tool.
  - Total or partial models from third party tools (in XMI format [XMI, 2006])
  - Database schemas
- Support for cooperative modeling
- Automatic generation of model documentation
- Automatic generation of model functional size metrics

In MDA terms, we could say that OLIVANOVA Modeler is a tool for the edition and validation of PIMs. The tool implements a model repository that can be exported to an XML (XML, 2006) format for interchange with other tools.

As discussed above, an OO-Method conceptual model comprises four model views: objects, dynamic, functional, and presentation. Thus, the tasks of the analyst typically involve the definition of the system from these four complementary viewpoints.

Defining the Objects Model View

The first task an analyst takes care of when creating an OO-Method conceptual model is the definition of the objects model view. This view captures the static aspects of the system in terms of which entities (classes) comprise the system (e.g., Vehicle, Client, Invoice, etc.), which are the relevant properties of each entity (e.g., InvoiceNumber, InvoiceDate, InvoiceAmount, InvoicePaymentDate, IsPaid, etc.) and the relevant relations between entities (e.g., each Invoice corresponds to one and only one Client, which can have zero or many invoices).

Integrity constraints can be defined for classes to state the conditions that must be fulfilled by instances of a class at any time in order to enforce the consistency of the data managed by the system (e.g., "InvoiceAmount > 0" states that the amount of an invoice must always be greater than zero and thus prevents the existence of an invoice whose amount is, for instance, negative).

Once the structure of the data to be managed by the system has been defined, the analyst typically moves on to define the services (the equivalent to UML operations) that will operate on that data. For example, in the Invoice class, the analyst will define services such as "newInvoice" to create an invoice, with arguments "invoiceNo" (invoice number), "client" (client to be invoiced), "invoiceDate" and "invoiceAmount"; or a service such as "pay" to mark an invoice as paid, with arguments "invoice" (the current invoice to be marked as paid) and "paymentDate."

If the execution of a service requires some conditions to be verified, these preconditions can be associated to the given service in this objects model view. For instance, if the payment date of an invoice must be later than its creation date, the analyst would associate the following precondition to the "pay" service: "invoice.InvoiceDate < paymentDate."

The complete specification of the objects model view is usually achieved through a series of iterations before moving on to the definition of the other three views or after a series of iterations covering the definition of this and the other three views.

Defining the Dynamic Model View

Once the analyst has defined (or after editing or deleting the definition of) services in the objects model view, s/he can proceed to define when the occurrence of these services can take place in the dynamic model view. This is done through the use of State Transition Diagrams that represent what states are reached by an object upon the execution of a service on it, depending on which state that object is in.

For instance, when an invoice is created upon the execution of its "newInvoice" service, that invoice reaches the "Unpaid" state. The execution of its "pay" service will change the state of that invoice from the "Unpaid" to the "Paid" state. An invoice can be destroyed either when it is in the "Unpaid" or in the "Paid" state, but it cannot be paid again if it is already in the "Paid" state. This example is illustrated in the (partial) state transition diagram in Figure 11.6.

Figure 11.6   **Partial State Transition Diagram for Class Invoice**

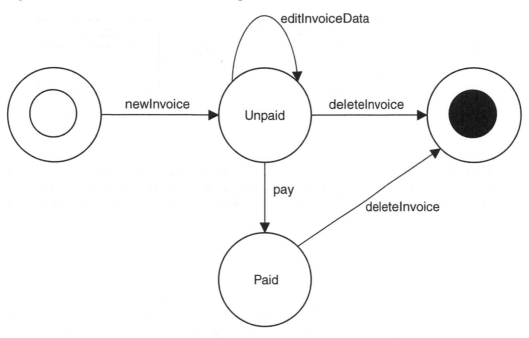

The analyst can also define the interobject communication aspects of the system in this dynamic model view, which in this case is supported by the graphical notation of UML communication diagrams.

For instance, in order to support the requirement that the creation of an invoice must always result in sending a notification to the invoiced client, the analyst decides to create a global service name "InvoiceClient" to encompass the execution of the "newInvoice" service of class "Invoice" with the execution of the "notify" service of class "Client" in a single execution unit. Figure 11.7 illustrates the communication diagram for the "InvoiceClient" global service, where these two atomic services are used to specify the resultant global service.

Defining the Functional Model View

As in the case of the dynamic model view, once a service has been added or edited for a class, the analyst can move on to define how the execution of that service will change the state of the object (in terms of the values of its attributes) on which it is executed. The definition of the functional model view does not have to take place after the definition of the dynamic model view, the only real prerequisite is that the related services must have been defined or edited previously in the objects model view.

As discussed above, services can be events or transactions, that is, atomic or molecular execution units; and the analyst can define how the occurrence of events changes the value of attributes of a class in the functional model view. The dynamic logic axioms used for that purpose do not have a graphical notation, but rather a textual, object constraint language–like one. Each of these dynamic logic axioms, called valuations, relates an attribute and an event of a class in order to state the value that this attribute will have when the event occurs.

Figure 11.7 **Communication Diagram for the InvoiceClient Global Service***

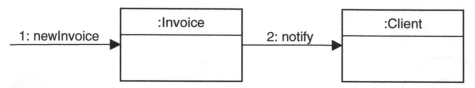

*Where two services of the class Invoice (newInvoice and notify) are encapsulated in a global execution unit (the global service called InvoiceClient).

For instance, upon the occurrence of the "pay" event on an invoice, the analyst determines that its "InvoicePaymentDate" attribute will have the value of the "paymentDate" argument of the "pay" event, and that the "IsPaid" attribute of the invoice will be set to true. This is illustrated in Table 11.1.

Defining the Presentation Model View

The aspects of user interaction with the system can be defined by the analyst as soon as its static aspects (classes, attributes, relationships) and the services that have been defined are in place. As discussed in a previous section, the catalogue of patterns to define the abstract UI are structured in three levels. This does not dictate, however, that the analyst must define the presentation model view in this fashion: either a top-down (going from the hierarchical action tree to the elementary patterns in the third level) or a bottom-up approach (even a combination of the two) can be used by the analyst.

For instance, when defining the interaction scenario to access (and interact with) the invoices in the system (using a population interaction unit), the analyst may well follow any of these approaches:

- First, define the population interaction unit for the "Invoice" class without defining its constituent third-level patterns. Then define each of its constituent patterns, for instance: a display set (to define which attributes of the invoice will be presented to the user), an order criterion (to specify in which order the invoices will be presented to the user), and a set of offered actions (i.e., which services will be available to the user for execution on the presented invoices). Then create a hierarchical action tree and select the population interaction unit previously created as one of its constituent elements.
- First, define the elementary third-level patterns to compose the population interaction unit (i.e., the display set, the order criterion, and the set of offered actions). Then create the population interaction unit and select the previously created elementary patterns as its constituent elements. Then create a hierarchical action tree and select the population interaction unit that was previously created as one of its constituent elements.
- First, define the hierarchical action tree, then the population interaction unit, and then the constituent elements of the latter.

As in the case of the dynamic model view and the functional model view, the order in which this presentation model view appears in this document does not mean that it cannot be defined until the other two views have been completely defined. However, the elements of the objects

Table 11.1

Functional Model in OO-Method

Attribute	Event	Valuation effect
InvoicePaymentDate	pay	paymentDate
IsPaid	pay	true

model view that are referenced from this view (classes, attributes, relationships, services) must already have been defined.

OLIVANOVA Transformation Engines

The OLIVANOVA Transformation Engines are implementations of different conceptual model compilation processes. Each transformation engine implements the following: a repository of the conceptual model, a repository of the application model, a set of mappings between the elements in the repository of the conceptual model and the elements in the repository of the application model, and the set of text transformations associated with each element in the repository of the application model.

The conceptual model repository is a common component that is common to all transformation engines. It is capable of loading an XML interchange file containing a model created with OLIVANOVA Modeler.

Mappings access the conceptual model repository and populate the application model repository. This application model repository is specific to each transformation engine and contains the elements that correspond to mechanisms that execute elements in the conceptual model as defined in the execution model, as well as those mechanisms pertinent to the platform, technology, and programming language at which the transformation engine is targeted.

Text transformations operate on the application model repository to generate the code fragments corresponding to each element in it.

In MDA terms, we could say that an OLIVANOVA Transformation Engine is the implementation of a tool that operates PIM-to-PSM transformations and PSM-to-Text (code) transformations.

Compiling OO-Method Models with OLIVANOVA Transformation Engines

Once the analyst has a version of the OO-Method conceptual model ready for implementation, s/he then moves on to choose the set of model compilers that automate that implementation task. Currently, OLIVANOVA Model Execution targets three-layered architectures (the presentation layer, the business logic layer, and the persistence layer) offering transformation engines that allow the compilation of an OO-Method conceptual model to (among others):

- JSP, ASP.Net, Visual Basic, and C# for the presentation layer,
- EJB, Visual Basic, and C# for the business logic layer, and
- SQLServer, Access, MySQL, Oracle, and DB2 for the persistence layer.

If, for instance, the analyst decides to have her/his model implemented in JSP for the presentation layer and EJB for the business logic layer using a MySQL database for persistence, then s/he would choose to use the JSP Transformation Engine and the EJB Transformation Engine using MySQL as database.

The JSP Transformation Engine, for instance, would transform each element in the presentation model view to its corresponding element in the JSP application model (such as JSP pages, servlets, validation scripts, etc.) and then each element in the JSP application model into the corresponding text (HTML, JavaScript, etc.).

If the analyst decides to target another platform (i.e., ASP.Net for the presentation layer, C# in the business logic layer, and SQLServer database for persistence) since her/his OO-Method conceptual model is truly platform-independent, s/he would only need to "recompile" her/his model again with the appropriate set of OLIVANOVA Transformation Engines (namely, the ASP. Net Transformation Engine and the C# Business Logic Transformation Engine using SQLServer as database) without making any change or modification to it.

CONCLUSIONS

Even though researchers have been talking about the "crisis of software" for the past few decades, producing an information system today is still a costly process (expensive resources are used over extended periods), much too slow for modern business conditions, very risky (hard to control, and with a high failure rate), and highly unsafe (due to the many hidden failure points). Considering that the software development process has not changed much in the past forty years and that it has basically centered on the idea of programming, it is time to consider whether there might not be a better way.

In line with the modern approaches based on MDA, Extreme Non-programming, Conceptual Schema-Centered Development, and the like, we have presented a method (the OO-Method) with a supporting set of tools (OLIVANOVA Model Execution) that is based on a different "concept": the idea that "the model is the code" instead of the conventional, programming-based idea where "the code is the model." This new framework provides a computer-aided software development environment that is designed to deal with information systems development through the required processes of model transformation.

Specifically, we have shown how to build a precise conceptual schema and how to convert it into its corresponding software product by defining the mappings between conceptual primitives and their software representation counterparts. These mappings are the core of a model compiler that makes the following statement a reality: "to develop an information system, it is necessary and sufficient to define its conceptual schema." The automation of systems building then becomes an affordable dream that is waiting for tools (such as the ones presented in this chapter) to justify its adoption in practice.

REFERENCES

Arcstyler. Interactive objects–business–IT transformations. Available at www.arcstyler.com (accessed June 2006).
CARE Model Compiler. CARE Technologies products: transformation engine. Available at www.care-t.com/products/transengine.html (accessed June 2006).
CARE Modeler. CARE technologies products: modeler. Available at www.care-t.com/products/modeler.html (accessed April 2007).
Care Technologies. 2007. Care Technologies: OlivaNova: the programming machine. Available at www.care-t.com (accessed June 2007).
Eakman, G. 2007. MOF Model-to-Text Transformation Language RFP. Available at www.omg.org/cgi-bin/doc?ad/2004–4-7 (accessed May 2007).

France, R., and Rumpe, B. 2007. Model-driven development of complex software: a research roadmap. *Proceedings of the Future of Software Engineering (FOSE'07)*. Minneapolis, MN: IEEE Computer Society, 37–54.

Grünbacher, P., and Ledru, Y. 2004. Automated software engineering: introduction. *ERCIM News*, 58 (July), 12–13.

Heaton, L. 2001. MOF QVT final adopted specification. Available at www.omg.org/cgi-bin/doc?ptc/05–11–01 (accessed June 2006).

J2EE. Java EE at a glance. Available at http://java.sun.com/javaee (accessed June 2007).

MDA. OMG Model-driven architecture. Available at www.omg.org/mda (accessed April 2007).

Mellor, S.J.; Clark, A.N.; and Futagami, T. 2003. Model-driven development: guest editor's introduction. *IEEE Software*, 20, 5 (September–October), 14–18.

Mellor, S., and Balcer, M. 2002. *Executable UML: A Foundation for Model Driven Architecture*. Reading, MA: Addison-Wesley.

Microsoft .NET. Microsoft .Net: driving business value with the Microsoft platform. Available at www.microsoft.com/net/ (accessed March 2007).

Miller, J., and Mukerji, J. (eds). 2003. MDA Guide Version 1.0.1. Available at www.omg.org/docs/omg/03–06–01.pdf.

MOF. OMG's MetaObject Facility. Available at www.omg.org/mof (accessed June 2007).

Molina, J.C. 2006. Technology: MDA. Available at www.care-t.com/technology/mda.html (accessed June 2007).

Morgan, T. 2002. *Business Rules and Information Systems: Aligning IT with Business Goals*. Reading, MA: Addison-Wesley.

Olivé, A. 2005. Conceptual schema-centric development: a grand challenge for information systems research. *Seventeenth International Conference on Advanced Information Systems Engineering, CAiSE 2005*. Porto, Portugal, June 13–17. Lecture Notes in Computer Science 3520. Berlin: Springer-Verlag, 1–15.

OptimalJ. Compuware OptimalJ: model-driven development for Java. Available at www.compuware.com/products/optimalj/ (accessed on June 2007).

Pastor, O.; Hayes, F.; and Bear, S. 2002. OASIS: an object-oriented specification language. *Fourth International Conference on Advanced Information Systems Engineering, CAiSE 1992*. Lecture Notes in Computer Science 593. Berlin: Springer-Verlag, 348–363.

Pastor, O.; Molina, J.C.; and Iborra, E. 2004. Automated production of fully functional applications with OlivaNova model execution. *ERCIM News*, no. 57 (April), 62–64.

Pastor, O.; Gomez, J.; Insfrán, E.; and Pelechano, V. 2001. The OO-Method approach for information systems modeling: from object-oriented conceptual modeling to automated programming. *Information Systems*, 26, 507–534.

Selic, B. 2003. The pragmatics of model-driven development. *IEEE Software*, 20, 5 (September), 19–25.

Teichroew, D., and Sayani, H. 1971. Automation of system building. *Datamation*, 17, 16 (August), 25–30.

UML. Unified Modeling Language: UML resource page. Available at www.uml.org (accessed June 2007).

Völter, M.; Stahl, T.; Bettin, J.; Haase, A.; and Helsen S. 2006. *Model-Driven Software Development: Technology, Engineering, Management*. Indianapolis, IN: Wiley.

XMI. MOF 2.0 / XMI Mapping Specification, V2.1. Available at www.omg.org/technology/documents/formal/xmi.htm (accessed June 2006).

XML. Extensible Markup Language (XML). Available at www.w3.0rg/XML (accessed April 2006).

EDITORS AND CONTRIBUTORS

K. Suzanne Barber is director of the Center for Excellence in Distributed Global Environments (EDGE), a cross-disciplinary center where departments throughout the University of Texas are working together to revolutionize how distributed engineering teams, distributed computation, and distributed information exchange ensure the effective and efficient use, delivery, and security of software systems. As director of the Laboratory for Intelligent Processes and Systems, she pursues her personal research interests with her students addressing (1) in-depth, iterative, and coordinated design and analysis of software systems among distributed teams, as well as (2) information assurance and coordination for distributed agent-based software systems. She has published over 300 articles in refereed conference proceedings, journals, and book chapters, and holds copyrights for innovative software engineering analysis and design environment. As director of Software Engineering academic programs at the University of Texas, she leads educational initiatives for undergraduates, full-time graduate students, and working professionals.

Nicholas Berente is a research fellow at the University of Michigan's School of Information. His research focuses on complex design processes and the role of information systems in supporting innovation. He has a bachelor's degree in finance from John Carroll University and an M.B.A. and Ph.D. from Case Western Reserve University. He is the founder and former president of Pentagon Engineering Corporation, a nationwide systems integrator that specialized in the information systems that support product development, which he sold in 2002.

Roger H.L. Chiang is associate professor of information systems at the College of Business, University of Cincinnati. He received his B.S. degree in management science from National Chiao Tung University, Taiwan; M.S. degrees in computer science from Michigan State University and in business administration from the University of Rochester; and Ph.D. degree in computers and information systems from the University of Rochester. His research interests are in data and knowledge management and intelligent systems, particularly in database reverse engineering, database integration, data and text mining, document classification and clustering, domain knowledge discovery, and semantic information retrieval. He is currently senior editor of the *DATA BASE for Advances in Information Systems,* and associate editor of *Journal of Database Management, International Journal of Intelligent Systems in Accounting, Finance and Management,* and *MIS Quarterly.* His research has been published in a number of journals including *ACM Transactions on Database Systems, Communications of the ACM, DATA BASE for Advances in Information Systems, Data & Knowledge Engineering, Decision Support Systems, Journal of American Society for Information Science and Technology, Journal of Database Administration, Journal of Management Information Systems,* and *Very Large Data Base Journal.*

Christopher J. Davis is assistant professor of information systems at the College of Business, University of South Florida Saint Petersburg. His recent research explores the impact of information technology on the process and organization of work and the efficacy of systems analysis and design techniques. His work has been presented at international conferences in Europe and the United States and published in a range of journals, including *Communications of the ACM, Journal of Computer Information Systems, International Journal of Technology and Human Interaction, Journal of Organizational Change Management, Systems Research, and Behavioral Science,* and *MIS Quarterly.*

Tharam Dillon holds the position of professor as Head of Research Development with the Digital Ecosystems and Business Intelligence Institute, Curtin University of Technology, Australia. His research interests include data mining, Internet computing, e-commerce, hybrid neuro-symbolic systems, neural nets, software engineering, database systems, and computer networks. He has also worked with industry in developing systems in telecommunications, health care, e-commerce, logistics, power systems, and banking and finance. He is editor-in-chief of the *International Journal of Computer Systems Science and Engineering* and the *International Journal of Engineering Intelligent Systems,* as well as co-editor of the *Journal of Electric Power and Energy Systems.* He is on the advisory editorial board of *Applied Intelligence,* published by Kluwer in the United States and *Computer Communications,* published by Elsevier in the UK. He has published more than 400 papers in international and national journals.

Yael Dubinsky is a visiting member of the human–computer interaction research group in the Department of Computer and Systems Science at La Sapienza, Rome, and for more than ten years has been the instructor of a project-based course in the Department of Computer Science at Technion Institute of Technology. She is also affiliated with the Software and Services group in IBM Haifa Research Lab (HRL). Her research interests involve aspects in software engineering and information systems. She has significant experience with guiding agile implementation processes in industry and academia. She has presented her work (since 2002) and co-facilitated tutorials (since 2005) in Agile and XP conferences.

John Erickson is an assistant professor in the College of Business Administration at the University of Nebraska at Omaha. His research interests include Unified Modeling Language, software complexity, and systems analysis and design issues. He has published in journals such as the *Communications of the ACM, Journal of Database Management,* and in conferences such as AMICIS, ICIS WITS, EMMSAD, and CAiSE. He has also co-authored several book chapters.

Robert M. Fuller is an assistant professor of information systems at the College of Business Administration, University of Tennessee. His research interests focus on the fit and use of collaborative technologies for decision performance and the adoption and use of communication technologies. His research has been published in the *Journal of the Association for Information Systems, Decision Support Systems,* and the *Journal of Computer Information Systems,* and he has presented at national and international conferences.

Paolo Giorgini is researcher at the University of Trento, where he currently leads the Software Engineering and Formal Methods Group of the Department of Information and Communication Technology. He received his Ph.D. degree from the Computer Science Institute of the University of Ancona (Italy) in 1998. Between March and October 1998 he worked at the University of Macerata and the University of Ancona as a research assistant. In November 1998 he joined the Mechanized Reasoning Group (MRG) at University of Trento as postdoctoral researcher. In December 1998 he was visiting researcher in the Computer Science Department of the University of Toronto (Canada), and more recently he was visiting researcher in the Software Engineering Department of the University of Technology in Sydney. He has worked on the development of requirements and design languages for agent-based systems, and the application of knowledge representation techniques to software repositories and software development. He is one of the founders of Tropos, an agent-based–oriented software engineering methodology. His publication list includes more than 130 refereed journal and conference proceedings papers and eight edited books. He has contributed, as chair and program committee member, to the organization of international conferences such as CoopIS, ER, CAiSE, AAMAS, EUMAS, AOSE, AOIS, and ISWC. He is co-editor-in-chief of the *International Journal of Agent-Oriented Software Engineering* (*IJAOSE*).

Thomas Graser is currently a systems analyst and has over twenty years experience in the software engineering field in both research and practice. He is a software architecture evangelist, helping organizations define architectures that add value to the software development life cycle and play an active role in decision making during system design and configuration. He emphasizes defining architectures in a rational manner where measurement is used to demonstrate that the architecture meets requirements and provides justification for architecture refinement. He has served numerous roles in the software development life cycle including project manager, requirements engineer, architect, and developer. His software development experience encompasses a wide range of platforms and environments from IBM mainframes to Microsoft .Net. He also shares his knowledge and experience by teaching and supervising students in the Executive Software Engineering M.S. Degree Program at the University of Texas at Austin.

Bill C. Hardgrave is the Edwin and Karlee Bradberry Chair in Information Systems and executive director of the Information Technology Research Institute in the Sam. M. Walton College of Business at the University of Arkansas. His research on software development (primarily people and process issues) has appeared in *MIS Quarterly, Journal of Management Information Systems, Communications of the ACM, IEEE Software, IEEE Transactions on Software Engineering, IEEE Transactions on Engineering Management, DATA BASE for Advances in Information Systems, Information and Management,* and *Educational and Psychological Measurement,* among others.

Orit Hazzan is an associate professor in the Department of Education in Technology and Science of the Technion Israel Institute of Technology. Her main research topic—human aspects of software engineering—deals with cognitive and social issues of software engineering in general and of agile software development in particular. She is co-author (with Jim Tomayko) of *Human Aspects of Software Engineering* (Charles River Media, 2004). She combines her academic research with consulting to Israeli software development companies with respect to the assimilation of agile methods and change management. She has presented her work at computer science and software engineering education conferences as well as at the Agile and XP conferences.

Brian Henderson-Sellers is director of the Centre for Object Technology Applications and Research and professor of information systems at the University of Technology, Sydney (UTS). He is author or editor of twenty-eight technical books, co-editor of the ISO standard 24744 ("SE

Metamodel for Development Methodologies"), editor of the *International Journal of Agent-Oriented Software Engineering,* and is also on several editorial boards. In July 2001, he was awarded a Doctor of Science (D.Sc.) by the University of London for his research contributions in object-oriented methodologies.

Alan Hevner is an Eminent Scholar and professor in the Information Systems and Decision Sciences Department at the University of South Florida, where he holds the Citigroup/Hidden River Chair of Distributed Technology. His areas of research interest include information systems development, software engineering, distributed database systems, health care information systems, and telecommunications. He has published more than 120 research papers on these topics and has consulted for several Fortune 500 companies. He has a Ph.D. in computer science from Purdue University, and he has held faculty positions at the University of Maryland and the University of Minnesota. He is a member of ACM, IEEE, AIS, and INFORMS.

Emilio Iborra spent most of his career working for multinational hardware companies, in particular at Tandem Computers (later acquired by Compaq Computers, now HP), where he was advisory analyst and project manager in finance and telecom. Specializing in business security, he was an active member of the European security team and principal specialist in Atalla crypto-technology products. At the spin-off of CARE Technologies, he accepted the CEO position, where he directed the creation of a set of products. He left CARE in 2006 to co-found AMI2, where he continues the research and development of software engineering in user interaction and ambient intelligence.

Karlheinz Kautz is professor in systems development and software engineering in the Department of Informatics at Copenhagen Business School, Denmark, and until recently director of studies for the course program on computer science and business administration. Previously, he was employed as a senior researcher at the Norwegian Computing Center and as a lecturer at universities in Germany, Norway, England, and Denmark. He is chairman of the IFIP TC8 WG 8.6 on Diffusion, Transfer, and Implementation of Information Technology. His research interests are diffusion and adoption of information technology (IT) innovations, evolutionary systems development and system development methodologies for advanced application areas, the organizational impact of IT, knowledge management, and software quality and process improvement. He has published in these areas in such journals as *Information and Software Technology, Information, Technology and People,* the *Scandinavian Journal of Information Systems, Software Process Improvement and Practice, IEEE Software,* and the *Journal of Knowledge Management,* and is a member of ACM and IEEE.

Arie Keren is a senior software engineer with more than twenty years of experience in software development. Currently, he is doing freelance work in analysis, architecture, and development of software-based systems. During the project described in this book, he led the systems engineering group at MAMDAS software development unit in the Israeli Air Force. He has a Ph.D. in computer science from Hebrew University in Jerusalem (1998), M.Sc. in computer science from Tel-Aviv University (1991), and B.Sc. in computer engineering from Technion, Haifa (1983).

Manuel Kolp is an associate professor in computer science at the Université catholique de Louvain, Belgium, where he is head of the Information Systems Research Unit and coordinator of the Center of Excellence in Management and Information Technology. He is also a visiting professor at the University of Brussels and the Universitary Faculties St. Louis of Brussels. His research work deals with agent architectures and ERP II systems. He was previously a postdoctoral researcher at the University of Toronto. He has been involved in the organization of international conferences and workshops on information systems and agents. His publications include more than 50 refereed journals or periodicals and conference proceedings as well as three books.

Richard Linger serves as manager of the Carnegie Mellon University Software Engineering Institute's CERT STAR*Lab, and the Survivable Systems Engineering group. He has developed technologies for survivable systems analysis (SSA) to improve survivability in the presence of intrusions and failures; function extraction (FX) for automated computation of the functional behavior of programs; flow-service-quality (FSQ) engineering for network system development; and Cleanroom software engineering for development and certification of high-reliability systems. Previously at IBM, he was co-developer of Cleanroom software engineering specification, design, verification, and certification technologies for creating high-reliability software. He has taught software and security courses at Carnegie Mellon University, and has published three software engineering textbooks and an extensive set of book chapters and technical papers.

Kalle Lyytinen is Iris S. Wolstein Professor at Case Western Reserve University, adjunct professor at the University of Jyvaskyla, Finland, and visiting professor at the University of Loughborough, UK. He currently serves on the editorial boards of several leading information systems (IS) journals including *Journal of AIS* (editor-in-chief), *Journal of Strategic Information Systems, Information & Organization, Requirements Engineering Journal, Information Systems Journal, Scandinavian Journal of Information Systems,* and *Information Technology and People,* among others. He is AIS fellow (2004), and former chairperson of IFIP 8.2 and a founding member of SIGSAND. He has published over 160 scientific articles and conference papers and edited or written eleven books on topics related to the IS discipline, system design, method engineering, organizational implementation, risk assessment, computer-supported cooperative work, standardization, and ubiquitous computing, among others. He is currently involved in research projects that study IT-induced radical innovation in software development, IT innovation in the architecture, engineering, and construction industry, design and use of ubiquitous applications, and the adoption of broadband wireless services in the UK, South Korea, and the United States.

Sabine Madsen is assistant professor in the Department of Informatics at Copenhagen Business School, Denmark. She was employed as a project manager in the Danish information technology industry before joining the Department of Informatics in 2001. She completed her Ph.D. research on process and method emergence in information systems development practice in 2004. Her research interests concern (emergent) information systems development processes, methods, and the relationship between research and practice.

Juan Carlos Molina has a degree in computer science from the Valencia University of Technology, Spain. He is research and development manager for CARE Technologies S.A., the company that develops the OlivaNova Model Execution set of tools, which fully support the MDA-based, conceptual model-centric software development approach described in this book. In this context, he has developed a strong background in advanced technological transfer from academia to industry that has produced both successful industrial products and relevant scientific publications.

John Mylopoulos has been professor in computer science at the University of Trento, Department of Information and Communication Technology, since September 2005. He received his B.Eng.

degree from Brown University in 1966 and his Ph.D. degree from Princeton in 1970, the year he joined the faculty of the University of Toronto, where he remains a part-time professor. His research interests include software requirements engineering, data semantics, knowledge management, and knowledge-based systems. He is the recipient of the first Outstanding Services Award given by the Canadian AI Society (CSCSI), a co-recipient of the most influential paper award at the 1994 International Conference on Software Engineering (ICSE'94), a fellow of the American Association for AI (AAAI), and a past president of the VLDB Endowment (1998–2003). He has served on the editorial board of several international journals, including *ACM Transactions on Information Systems* (*TOIS*), the *ACM Transactions on Software Engineering and Methodology* (*TOSEM*), and the *ACM Computing Surveys*. He is co-editor-in-chief of the *Requirements Engineering Journal* (Springer-Verlag). He has also contributed to the organization of major international conferences, including program co-chair of the International Joint Conference of AI (1991), general chair of the Entity-Relationship conference (1994), and program chair of the International IEEE Symposium of Requirements Engineering (1997). He is currently leading a number of research projects, and has been principal investigator of national and provincial Centres of Excellence in Canada.

Kinh Nguyen is a lecturer in computer science at La Trobe University, Australia, and is a member of the Software Engineering Research Group. He obtained his B.Sc. 1st Class Hns. and M.Sc. with Distinction from Canterbury University, New Zealand, and Ph.D. in computer science from La Trobe University. He has been actively working in the area of data-intensive systems development, covering conceptual modeling, relational databases, object databases, Web information systems, aspect-oriented programming, and model-driven engineering. One of his main interests is the practical application of formal notations in rigorous software development processes.

Oscar Pastor is professor for object-oriented development methods at the Valencia University of Technology, Spain. He has a Ph.D. in computer science and a degree in physics. He has taught software engineering for more than fifteen years, during which time his research has focused on object-oriented conceptual modeling, requirements engineering, Web development, and model-based software production. He has headed prestigious scientific events such as the World Wide Web Conference in 2007 (Web Engineering Track) and the International Conference on Conceptual Modeling in 2005. In addition, he is the principal creator of the OlivaNova Model Execution, an advanced MDA-based set of tools that produces a final software product starting from a conceptual schema where the system requirements are captured.

Mark Pleszkoch is a senior member of the technical staff of the Software Engineering Institute (SEI). His research interests include automated proof checking and its application to formal verification of programs. Prior to joining the SEI, he worked for IBM and was an original member of IBM's Cleanroom Software Technology Center, where he educated and consulted with clients on software process, formal verification, and statistical testing of software. He was the principal architect of the IBM Cleanroom Certification Assistant tool set for statistical testing automation. He holds a Ph.D. in Computer Science from the University of Maryland, as well as an M.S. in mathematics from the University of Virginia, where he was a Putnam Fellow of the Mathematics Association of America. He is a member of the Association for Symbolic Logic and the IEEE.

Stacy Prowell is a senior member of the technical staff of the Software Engineering Institute (SEI). His research interests include rigorous software specification methods, automated statistical testing, and automated analysis of software behavior. He has managed both commercial and academic software development projects, and consulted on the design, development, and testing of applications ranging from consumer electronics to medical scanners, from small embedded real-time systems to very large distributed applications. He holds a Ph.D. in computer science from the University of Tennessee, and is a member of the ACM, IEEE, and Sigma Xi.

Keng Siau is the E.J. Faulkner Professor of Management Information Systems (MIS) at the University of Nebraska, Lincoln (UNL). He is the director of the UNL-IBM Global Innovation Hub, editor-in-chief of the *Journal of Database Management,* and co-editor-in-chief of the *Advances in Database Research* series. He received his Ph.D. degree from the University of British Columbia (UBC), where he majored in management information systems and minored in cognitive psychology. His Master's and Bachelor degrees are in computer and information sciences from the National University of Singapore. He has over 200 academic publications. His research has been funded by NSF, IBM, and other IT organizations. He has received numerous research, teaching, and service awards. His latest award is the International Federation for Information Processing (IFIP) Outstanding Service Award in 2006. He served as the organizing and program chairs of the International Workshop on Evaluation of Modeling Methods in Systems Analysis and Design (EMMSAD) (1996–2005). He now serves on the EMMSAD Steering Committee and SIGSAND Advisory Board. He also served on the organizing committees of AMCIS 2005, ER 2006, and AMCIS 2007.

David Talby has recently become a senior manager of software development at Amazon.com, after a long period of work in software development and management in the Israeli Air Force. He is also a lecturer and doctoral student of computer science at the Hebrew University, Jerusalem. His research interests are in software engineering, focusing on agile methods and large-scale enterprise software development, as well as parallel computer scheduling and workload modeling. He received his M.Sc. in computer science and MBA in business administration from Hebrew University.

Gwendolyn Walton is a faculty member in the Mathematics and Computer Science Department at Florida Southern College. Her research interests include theoretical foundations for computation of nonfunctional software attributes, and rigorous methods for specification and evaluation of large-scale software systems. Previously she held positions as a senior software engineering researcher in the CERT Program of the Software Engineering Institute, president of Software Engineering Technology Inc., assistant vice president for Science Applications International Corporation, senior data systems programmer for Lockheed Missiles and Space Company, and research associate for Oak Ridge National Laboratory. She received her Ph.D. in computer science from the University of Tennessee. She is a member of ACM, IEEE, and the Society of Women Engineers.

SERIES EDITOR

Vladimir Zwass is Gregory Olsen Endowed Chair and Distinguished Professor of Computer Science and Management Information Systems at Fairleigh Dickinson University. He holds a Ph.D. in Computer Science from Columbia University. Professor Zwass is the founding editor-in-chief of the *Journal of Management Information Systems,* one of the three top-ranked journals in the field of information systems; the journal has celebrated twenty-five years of its publication. He is also the founding editor-in-chief of the *International Journal of Electronic Commerce,* ranked as the top journal in its field. More recently, he has been the founding editor-in-chief of the monograph series *Advances in Management Information Systems,* the objective of which is to codify the field's knowledge and research methods. He is the author of six books and several book chapters, including entries in the *Encyclopaedia Britannica,* as well as of a number of papers in various journals and conference proceedings. He has received several grants, consulted for a number of major corporations, and is a frequent speaker to national and international audiences. He is a former member of the professional staff of the International Atomic Energy Agency in Vienna, Austria.

INDEX

233